# Beamish Boy

## ALSO BY ALBERT FLYNN DESILVER

Poetry

*A Field Guide to the Emotions*
*Letters to Early Street*
*Walking Tooth & Cloud*
*Some Nature*
*A Pond*
*Foam Poems*
*The Book of Not*

# Beamish Boy

*(I Am Not My Story)*

*A Memoir of Recovery & Awakening*

Albert Flynn DeSilver

The Owl Press

Woodacre, California 2012

## NOTE

This book is true to the letter of my heart, a true account, as in true as truth can be given the vagaries of the mind (especially one at times severely "under the influence") and the beclouded nature of memory drunk on time. Names have been changed to protect privacy, and one person (character) is an amalgam of two from "real life." This was intended to cut down on confusion and enhance the clarity of the story without compromising its overall integrity.

for Magpie and Serena

*"And, has thou slain the Jabberwock?*
*Come to my arms, my beamish boy!*
*O frabjous day! Callooh! Callay!"*
*He chortled in his joy.*

—Lewis Carroll,
from "Jabberwocky"

*I cannot tell what I am, because words can describe only what I am not.*
—Nisargadatta Maharaj

# CONTENTS

**Part I**

**Part II**

**Part III**

# *Beamish Boy*

Part I

PROLOGUE:

# Sunday Bloody Sunday

The air is heavy and wet, cicadas grating, trees drooping with the burst of fresh leaves; a new moon at dusk is spilling forth its shadow like a sea of lost ink. A dense haze is smudging out a shy glint of stars. Inside, "Sunday Bloody Sunday" is cranked on the stereo. It is, in fact, a Sunday night, and there I am at nineteen in 1987, just back from my first year of college, looking out the open window from the crowded kitchen of a party at my friend Patrick's house in Connecticut. Old friends from middle and high school are milling about smoking, talking loudly. Everyone is coupled or grouped up. Allison and Ryan, so skinny and beautiful, are leaning against the stove, pressed together like sheets of seaweed. They're making me jealous, and I feel a gnawing longing for Amy. A blurry crew is seated at the kitchen table playing "quarters" and laughing. I've got both hands wrapped tightly around my red plastic cup of beer—my seventh or eighth of the night. It's the way I would have wrapped my hands around Amy's waist. Possessive and clingy.

I am standing alone again. Eyes darting around, fingering the rim of my cup, feeling the absence of Amy, trying not to hear her resistant voice ringing in my head as echo. *You're going to Colorado next year, and I'll be back in Ohio, and I just don't see how this can work. I know, I know I had an amazing time too. I'm confused. Love is a big word. I need time to figure things out.*

So I make myself fake-occupied staring at a grease-splattered photo to the right of the stove. It's of Pat and his family at the Grand Canyon, and I am struck by their matching postures when standing in profile, looking like an innocent family of seahorses. They seem to all fit in snugly together. While looking at this picture, I can't help but wonder: Where is the strict and violent German governess? The schizophrenic aunts and uncles? What about the fleeting mom who tells outrageously dirty jokes at fabulous parties, with a perpetual Benson & Hedges hanging out of her mouth? Did Mr. Daley truly have just one wife, perfect little Mrs. Daley? She looks a little like Amy, albeit an older version, with her straight blond hair, athletic build, and small sage-light eyes.

A pang of longing ripples through my belly. I turn away and find myself standing uncomfortably still alone, swaying. I shuffle over to Mike Castleton, interrupting him mid-sentence with what's-his-name. Mike's the biggest guy here: six feet tall, sandy blond hair, muscular, practically a full beard shadowing his face. I'm feeling bold and edgy. I need a ruckus, an audience, something to take me out of this longing and missing that's chewing at my heart. I take a giant pull from my beer, then pivot and swerve in an instant into Mike's personal space, mouth good and full. I spit it right into the breast pocket of his blue and white striped oxford shirt. Foam spills drowsily out of his pocket and down his shirt.

"What the fuck . . . you idiot asshole," he says with a solid punch in the arm and a swift kick in the ass, which sends me flailing out the door, onto the deck. My ass is throbbing, but there is laughter, and I assume it's *for* me. I am yearning for it to be for me.

The deck is a dark boat—blackness washing up against the gunwales, leaking in among the gaping spaces around my feet and legs. The planks are creaking. Voices. Are they talking shit about me? Time folds in on itself, fades in and out, inspires another beer from the keg. My tenth, twelfth?

Things are getting unmanageably hazy. I weave inside and out among the chattering masses. A person appears before me swathed in a black trench coat, hands me a shot of something liquid and golden. I knock it back and drop the glass at my feet, my hand having gone limp at the wrist. Trench coat says things, mumbly underwater things, then vanishes like vulture shadow. A yellow room appears with dizzying stripes and red angry flowers, tilts uncomfortably on its side, inspires another visit to my dark boat for air. But the darkness is rising up to my chest, threatens to drown me out. At some point, I find myself stumbling off the deck, drawn to voices out in the driveway. The asphalt rears up at me like a shadowy horse; the trees above me spin.

I approach the circle of people, drawn as if to a white life preserver thrown out in a sea of choppy dark. I join them, swaying, noticing a triangular flood of light between the garage doors. Someone's head is backlit, the outline of it glowing as if they are about to get sucked into the light. I wish that was me, getting sucked into a vast yellow brightness of warmth, of acceptance. I'm trying to think of a joke, or even a quick anecdote about how friggin' cute Sarah Brenner looks in her tight orange tube top. Something, anything, to announce my presence. Nothing.

My brain is numb. My mind gone blank. Though I'm standing in this circle of "friends," no one seems to notice that I'm there. The circle of people begins spinning, like an Impressionist painting of a merry-go-round, colorful shirts blurring, pulsating, bloating into strange shapes. I feel as if I'm going blind and turning invisible simultaneously. With the next wave of dizziness, I am about to fall when I right myself by reaching for my zipper. It's a gesture of epiphany. This will be my announcement that I'm here, my golden greeting, if you will. The group's eyes widen as I pull out my penis and proceed to pee right then and there on the forest of feet and legs before me, twirling my dick so its golden stream blooms in lasso-like circles.

"Hey, fucking DeSilver, put that thing away." "Yo, scumbag." "What the fuck, you loser." "Holy shit, that's so gross." "Who is that sick fuck?"

In that moment, my vision goes from double blurred to a pixilated hall of mirrors. Shame and embarrassment swoop in and envelop me, seep into my skin like a cold dew, as the crowd scatters and I stumble off into the bushes to throw up. I'm being poked and scratched and rejected by the bushes. I need out. Out of this skin, this body. I find myself crawling, seeking cover, a kind of embrace toward a stable surface that can orient me in space. There is the faint scent of oil and tar. The skin of my cheek is smushed into the pavement, pebbles imprinting on it. The warmth from the day's sun is almost soothing, yet not at all like a woman's face, rather a thousand times harder and a thousand miles farther away. I'm drifting into a nauseating void. And then I black out.

And just as suddenly, I'm torn awake, first by the excruciating roar of an engine, though it's so loud that I can't locate it. It's a swarm of vibration, so loud, in fact, that it feels as if it's coming from *inside* me—and it's magnified by the immense sensation of being trapped under a great metallic weight like the steel lid of a casket, or of being pinned to the tracks beneath a freight train. The panic is piercing. It's an instant of violent prickling over the entire length of my body. And then the pain cuts in, is searing and hot. It's my left leg, and it feels as if it might get torn off.

A ferocious scream issues not so much from *me* as from the molten core of middle earth, nothing less than a life-jarring howl. And it comes with a message: STOP THE FUCKING CAR. I'm under a car, Mike Castleton's rusty yellow Jetta, CSN blasting on the tape deck, Mike good and drunk and filled with lust for Deirdre whom he's just kissed as he's backing over me.

1

# The Clock Tower

I grew up in a clock tower with bats in the belfry. Bats in the bedroom, the drawing room, out on the loggia, hanging upside down gripped to a fold in the yellow dining room curtains, floating dead in the swimming pool. Bats in pieces on the front stoop, compliments of the cats. Bats hidden in my baseball mitt, clinging to the branches of my magnolia tree. Bats in the bathroom, the Blue Room, the boiler room, stuck to a thin brick in the chimney. Bats in the kitchen, filling up the windows and every last shadow—bats in the white spaces of Mom and Dad's eyes.

The house was actually called the Clock Tower. It said so on the metal plaque on the brick pillar by the front door, on the mailbox, and even on the door of the old Volvo station wagon in faded red Gothic lettering, as if we were an exclusive country club or remote English estate. This was the same Volvo that had perpetual flecks of confetti sprinkled between the seats (from a New Year's Eve party before my time) and a hole in the floor, and which caught fire one early morning on the way to school. This car was the locale of my earliest memory of Mom: me at four or five, falling asleep on her lap in the back seat after too many Shirley Temples at the Red Coach Grille, as Mom sang "When You Wish Upon a Star" and "Somewhere Over the Rainbow" to me. I was in heaven. I was, in fact, somewhere over the rainbow, floating through an endless sea of stars, being transported "way up high" into the vast space of bluebirds and lullabies, high above the chimney tops where my dreams would come true. Dreams of seeing and being seen, blurred dreams of color and light, voice and sound, a poetic vagueness of birds and trees and the endless sky that held them. Or perhaps, being a boy in America, they were dreams of being a hockey or baseball player, not so much for the game, but for the spectacle, the community, the script of players swirling about in a secret language across ice or field.

And this song was being sung into my tiny impressionable body, and I was soaking it in as I drifted off, caught in the safe, fantastic realms of my imagination. This is the place I would go to again and again in my life as refuge, as a safe haven of truth, where I dared to dream.

But that glorious feeling was soon squelched by the fact that as we pulled into the driveway I knew I would once again be turned over to Miss Hedy, our German governess. I would be torn from the space of rainbows and bluebirds, and my dreams would be crushed by the weight of this dark, alien creature and her smothering chubbiness, harsh commands, grating control, and eventual violence.

As I try and place my dad in this memory or even find a first, separate one for him, I go blank. There is no pivotal tell-all memory that arises in my mind. He was just kind of there, almost an apparition, a specter of fatherhood, a fleeting volley between presence and absence. Otherwise, I can see him stomping back to the base line on the tennis court after losing a shot, swearing at himself. I can see him munching on peanuts, Carr's Water Crackers and blue cheese during "drinks time" in the early evening, seated in his favorite purple chair in the library, martini in hand. Or staring into a glass of wine held up to the light at the dinner table with his thin graying hair, plaintive round face creased with curiosity and regret, his pudgy belly and skinny legs, his perfectly average height and build. There are visual clips, but no song, and very few words.

Mom and Dad's first child, Carlos, my ghost brother, died within minutes of his birth in 1963, after being strangled by the umbilical chord. Mom was devastated and bewildered, yet armed with plenty of cocktails and "ciggies," she persevered to successfully give birth to my sister Margaret in 1964, Serena in 1966, and me in 1968.

Dad, having grown up in Brooklyn and become an architect, was drawn to Connecticut because it seemed the ideal place to find architecturally unique and quiet properties on which to raise a new family. Just an hour north of New York City, New Canaan was still fairly rural in the sixties, with a number of farms and large estates. Philip Johnson, of the famous Glass House, and other innovative architects had built houses there. Eventually, Dad found an amazing Dutch Colonial white brick house called the Clock Tower, which had been built in 1900. The Clock Tower was an architectural anomaly in the neighborhood, so much so that it drew the attention of *House & Garden* magazine, which did a feature on it in the early seventies after Dad had designed and built two dramatic brick wings on each side of the tower.

The Clock Tower was a huge, white brick expanse with no windows in the front. The wings were solid white brick as well, with a series of three slightly recessed arches. The back was opened up by two-story porches on both sides. The roof was shaped like half of a giant stop sign. And there was, in fact, a huge clock on the front, with an interior bell in the center that didn't ring.

The Clock Tower sat on an enchanting property, with honeysuckle tangled atop the tennis court fence, great beds of roses along the nineteenth-century stone walls, and vast peony gardens next to the pool area. In front of the house was a huge open brick porch that stood like an island between the peony gardens and the driveway. It had waist-high walls and two openings at each end that you could walk through. The walls were topped with thick slate. This was my imaginary baseball diamond, and I had many a major World Series rally here, mostly between the Red Sox and Yankees. I loved to pitch like Catfish Hunter, his sidearm making the ball swerve like a rounded bird whose wings were secretly tucked into the ball's fiery stitches.

A recess cut halfway along the length of each wall acted as first and third bases. Home plate was the entrance, second base the exit behind me. Halfway up the front and back walls was a sloped edge of cement, which if hit just right with a fastball, would launch the ball into the air. I used Dad's bright yellow Slazenger tennis balls with the black cheetah imprinted on the side. These had the most rebound action. Phil Rizzuto's voice echoed in my head constantly, but especially when Reggie Jackson knocked one out of the park. Phil Rizzuto loved me, was constantly in awe of me, whether I was pitching as Catfish or batting as Reggie, he became my default cheerleader. I would play alone for hours, often going into extra innings. The sound of the crowd was always incredibly loud in my head, always focused on celebrating me and my heroic feats of athleticism. I would beam toward the imagined crowd, soaking in the attention, the adoration. At a certain point I carried the crowd around with me wherever I went. It was most vocal at my virtual baseball games, but I developed the habit of imagining the crowd with me at all times, always listening and cheering me on. It was like I was in a perpetual sitcom. I was like Alan Alda in *M*A*S*H* or John Ritter in *Three's Company*, who always had a crowd around them laughing and celebrating their every move. I would say something out loud to my sisters or a friend that I thought was either funny, irreverent, outrageous, or random—anything from telling my sisters, "fuck off sleezy heads," to sharing a joke with my best friend that I heard my mom tell: "So this terribly homely woman stumbles into the Ritz bar with a parrot on her shoulder and slurs, 'Anyone who can guess this parrot's weight can fuck me.' A gentleman sitting next to her replies, sarcastically 'uh,uh, 750 pounds?' 'Close enough,' says the woman." At which point I would snort softly, click my teeth, and swing my jaw from side to side, hearing a roar of laughter from "the crowd" in my head. No matter that my friend didn't laugh, looked at me blankly, and replied, "That's fucking stupid." This quietly aubible snort, jaw swing, and roar of laughter in my head became more and more pronounced to the point where a close friend once asked, "What are you doing there with that snort and teeth clicking?" I would flush slightly pink with embarrassment and say, "Nothing, what are you talking about, I was just laughing a little." It became a kind of tic, an unconscious response to imagined humor, or my response to an awkward or lonely moment that for me needed some company.

Another favorite spot on the property was the Dungeon. It was jail cell and playground for my sisters and me, our war zone and safe house. This stone ruin had long been abandoned. With high walls, separate rooms, and even a broken chimney, it extended above a low, dank garage on a small hill. Every autumn, my sisters and I filled it with fallen leaves from the surrounding maples, oaks, and elms. Then we would launch ourselves off the high walls, plunging into the deep leaf piles as if into a sea of crimson, gold, and tangerine. We would bury ourselves in the silence, softness, and sumptuous smell of dried and dying maple, musky oak, and grassy elm.

Climbing the trees around the Dungeon was perhaps my first addiction, or love, or perhaps first foray into poetry. I found reverie in the canopy. I saw a kind of script in the erratic reach of branches, a mysterious language that seemed to initiate a conversation with beauty. The higher I climbed, the more ethereal the light, the more distance between me and Miss Hedy, and the more distance from the distance between me and my parents. I was reaching for a glowing green kindness I saw among the leaves, perhaps an emotional vernacular in the flickering gauzy light that was like an eternal emerald bed I could be gathered up in and embraced by.

One of my favorite photographs from the Clock Tower is of Mom and me standing together on the back loggia with the Dungeon in the background. I'm about four or five. It's October, my birthday month. The trees are bare. I'm in blue corduroy floods, a Norwegian sweater, and red snap-over shoes. Mom is standing beside me, her long strawberry-blonde hair curling below her shoulders. She's wearing a brown blouse with a gigantic collar, red trousers, a thick belt with gold Hermès buckle, and a pair of white, strappy, high-heeled shoes. Mom's smile is tentative, distant. The neighbor's splotched collie is looking away through the railings. I'm holding Mom's hand, as if we're practicing holding hands, as if this is almost a new thing, or at least too rare a thing, and my slightly strained expression shows that all I want is to hold on forever, for dear life.

There were three floors in the Clock Tower. The first floor was the kid's realm, where we had a separate kitchen, a playroom, TV room, and all our bedrooms. The third floor housed two guest rooms, the Blue and Pink Rooms, and a small bathroom. Mom and Dad spent most of their time on the second floor, which was largely off limits to us kids and was the main front entrance to the house. The second floor had an elegant "drawing room" (separated from the grand entrance room by arched brick columns, which my mom loved to coil with pine boughs at Christmastime), which featured several sofas you were not allowed to sit on, unless you were an esteemed guest. There was a master bedroom and suite, a library, a bar/utility room, a living room, a dining room (complete with circling bats), and a full-sized kitchen with an eight-burner restaurant stove. My mother hosted fabulous parties in the drawing room, for which she would dress my sisters in Laura Ashley dresses, and me early on in a sailor suit, and later in an oversized Brooks Brothers suit. She paraded us around as if we were showpieces, making us pass hors d'oeuvres of pâté and puréed broccoli on white toasts with the crusts cut off.

"Now, look Mr. Cadbury in the eye and grab five," Mom would insist, shoving me abruptly into Mr. Cadbury's personal space.

"Hi," I'd say shyly.

"No, no, love, it's 'How do you do, Mr. Cadbury? How perfectly delightful to meet you!'"

"Hello," I'd repeat awkwardly.

And on it went for hours, late into the night, with Mrs. Druxbury, Mr. Stoddard, Cousin Rupert, and Aunt Louisa, and always Mr. and Mrs. Nutcake. Whenever Mom couldn't remember someone's name in the moment, and after several martinis, she would say, "Now, Albert, you remember Mr. and Mrs. Nutcake." She presented all these people as if they were great luminaries of industry and culture, gods of extreme importance and consequence, and the message was *you want to be like them, you want to beam with substance and significance.*

Mom, who relished the opportunity to call herself a "recovering Catholic," was surprisingly fanatical about the Christmas decorations complete with angels, baby Jesus, and nativity scenes. Maybe it didn't matter the holiday, what mattered was the celebration and chance to lavishly decorate. She even set out a crèche on the dining room sideboard surrounded by pine cones and red and green ribbon. When anyone commented she'd reply in her best New York Jewish accent, "What's the sound a Hanukkah bush makes when it falls to the ground? (silence) A Crèche."

The grand entrance room housed a twenty-foot-plus Christmas tree. To me, it looked bigger than the one they hoisted up with a crane at Rockefeller Center every year. Finding the right tree and having it delivered and properly placed was always a "shitstorm," as Mom liked to say, because Dad would stumble around wrestling and cursing "the goddamn sonofabitch tree," allthewhile banging up the front door and scratching the floors. He eventually installed a pulley system so the tree could be raised up with help from Pasquale, the gardener. There it stood, bare and tall, until a random night a couple of weeks before Christmas, when we would all gather and open the huge boxes of ornaments my mom had collected for years.

Decorating the tree was always nerve-wracking, as Mom was sure we'd drop and break her favorite glass reindeer, which she had bought in Paris twenty years before. "Keep this away from those fucking cats, they've already smashed eighty-seven of my most precious ornaments," she'd say, reluctantly handing me an enormous Space Age silver ball dusted with green sparkles and indented with a crazy pink and orange chasm of ripples that would break my reflection into strange shapes. The cats loved to bat these off the tree, and took advantage of the fact my sisters and I were too short to reach very high. Sometimes, after hundreds of ornaments had been placed, lights draped, and tinsel woven in, the cats would even climb the tree. Then Dad would freak out and take a broom to the cats, who would skitter out from under the tree, hissing and trailing scarves of tinsel around their necks or with a mouse ornament dressed as Santa Claus in their maw, glass ornaments shattering in the mayhem.

One of my favorite spots in the Clock Tower was the large utility room upstairs just off the library. One of the reasons I loved this room was the bright whiteness of it, the way it beamed in contrast to the darkness of the rest of the house, and the fact that at Christmastime it doubled as Santa's Workshop. A week before Christmas every year, this room was off limits, with a scrap-of-paper sign crookedly taped to the door that said, "Do not enter/Santa's Workshop" in my mom's lasso-tangled handwriting. For much of the year, the corners were piled with tubes of wrapping paper and baskets of multicolored ribbon. The rest of the time it was the bar.

I can still remember the piercing scent of lemon peels trapped in the sink from my parents' multiple evening martinis. The little square stainless steel bar sink was perpetually crammed with them. There was always a small collection of haphazardly peeled lemons in the fridge, like the preserved heads of some badly scarred family of rodents—they were always the first thing to greet you when you opened the fridge door.

The utility room/bar had white walls, white cabinets, and white counters, with a skylight tucked into the ceiling. It was cluttered on one side with liquor bottles and cases of wine, and on the other with junk, paper bags, ribbon, tools, fabric, and magazines. Every night, my parents went to the side with all the bottles and clinked around a lot and came out drinking things, adult things. This room was a great mystery to me at the time. It appeared as some kind of laboratory where magical potions were made. Perhaps these potions could give you some kind of special powers.

Mom and Dad often traveled to Europe to visit friends and for leisurely vacations, mostly together, but I also remember Mom traveling to Africa alone on a couple of occasions. It was always unclear why she went and never took Dad. There was talk of visiting friends spending time with "The Hemingways," whoever they were. When my parents were home, they spent much of their time "upstairs." It was a rare evening that we would all gather for dinner as a family in the poorly-lit upstairs dining room, which was usually reserved for Mom's "smart parties." But this did happen occasionally.

We were finally all gathered together on a sticky, cricket-drenched night in July—Mom and Dad, my two sisters, Margaret and Serena, and me. I was all of five or six. Miss Hedy, the governess, was either away or sequestered in her quarters downstairs. Suddenly, Dad leapt up out of his chair and shouted, "Oh for Pete's sake, it's the goddamn bats again!"

Tennis racket in hand, as if it were a bow and arrow or a gun, he was off and running, his eye fixed on a small fruit bat that had flown down from the tower and was circling erratically.

"Albert! Watch out—duck!" he shouted, rushing over to me and swatting. It was an overhead serve, à la Bjorn Borg. I scrunched into a ball, shutting my eyes tight surrendering to the dark behind my eyes and a searing burst of fear, and prepared for the blow. I felt the wind slightly ruffle the hair on the very top of my head. My sisters shrieked. "Look out, girls!" Dad roared, as his backhand took out Mom's favorite candlestick holders on the antique sideboard.

"Harrison, the silver, for Christ's sake!" Mom shrieked, clearly alarmed. *Smash!* Candlesticks knocked to the floor, candles broken in half, flame out, leaving a ribbon of smoke I followed with my eyes until it disappeared.

"C'mere, you son of a bitch," Dad mumbled, bouncing off the walls, a little drunk. Mom shifted uneasily in her chair. A wash of Rive Gauche perfume blending with the scent of cold ham and asparagus wafted from my plate. Mom's perfume was the perfume of parties, of traveling, of leaving the house. It was the smell of distance.

"Open the porch door, would you, Margaret?" Dad said, motioning to my oldest sister, who cautiously crawled over the parquet floor as if wiggling though a minefield and pushed the door open with her foot. Another bat swooped in.

"Oh Jesus, now look what you've done. Goddamn it!" My sister slumped back in her chair, and I could just barely see her eyes, filled with guilt and alarm. This was where I'd been hiding ever since bat No. 1 had made its appearance. Missing by a mile with every swing, Dad finally collapsed back in his own chair and poured Mom and himself another glass of wine from their second bottle.

"Okay, then, I guess bats are us," Dad exclaimed, with resignation and fatigue in his voice. He had lost another tennis match, this time to a pair of bats.

We found dead bats everywhere around our property, dead from old age, dead, from banging into a chandelier, dead from getting swatted out of the sky by my barbaric black cat, Snowy. Early one hazy hot August morning when I was six or seven, I was wandering around alone outside along the brick porch beneath the loggia, when I noticed one of these dried and desiccated bats. Normally, I wouldn't have thought much about it, but as I walked by I heard it peep. This bat was clearly dead—dried and stiffened by days of exposure to the sun, with even a few ants crawling around it. It peeped again. The closer I got, the louder the peeping. Though spooked and perplexed, I was curious enough to grab a stick and poke at the carcass. It scraped against the brick like a thick dried leaf. More peeping. Finally I flipped it over, and there, clinging ever so tenderly to its dead mother's breast, was a baby bat crying out for help. Not able to see what else to do, I left it there in the blazing sun, vulnerable and alone to fend for itself.

## 2

# Das Hell Frau

Stern, dour, controlling, and fat, Miss Hedy was our Swiss-German governess from Zurich, and there from the very beginning. She was probably fifty-something when I was born. Mom and Dad were referred to her "from a friend." I'm sure they got references and did a comprehensive background check. I imagined they found her waddling around down by the Stamford train station gripping onto her large plastic shopping bags, looking lost and bewildered, and for a job with a nice suburban family. I imagined Mom and Dad cruising by in their Mercedes, and as they saw her, thought, "Oh, hey, now there's a nice looking lady, perhaps she could help with the kids." They pull up asking if she needs any help, and she says, "I unt a governess, looking for verk."

"Oh, terrific, we're new parents looking for help with our kids, jump in."

Atop her plump, fleshy head was a mash of gray curls, like what you might find while sweeping up at a charnel ground. She wore a starched, ribbed, white nanny suit, and often dark brown nylon "socks" that rolled up just slightly below her knees. I can remember all too clearly her pressing me into her gargantuan breasts to give me a hug, her ribbed suit imprinting striations into my cheek like a metal grate.

Miss Hedy spoke in a heavy, accented monotone, except when she was yelling at us, which was often, at which point her voice would turn to a harsh metallic growl. "Take zeiss bull cap uff ver head in da house!" she'd snap, swiping my prized Red Sox hat right off my head. The highly coveted one that Grampy brought me straight from the head of Rick Burleson at Fenway Park. Or, if we left a loaf of bread out or a box of cereal on the counter: "Don't put me the food here down, odderwize da mouse is on." Apparently, when my sisters were being potty trained, Miss Hedy would bring my mother the potty training pan for an update and say, "Today she make me tinkle, tomorrow she make me poo."

My sisters and I had pretty foul mouths growing up, having listened to Mom tell outrageous jokes sprinkled with expletives at the dinner table and at her lavish parties. Miss Hedy didn't approve, and so when *shit* and *fuck* inevitably came bursting from our mouths, she would sputter furiously in her German accent, "Veel hav nussing from fuck and stop me vit the shit!" After nursing our smacked heads, we would roll with laughter, making fun of her butchered phrases.

Miss Hedy was fanatical about cleanliness. Everything needed to be disinfected daily. She practically wore a can of Lysol spray on her hip in a holster. She never knew when a stray germ might appear out of nowhere. Seeing us as poorly raised, if not altogether abandoned, Miss Hedy set out to fix us unruly kids, and to control us at all costs.

She also started in on the cats. She had it in for my black cat, Snowy, who had bladder issues and would often pee in the house. One day, Snowy peed in my sister's closet, and when Miss Hedy got wind of it, she angrily snatched up the cat, which yowled and clawed at her, then ran it to my sister's closet and forcefully rubbed the cat's face in its own mess. However, between the time the cat had peed and Miss Hedy had heard about it, my father had already poured a pool of super-concentrated extra-strength Lysol cleaner on the spot. The cat screeched, clawed, squirmed, and ran off to hide for days. When she finally came out, she was gravely ill, all the hair on her face and neck was burned off, and she had a gravelly, hacking cough that lasted for years. I can still hear that scratchy, elongated cough echoing in my head like a death rattle.

We humans weren't treated much better. Miss Hedy loved bath time, the opportunity to scrub us "dirty-mouthed" children clean from the outside in. She'd drop me in scalding hot bathwater like some kind of impervious crustacean, and no matter how many tears of resistance there were, she would start scrubbing with brushes and loofahs and all manner of grating tools. She was big on scrubbing under my fingernails with a baby blue plastic brush until my fingertips were bright pink and bleeding. She left no body part unscrubbed or unscalded.

Once when I was five and left my favorite brown and yellow honeybee shirt and red swim trunks in the bathroom, she came at me in a maelstrom of rage. "Vass is dees leavink clothes as mess in da batroom? Zee go in hamper, here!" And with that she dragged me by the ear screaming into the laundry room. I wailed in response and swatted at her, begging her to leave me alone. She retaliated by grabbing my arm and smacking me upside the head repeatedly. "You von't talk back to me, ever, ever again! Shame, shame on you—you von't come out vuntil I say!" she yelled, between pursed lips and tightened jaw, as she dragged me across the hall by my hair, threw me into my room and slammed the door. I laid in my bed face-down in my Bozo the Clown pillow, watching the weird pink flames of his hair redden with my tears, trying to elicit some sympathy or response. He just looked away into some unknown distance, smiling his hollow toothless smile as I waited for Mom and Dad to appear, to tell me it would be all right, to save me from Miss Hedy. They never showed up.

One day when I was around seven, I found myself sitting alone in my favorite dirt patch beneath the ratty sprawling rosebush, just off the driveway. It was a little after dawn, late August, the air fairly cool and dry after the previous day's rain. The roses had long before bloomed and died, and their curled brown petals were arranged in funny piles by the wind. They looked like small, partially torched pieces of paper on which a short note-to-self might have been written. I was staring into the thick trunks of the rosebush, which were studded with large thorns spaced nicely apart, like the teeth of a goofy alligator. Some of the thorns were bright green, some brown and brittle, ready to break free of the stalk.

I was lazily running my hands through the dirt, fingering the grains and pebbles. A collection of dusty, wrecked Hot Wheels sat in a heap nearby. They didn't interest me in the moment, as I was busy having a mindless sensory experience with my hands. The time dragged on, the light bloomed. I almost hoped one of my sisters would appear at any moment. They didn't. Perhaps Dad? Nope. The friendly garbage man? Oh yeah, it was Sunday. A wave of loneliness spilled in, sloshed around, got absorbed. Soon I found a favorite pebble, a kind of friend who would listen to me, and I to it. It wasn't even a real pebble, more like a piece of black asphalt, but it was dark and round and rugged, and it felt somehow alive between my small, tender fingers. I liked the uniformity, the predictability, how it rolled easily between thumb and forefinger.

The silence this time of morning was deafening. A good sound could keep me company, but even the birds seemed distant and far away. I reached up and placed the pebble gently in my left ear. Perhaps it would act as a hearing aid, bringing the birdsong, the crickets, my sister's voices closer to me. But it had the opposite effect, which was actually more soothing. It dampened the world, silenced the silence, amplified the solitude, brought me gently inward. I fiddled with my new earwear as if arranging a puzzle piece, and tweaked it a bit so it would click more perfectly in place. It did. It was now lodged firmly in place. A wave of panic sank in, and I reached in to pull it out. No luck. I found I couldn't get a grip, and the more I tried, the deeper it sank. Wow, now it was completely stuck.

I stood up and began pounding the opposite side of my head the way I did after a big swim at Kiwanis Lake when the water had swirled deep inside my ear. I pounded and shook and stomped up and down with my head tilted until it felt as if my brains would spill out, but the pebble was fixed, cemented in place. My mounting panic wasn't so much from injury as it was from fear of consequences.

I snuck back to the house and in through the outside door of the bathroom. No one was up. I looked in the mirror and was alarmed by the grave look on my face. I scrunched my ear around a bit, trying to tilt my head just so to get a better look. I couldn't see anything. I climbed the blue stool, hovering above the sink in a dizzying panic over what I'd done. I fingered around until my ear started to ache. I worried. Finally, Serena came to the door. I was half relieved and half troubled, as I knew I would be found out. By Miss Hedy. I started shaking. Then told her right away, "I have a pebble in my ear," and she laughed.

"How did you do that?"

"I don't know, I was bored." She laughed again.

"It hurts!" I told her. She tried to peer in, but could only see a dark blob.

She ran out and met Miss Hedy in the hallway, promptly shouting, "Albert has a rock in his head!"

Miss Hedy rushed in. "Vuss is dees rock in hed?" She was dressed in a nightgown and smelled musty, her hair pinned down flat to her head. She looked sleepy and somewhat vulnerable, less of a brute. Hesitating a bit, I told her. She immediately became agitated and started rifling through drawers to find the exact right implement to try and extract the pebble. I half expected her to pull out a chainsaw. She came up with tweezers that were too short and sharp, but started prodding around in her familiarly aggressive manner anyway. The pain kicked in, and my ear started to bleed. She was determined and dug deeper. I screamed. She tried another implement and drove the pebble further into my ear canal. It was not until the blood began trickling substantially down my neck and after my screaming and whimpering pleas started to affect her own ears that she finally gave up and we went to the doctor.

The doctor took one look and said, "This needs to be surgically removed!" I was in the hospital for three days. When I woke up pebble-free after the surgery, I remember being led down the hallway in an anesthetic daze by a sweet nurse. I was hallucinating wildly: visions of peonies and roses in pulsating blotches bloomed and dissolved across the halls and floor. Albeit bewildered, I was mesmerized and enchanted by an alternate experience, or reality, one that could soothe me from a growing alienation and unpredictable rage. When the nurse asked me how I felt, I said, "Fine! Look at all the beautiful flowers!"

Around this time, my cousins came to visit for the first time from Paris. Mom's sister Barbara had three boys: Johnny, who was Margaret's age; Nicky, Serena's age; and Andreas, or Bundini, as he was affectionately known, my age. Uncle Tristan and Aunt Barbara had taken the boys first to Boston to see Grampy, a Red Sox fanatic. Grampy took them to a ball game at Fenway Park, home of the great "Green Monster," the famous high wall in center field. It was bat day, the boys were ecstatic, and each got his own twenty-inch replica bat, complete with Red Sox insignia and top player signatures.

At the Clock Tower, my sisters and I were excited to see our cousins and planned to stay up late hearing about the big game, as well as their adventures in Paris. The adults were off to a party for the night. The boys were to sleep upstairs in the Blue Room, which was right next to the Pink Room on the ever-mysterious cobwebby third floor. These rooms were in the heart of the tower, complete with all the dusty clock machinery, low ceilings, peeling paint, creaky floorboards, small dirty windows, cobwebs, and of course lots of bats. Whenever I read Poe or Kafka, I think of the Blue Room. There easily could have been a raven permanently perched on the windowsill of the room, and I wouldn't have been surprised if Miss Hedy had buried some neighbor kid under the floorboards. It was a great place for ghosts.

Miss Hedy was in charge that night and on foot patrol, making sure we were in bed by 8:30. The cousins were ready to play and hang out. They weren't afraid of Miss Hedy and her rules. My sisters and I, on the other hand, knew better, and were terrified, yet our childlike desire for adventure and play quickly outweighed the fear. So after we were sent to bed, Johnny and the boys came to our bedrooms on tiptoe, whispering and giggling. There was lots of shushing and "Oh, come on!" as they lured us up to the Blue Room. Margaret was particularly hesitant, but Johnny insisted, and up we went.

It wasn't but a few minutes into an epic pillow fight that we heard the footsteps, each thump inspiring an incision of terror in my belly. And then the wrathful yelling. "Vass is diss I hear upstairs?" I jumped into the closet beneath piles of my cousins' musty trousers smelling of French cologne and jet fuel. Between the sound of her voice and the thickness of the closet dark, I felt like I was descending into a pit of boiling black tar. Margaret and Serena slipped under the bed as if sucked under by a gigantic vacuum cleaner, completely oblivious to the potential for spiders and bats. Johnny, Nicky, and Andreas continued to play and giggle. They figured it was a game. Johnny ran to the door as Miss Hedy stammered up the stairs, wheezing.

"Vas are you doing in dare? It's bedtime now—you vill get back to bed immediately!" she bellowed.

Just as I heard the hand on the doorknob, Nicky screamed, "Lock it, quick!" Johnny pushed in the handle.

Miss Hedy started pounding on the door. "You vill open zees door right now or I vill call zee police!" She yelled against the wood, her angry breath about to burn a hole right through the door. Johnny hesitated for a second or two and then I heard the door open. Miss Hedy burst through the door, pinning Johnny behind it, and beelined straight for Nicky, who at this point was sitting on the bed in front of her. She started immediately smacking him with both hands, saying over and over, "You are a very bad boy, shame on you!"

Johnny jumped to his brother's defense, grabbed the nearest Red Sox commemorative baseball bat, and started batting at Miss Hedy, screaming, "Get off my brother, you scary hag!" She backed away, visibly startled and disturbed, shaking her finger violently.

"I vill be back to get yoo, I vam not stoopit," she spit as she stammered back toward the staircase.

Johnny yelled back at her, "Oh yes, you are!" and slammed the door, locking it for good this time.

There was another time Mom and Dad were out at a dinner party when my sisters and I had some neighbor kids over and we stayed up later than normal in the drawing room getting a bit rowdy. After a fiery request or two, Miss Hedy ordered everyone downstairs "for zee last time," then caught and dragged my sisters into the upstairs coat closet, locking them in with a chair while she rustled up the rest of the strays. I tore off and hid in the boiler room.

Filled with more cobwebs than a Halloween window display down at Brezlow's variety store, the boiler room was dank and ominously lit by a weak and flickering single naked bulb. It was cold to the bone, echoing with metallic creaking sounds and teeming with centipedes and spiders. I tried to distract myself by dreaming of the rows of Butterfingers, stacks of Bubble Yum, the forests of candy sticks at Brezlow's counter. And yet before me were brick walls coated in soot, a cement floor littered with bat and mouse turds. Somehow, in that moment, the boiler room felt cozy and safe compared to a black, locked closet. I crouched in the corner shivering, as I heard Miss Hedy calling out after me, yelling in a withering German whine, akin to the straining engine of an old Mercedes, the V's and Z's of her accent whizzing by like sharp arrows pinning the terror to my heart. Something about how she was going to tell Mr. and Mrs. DeSilver how terribly behaved we were. She left my sisters locked in the closet weeping for a couple of hours until just before Mom and Dad returned home.

I'm not sure if it was from the incident with my cousins or another Miss Hedy run-in, but my dad confronted me one day in the downstairs hallway made of dingy yellowy-white brick, demanding I pick up some mess in the playroom I may or may not have even made. I squirmed, blamed my sisters, and then he brought up how we had been giving Miss Hedy a hard time lately, which I denied, then called her some hateful name. "Don't you dare say that about Miss Hedy, goddamnit." I started wailing and tried to make a run for my room when he grabbed my right arm and pulled me into the corner of the hallway. With his free hand he started unbuckling his belt saying, "Stop being so fucking intransigent. ...Is this what you need to behave?" He slipped the belt out of the loops with a thick hissing sound, pulled his arm back and froze for a second as if cast in stone. "Go to your goddamn room, NOW!" Hunched in a terror-chilled ball, I braced myself for the blow, felt no contact and my arm drop free. Then, as if electrocuted, I sprang to my feet, ran down the hall crying, blasted into my room and pounced onto my ever-absorbent Bozo pillow. I asked Bozo why the adults were yelling all the time. Bozo just looked away and smiled.

I was amazed by Johnny's courage. The thought of physically fighting back against any adult, but especially Miss Hedy, was unimaginable. She was too brutal a force, and inspired too much fear. To see Johnny fight back was to have some slight sense of oppositional power emerging— the possibility of good triumphing over evil—something beyond mere cowering and obedience, which were my default responses.

* * *

A couple of years later, Miss Hedy was abruptly fired after she and Dad disagreed one too many times about how to raise children. My sister Margaret, thirteen or fourteen at the time, remembers Dad standing at the top of the main staircase at the Clock Tower yelling down at Miss Hedy, and she, in turn, yelling up at him. This steep, dark staircase was the setting for many of my nightmares as a kid, especially my dreams of falling, where I perpetually tumbled into a hellish tangle of flames, a snake pit, or a sweaty pile of crocodiles. "Don't tell me vow to do my job, dees children unt *my* children, you von't spend not any time mit dem," screamed Miss Hedy.

"Don't tell me how to raise my kids, goddamn it, and for the last time, these are my goddamn kids and I'll spend plenty of time with them from now on, because you're fucking fired!" roared Dad.

And with that exchange, poof, she vanished. One day she was there and the next, not. I think Mom and Dad told us she went on a trip back to Switzerland to see her sister and then just never came back.

All I know is the vacuum it left for all of us was bewildering. I didn't realize until she was gone how much of a sense of order her presence had provided. There were times when she could be somewhat caring and protective, almost affectionate, and then suddenly turn nasty and domineering again, so that when she left, there was a mix of relief and, if not sadness, then a melancholy confusion. And it wasn't as if Mom or Dad suddenly jumped in to fill the void.

A few years after Miss Hedy was fired, in 1983 or 1984, Mom and Dad proposed a ski trip to see Cousin Plop in Verbier, Switzerland. Margaret and I were excited, being avid skiers at the time. Serena opted out of this trip, and for good reason, as my parents insisted that we visit Miss Hedy and her sister for lunch in Bern.

The hotel had a grim, almost haunted look to it, dimly lit by wall sconces flickering against dark wood paneling and black tablecloths. There were bleak, dingy windows looking out onto the main square, which featured a fountain with a bronze figure atop a rearing horse. Because of the distorted old window glass, the figure looked twisted, as if he had just been shot and was just about to fall off his horse. This is how I felt sitting opposite Miss Hedy and her sister: frozen in a state of agonizing discomfort, ready to drop dead.

Miss Hedy and her sister sat side by side, looking like a pair of mean albino elephants in their oversized, starched, white nanny suits, with napkins roach-clipped to their collars. They both had slight mustaches. A little shaving off the outer edges would have made them look like female twin versions of Hitler, I thought. Were they twins? Twice the wrath. Was her sister assigned to the torture of some other family, God knows where? Miss Hedy's sister didn't speak English, so we just exchanged fake smiles and uncomfortable head bobbing. Otherwise, what did we talk about over bratwurst and pickled cabbage?

The only other thing I remember of that lunch is Mom falling in love with the giant glass ashtray the waiter had brought, and how after lunch she ever so casually slipped it into her purse. I had never thought of Mom as a thief. But there she was, cheerfully snagging an elegant glass ashtray with the words "Hotel Bern" printed on its side.

Thinking back on it now, it's incomprehensible to me why my parents would subject us to such a visit. Could they have been that oblivious? Did they honestly feel such regard for and obligation toward Miss Hedy? Or was it guilt at having fired her just a few years earlier?

Wherever she lived, Mom has always kept dozens and dozens of photographs perched on every conceivable surface, all in different styles of frame. I had grown up with some of the classics: the color photo of Margaret in a pink T-shirt and bright green shorts, her freckled face beaming as she sprawls on the polished deck of a Sunfish sailboat in the Bahamas, circa 1976. In a tortoise shell frame, a faded and curled head shot of me at five, with a bowl haircut and wearing a yellow and brown striped polo shirt. In an elegant sterling silver frame, there's Mom in black and white "in olden times," as she used to say, wearing a flowing white ball gown at a coming-out party in Boston around 1950. There's the faded and cracked black and white picture, framed in carved wood, of Grandma Margaret and Carlo Tresca, the famous labor organizer and anarchist, at her house in Brooklyn. And the highly coveted black and white of Mom's dad, Grampy, and Rosemary, his second wife, in the mid-sixties, just before church, no doubt, standing upright and looking debonair yet restrained. He's wearing a parade hat and an ascot with a dark suit; she, a proper, plain dress. The thing I remember most about Rosemary is that she once asked my mom how she was able to get the water on the stove to "boil like that." She wasn't much of a cook.

The placement of the photos followed a hierarchy, even at her condo and last residence, beginning with her bedroom and walk-in closet, followed by her bathroom, the living room, and finally what she loved to call the drawing room, AKA the den. Atop the most coveted location, the dresser of her walk-in closet, she prominently displayed next to some of her other highly prized photos, an elegantly silver-framed, full-sized 8x10 photo of Miss Hedy. She's standing alone next to a fountain, presumably in Zurich or Bern. She's wearing a round governess-looking black cap, and a formal, almost military-looking black suit. She's standing tall and proud, and smiling. Mom might have even taken this picture.

For the life of me, I couldn't fathom why Mom would display a photo of such an evil woman in such a sacred place on her dresser. That is, until my sister insightfully reminded me what a prized possession Miss Hedy truly was to Mom. Having a governess imparted an extraordinary level of social status in Mom's eyes. Miss Hedy was Mom's ticket to success, a sign that she was a member of the upper class. In those days, only the most socially refined and elite people had a governess, and having one was of utmost importance to her, no matter the repercussions.

# 3

# Aggravated F-ing Meatheads

"I want to play," I whined to my sisters one day back when Miss Hedy was still around, and I was about seven and they were nine and eleven. They were putting on the prized spacesuits Mom and Dad had brought back for us from one of their trips to Europe. They were excitedly gearing up for a scene from *Star Trek*, suburban style.

"Sorry, Albert. There isn't a suit for you."

"Yeah, there is. I know Mom got me one, too."

"No, she didn't. She only got them for Margaret and me."

"Yeah, she did. You guys took my suit! Where is it?"

I reached out to grab one of the suits.

"Don't fucking touch that," Margaret snapped.

" 'Don't fucking touch that'—naaa naa naa naaa, naaa," I mocked.

"Go away," they said simultaneously in their best disgusted tones, "or I'm going to tell Miss Hedy on you."

"I dare you!"

"Miss Hedddyyyyy!" Margaret started screaming half-heartedly as she slipped on her helmet and suit. They continued to ignore me and went on planning their adventure. I reached out and grabbed one of their space guns. Serena grabbed my arm, digging her nails into my skin to make me let go.

"Let go, you bitch," I screamed. Margaret jumped in and swatted at me.

"Albert, let go, you spoiled brat," Serena said, cutting into my arm with her nails.

"Owwwwwwww! That hurts, you bitch!"

I dropped the gun and ran off crying, stumbling down to the brick path behind the house. In an instant, I looked down and noticed a loose brick turned a bit in the sand, just asking to be picked up. I felt my hand throbbing against the brick, the words "Black's Brick Co." imprinting itself into my angry palm. I rushed back in a blind rage to where my sisters were playing. Rounding the corner, I heard their voices as if underwater, while inside I could hear my heart blasting against my chest, and everything went into a blurry slow motion. I aimed at Margaret, because she was closest and her back was turned. I launched the brick into the air, hitting her in the side of the head. Down she went with a light thud in the grass. I gazed in shock as she screamed and cried and threw her helmet at me. She was fine.

Another time, I chased after Margaret with a heavy red milk crate. "Heavenly Farms" read the faded white lettering on the side, blurring before my eyes as she dove into her bedroom to escape my wrath, and slammed the door just as the corner of the crate came down, smashing a huge reverse pyramid divot into the center of the door. My bright white knuckles were stuck in the tight matrix of the red crate, my hands glowing with rage as if trapped in a giant brittle spiderweb made of frozen blood.

Once when Serena drove me into a violent rage, for God knows what reason, I chased her out of the house with a giant butcher knife, raving like a devil child, screaming, "I'm going to kill you, you fucking bitch!" She tore through the backyard far out of reach, as I blindly hurled the weighty knife into oblivion, missing her by a considerable distance. The knife spun wildly like a helicopter with liquid blades, and then stuck in the grass at an extreme angle, vibrating. At that moment, had I rushed up to the knife to retrieve my weapon and try again, I would have seen my manic, buzzing tear-striped face twitching demonically in the murky blade. But I ran in the other direction, frightened by my own loss of control and my own rage-drunk power, knowing instantly that the knife and I should be as far away from one another as possible.

I was always severely punished for these extreme outbursts. Miss Hedy would swat and spank me, and then throw me in my room like an unruly zoo animal, where I would sulk behind my slammed bedroom door for hours. Mom never got involved, and Dad seldom did, but when he did, he always seemed more upset by being interrupted than by what I had done, and he had little interest in what was actually troubling me, or else he was just too oblivious to ask. I was terrified of adults at this point, yet subconsciously craved their attention and care. I wanted so desperately to be acknowledged and to exist in their eyes, and it only seemed to happen during a dramatic violent outburst to the point where that became my cue for how to get seen. It was somehow worth all the punishment and negative response, because without it, there was just a cold, empty void.

\* \* \*

I hated J.T., and yet he was my best friend growing up. Or more like my default best friend, because he was a convenient neighbor always up for playing. He was adventurous and willing, and always around. He lived down the street from the Clock Tower, in an out of place modest ranch house with a spacious front yard. Mom found him obnoxious and full of himself and his parents "common" and "lower class," even though they lived on our street, which was pretty upscale. J.T. was thick and beefy, with jet-black hair, brown eyes, big strong teeth, a chunky neck, and a large smile. He was always bragging and boasting, always brazenly confident beyond his years. The adults saw right through him, but I thought he was cool even when he treated me badly, telling me I swung like a girl when we played whiffle ball, never letting me shoot his BB gun when we went to the nature center to shoot frogs, never buying me Pop Rocks at the store when he had extra money and I didn't. He loved to keep tabs on how often his mom made us lunch and how my mom never did. I had a hard time explaining that she didn't like him, and wasn't much for making lunch in the first place. Sometimes Miss Hedy would make us lunch, but usually she would scare J.T. off with her liverwurst sandwiches.

He was big for his age, and more physically mature than the rest of us boys. He was always "better" than me in every way: stronger, faster, taller, even hairier (which meant a lot right around puberty). Mr. J.T. was the VP at some furniture giant, and Mrs. J.T was an embittered social-climbing housewife who got caught on the broken lower rungs of the ladder to suburban bliss. Both of his parents were in a constant state of anger, always yelling at J.T. to pick up his room, do his chores, get in the car already, do this, don't do that. They might have been born angry, but they seemed extremely frustrated by their circumstances and the general lack of control they were able to impose on the world and their children in particular. But at least they were around.

I liked to hang out at J.T.'s because his mom would always make us lunch, and drive us to school, to the nature center, or the Winter Club to go skating. My mom never drove us anywhere. Even though we played together all the time and Mr. J.T. knew my sisters perfectly well, we always got yelled at for cutting though their yard on the way to the nature center. They had a giant front lawn, and every weekend Mr. J.T. would be out there bouncing around on his fancy red tractor/mower in his undershirt with his toupee flapping up and down on his prematurely balding head. Whenever I was over at J.T.'s house for lunch (PB&J on Wonder Bread), Mrs. J.T. was always banging around in the kitchen in a fit of rage about something going on with her kids, who were making her "so aggravated." That was her favorite word: *aggravated*. She used to drive like a madwoman, late to pick up J.T.'s sisters at their after-school program—tearing through the windy back roads of New Canaan in their chocolate brown Ford Country Squire, muttering under her breath—"You fucking kids make me so *aggravated.*"

Eventually, by the time we were in high school in the mid-eighties, J.T.'s parents divorced and his mom became a serious alcoholic. I remember going over for a visit one Christmas morning, and she was already passed out drunk on the couch at 11 A.M. after drinking one too many Scotch and lemonades. I was only mildly embarrassed for J.T., as I could almost see my mom doing the same thing, although no matter how much my mom drank, she thought passing out was "very lower class." Stinking obnoxious drunk was fine, as long as you came off as witty and refined; passing out was tacky, very "non-U," as Mom would phrase it.

It seemed as if all the adults in our neighborhood were always yelling. J.T. and I spent much of our childhood in the mid- to late-seventies either buried in leaf piles or in closets crammed with pillows, first playing hide-and-seek, then spin-the-bottle and giving each other hand jobs by the time we hit puberty in the early eighties. Soon after that, we were actually kissing girls, and simultaneously being introduced to the numbing wonders of drinking and smoking cigarettes and pot—all to escape the wrath of the constantly yelling adults in our lives.

J.T. lived behind the nature center, and we grew up ice skating in the winter, fishing in the summer, riding bikes in the fall, and shooting bullfrogs in the spring. J.T.'s dad bought him a BB gun in the fourth or fifth grade, and we loved to go out shooting in the nature center, avoiding "Ranger Rick," who rightly would have punished us severely for harming the wildlife. J.T. was the first to get everything. The first to get a "Johnny Bench Batter Up" T-ball stand, the first screen TV, the first BB gun, the first dead bullfrog.

With a gun in our hands, we had the power of destruction. This was an outlet for all the growing pent-up energy of sadness and confusion that went largely unexpressed. It helped to fuel a destructive fire. I began to fall in love with the sound of shattering glass. In the summertime, baseballs were constantly breaking windows in our respective houses, which always threw the adults into a yelling frenzy. The more they yelled, the more we wanted to break stuff. We used to throw dirt bombs at the huge brick façade of the Clock Tower, just to watch the tiny brown explosions against the white brick. We eventually broke all the outside glass lamps.

It was 1978, and I can still see my mother in her yellow T-shirt, Kelly green floral Lilly Pulitzer skirt, and pink espadrilles, swinging open the huge wooden front door and yelling "What the hell are you doing, you fucking meatheads!" as we ducked behind a thick peony bush in the garden. We smashed the Erickson's elegant welcome sign at the end of their long gravel driveway; we smashed the big huge rainbow-colored Christmas bulbs my dad left on the lone pine out in front of the Clock Tower for months after Christmas. They made an exquisite popping sound on the asphalt, not unlike a shotgun going off.

After J.T. got a BB gun, I had to have one. I begged my dad and he resisted, then refused, then resisted again, and then broke down and gave in to my constant badgering. I can still feel the weight of that first squat carton of BBs in my palm. It was exactly the same shape and size as the milk cartons they served at school. The BBs were shiny orange copper pellets, and they felt good rolling around between my fingers, almost like spherical little coins.

I started shooting cans and bottles, sometimes breaking a bottle but not quite shattering it, which was much more preferable. I became a little disappointed with the gun's flimsy firepower in trying to shoot an occasional rabbit, until I started killing frogs at the pond, an easy target. At the time, this sick behavior induced only slight remorse and guilt, as I was consumed with trying to keep up with J.T.'s macho warrior-boy persona.

One day, I was wandering our property alone after school, the bare trees spider-webbing their way across the late autumn sky. A bird alighted on a branch nearby, and in an instant I swung into position and brought the gun up to my eye. I pulled the trigger, thinking there was no way I would actually hit it—but the primal warrior rushed in and I did hit it, knocking it right off the branch. It fell to the leaves with a deafening, unholy crunch and then rustled around helplessly in the yellow and red leaves, each movement growing louder as if someone had taken two huge sheets of crisp paper and was crumpling them in their fists against my head. I was immediately filled with horror and remorse at what I had done.

I ran screaming and crying to my sister Serena, who was the perfect person to spill a confession to. Like me, she had made it through the battlefields of Miss Hedy alive and had already at this point begun to pull away from the family, literally and emotionally. I sensed she would somehow understand my pain and remorse, because she had an extreme sensitivity and was also removed enough from the others that no one else would be told. So I wailed and begged forgiveness, and she just sat there and listened, a bit baffled by my anguish as I went on and on expressing such deep regret for hurting such an elegant and innocent bird, knowing on some level I had killed a piece of my own innocence, a part of my own flight, a portion of my own distant freedom.

# 4

# Crystal Street

Around 1978, Dad started to become overwhelmed with the cost of maintaining our lifestyle at the Clock Tower. Between family trips abroad, rising heating oil prices, and a real estate deal gone sour, Dad felt pressured, at the bottom of the market, to sell our "beloved" Clock Tower for virtually nothing. Even though he was working as an architect, it wasn't as if he made any money at it, as he mostly did remodels for friends at a discount. He thought he could make up for selling the Clock Tower by building us a newfangled prefab that he had partly designed. For the first time in his life he had to borrow money for the new house. He bought a woodsy acre and a half just across the border in New York State in an unincorporated area of Westchester County called Vista. In the meantime, we rented a house in Connecticut on the "other side" of town, on Crystal Street.

"This is not what you'd call *House & Garden*," Mom said, shortly after we arrived.

"Collettee, it's just for a year or two!" (This was Dad's term of annoyed endearment when trying to mollify Mom.)

"A week is all I can take of this dump," she replied.

"Goddamn it, Collette, I'm doing the best I can."

"The best you can do would be putting me up at the Ritz."

"For Christ's sake, Collette, you know we can't afford that right now. Don't be ridiculous."

"Ridiculous is this kitchen. Julia Child wouldn't be caught dead in this place. This makes Silver Hill ["the loony bin," as Mom liked to call it, where my Aunt Anne stayed periodically] look pretty good."

"I didn't hear that, goddamn it," Dad said.

"Nothing, dear," Mom said, and she pursed her lips and wandered into the next room to fish out a soft pack of Benson & Hedges 100s from her Gucci handbag.

Crystal Street, true to its name, seemed to illuminate all the multiple traumatic facets of our family life. Mom was aghast from the get-go. There was no dishwasher, no cleaning woman, no gardener, no governess, no "help." In their place were yellowish stucco-textured walls on the interior, stained wall-to-wall light blue carpeting, and olive and mustard paisley linoleum in the kitchen. A décor disaster, with no one to help cushion the blow.

Everybody was stressed out and unhappy about the move: my father, who was drowning in the guilt of it all; Mom, with her shattered high-society dreams and disappointing children—girls who wouldn't wear Laura Ashley dresses anymore, and a son who couldn't get into Hotchkiss or Exeter—and my sisters and me, reeling from the violence of our German governess and the general distance and sense of abandonment from our parents. It seemed as if my parents never gave much thought to parenting. It just wasn't one of their interests, which is why they hired a governess in the first place, but ever since Miss Hedy had left, they were on their own.

One illuminating facet of our family life was my father's frightening temper. When he lost his glasses or misplaced his car keys, all hell would break loose and he would stomp around the house yelling and whining at himself in this abrasive inquisitive shriek. "For Christ's sake, Harry, you've really done it now." Sometimes, I would think maybe something truly bad had happened, like maybe he had poisoned one of my sisters by insisting she eat the frightening leftover meatloaf that had been "curing" for three weeks in the back of the fridge. Or perhaps a Hell's Angel had just broken into the house and beaten up Mom, and then raided the fridge, eating all the perfectly chilled cantaloupe Dad was saving for his lunch. But usually it was as simple as him dropping a fork on the kitchen floor. "Goddamn it, Harry," he would yell into thin air. "Can't you even hang on to a f-ing fork?" He would ramp it up even more in volume and intensity if it were directed toward someone else.

When driving, he loved to rant about the stupidity of all other drivers on the road. They were always "this guy." "This guy's driving with his goddamn eyes closed." Or "This guy obviously has a goddamn blinker phobia." One time, when we were driving back from New York, up Madison Avenue, we got stuck behind a slow Pontiac Grand Prix. Dad was sputtering and cursing under his breath, getting more and more frustrated, until he finally yelled out, "That's what this guy is, a big prick!"

One day, when my sister and I got in a screaming match about whether we were going to watch *Three's Company* or *WKRP in Cincinnati*, Dad said, "Why the hell doesn't one of you do the dishes and the other get some goddamn homework done?" I said it was Serena's turn for the dishes and that I didn't have any homework, and then Serena told me to fuck off and we started in on each other again. Dad went into such a yelling rampage that he finally collapsed on the floor behind the couch. He was sprawled out on the lumpy blue wall-to-wall carpeting, moaning.

I had never heard my father moan before. He was almost sobbing, saying how we kids were going to give him a heart attack. Mom's response was to reach for the bottle of chilled Folonari white in the fridge and to knock another Benson & Hedges from her soft pack. She was appalled by the whole situation, freaked by Dad's overreaction, and panicked that he might actually have a heart attack. He was almost seventy. He eventually got up and went back to his crossword puzzle, as if nothing had happened.

The house and neighborhood were embarrassment enough to Mom, not to mention a disturbed husband and forced motherhood. We were rapidly becoming a version of *Dynasty* gone south.

"Crystal Street is where all the workmen live," Mom would tell her friends. She promptly named the house "La Masure," French for "The Hovel." She went to all the trouble to have expensive, though tacky, light blue stationery printed up that said "La Masure" at the top in red lettering. This was just to get a good laugh from her sister and her socially elevated friends.

One time, my parents were discussing decorating the living room "to tart the joint up a bit" as Mom put it, when Dad said something like, "Honey, whatever drapes you'd like in this room you can have; that's your department."

She winced, and replied, "Please don't use that word *drapes*, it's so blue collar."

"Goddamn it, Collette, *I'm* so blue collar!" my father roared.

Mummy (as she insisted we call her) had great aspirations for her "station in life" as she put it. It seemed that her one goal was to rise above her ordinary middle-class Irish Catholic upbringing on the fringes of Boston's high society. She had a habit of referring to people she didn't like as "peasants." They could be the nicest people in the world, but if they were shy and quiet and "uncultured," they were peasants. And when reactionary conservatives like Rush Limbaugh showed up on TV or in *The Times*, she would shout with disgust, "Oh, he's such a Visigoth!" I don't know if it was Mom or one of her good friends who came up with the phrase "N.Q.O.C.D." to describe a perfectly nice person they knew, but who didn't quite cut it socially. It stood for "Not Quite Our Class, Dear." And it was often uttered in an exaggerated English accent. Mom would often drop into her English accent, especially when talking to her friends from Europe. My friends used to ask me, "Is your mom from England?"

Mom's primary values revolved around table manners ("Please don't eat like a peasant, dear," she would sometimes scold), exclusive places (Park Avenue, the Upper East Side, the Ritz Bar in Boston, and the finest addresses in London, Paris, Rome, Johannesburg, Southampton, Pebble Beach, St. Helena), fine estates and interiors (preferably English or French castles and Italian villas), where one went to college (Ivy League), belongings such as clothes, luggage, jewelry (Hermès, Louis Vuitton, Tiffany & Co., etc.), and people you knew (the Hemingways, the Cadburys, the Luces, etc.).

Mom was a devout name dropper. Being listed in the social bible of all bibles, the *Social Register*, that thick black book filled with a who's who of the social elite in America and beyond, was an absolute must. She used to send in fake addresses and school names for her peasant children, since none of us made it into a decent private school or lived at an exclusive address. Supposedly, I went to Hotchkiss and lived in Greenwich Village in the early eighties. (I did actually interview at that school, but I failed the secondary school admission test and was rejected. And my father did, at one time in the seventies, have an apartment in Greenwich Village, though he sold it at a loss around the time he sold the Clock Tower.) Mom also longed to become a member of the Colony Club, but never made it. Either she couldn't actually afford it or, God forbid, she was never recommended. The Yale Club would have to do. A hilarious article in the *New York Post* in 2008 pretty much says it all. The title was "Snobs in a Snit at Ivy Club: City Yalies Rip Riffraff."

> The posh Yale Club in Midtown is fast becoming a cheesy wedding hall, with old-money members complaining of steady invasions of crowds from such lowbrow places as the Bronx.
>
> "It's crappy," said a woman who insisted *The Post* identify her only as "Mrs. Harrison DeSilver."
>
> "I just want to put my feet up here, but instead, weddings are being shipped down from the Bronx," groused DeSilver, a member for 50 years.
>
> "On the weekends, it just gets ridiculous."

DeSilver said the majority of the weddings at the club seem to involve people from the Bronx.

I'm surprised she didn't say "peasants" from the Bronx. The funny thing is Mom didn't even go to Yale. And Dad went for only two years before dropping out. I think she was actually a little jarred by the article, but then quickly defended herself by saying, "I mean really, the people, it is soooo embarrassing when they show up to the wedding in their T-shirts and underpants, or worse in their ruffled baby blue tuxedos and poofy hair. Oh Jesus, and the makeup on these ladies, you'd think they just walked in off Seventh Avenue."

None of this was lost on me. Throughout my adolescensce I rebelled against it, found her attitude judgmental, snotty and exclusive, and yet there was a tinge of, if not pride, then at least some semblance of elevated identity. I learned that I was different; I came from different stock, better stock than "those" peasants. This was tied in with the need to be seen and included, to be part of something shiny and bright, to garner some kind, any kind of acknowledgement, no matter how abstract and illusory, no matter how absurd.

The curious thing about Mom was that she placed such a huge priority on who you were related to, what school you went to, and who you knew, no matter who she was talking to. She would just as quickly drop the name of some famous anthropologist to a bum she was smoking with on the street as to a curator at the Met she was introduced to at a cocktail party on the Upper East Side. Whenever we went out to dinner, she would always leave the table right after she got her martini. Off she'd shuffle, riffling through her handbag for her "ciggies" and lighter and then out in to the street, even in the gnarliest blizzard. She inevitably came back to the table with a story.

"I just met the most marvelous man outside," she would exclaim. "He was from Bridgeport, the poor thing. Said he was in the Navy and spent a lot of time in France. So I said, oh BLAH BLAH BLAH in French. He just looked at me and said 'Huh?' Oh the poor thing, he was as nice as pie."

\* \* \*

To help distract us from the trauma of our move to the new house, Dad would take us up to Vista to witness the progress on the building project. Mom generally wasn't impressed with the blocky, angular modern design, with its severe roofline and vertical blue-gray siding. But she was happy designing the décor, when she could pick out Brunschwig & Fils wallpaper, and pricey fabric for curtains, (all-the-while ignoring Dad's shouting about the expense) and the famous cantaloupe color she chose for the dining room, which came out too dark, looking like baked pumpkin. From then on, anytime anyone mentioned the color, she'd reply, "Trick or treat?" This room was a strange transition from the kitchen, with its blue cabinets, blue fridge, and blue dishwasher.

At one point, my dad and she were discussing the finishing floor tile to be used in the basement of the new house, and what it would cost for the material in addition to laying the tile. Mom burst out with, "Jesus Christ, Harrison, you could lay me for half that!"

Mom the contrarian. One minute a ritzy snob carrying on as an erudite in an English accent, the next a low-brow commoner shit-talking like a trucker. This was both endearing and embarrassing. My friends thought she was hilarious. I was confused. At the time I could never quite figure out who she was or who we were as a family. Were we rich or poor? Middle or upper class? Social drinkers or drunken wrecks headed for the precipice?

# 5

# Coming of Age in the Derelict Den

One day a few years earlier when we were still at the Clock Tower, I was eight or nine and Mom and Dad were out somewhere, J.T. came over to play floor hockey. After a couple of games, we were bored. We wandered upstairs to do some exploring, and I showed him our special laboratory in the utility room. J.T. took in the sculptural display of differently shaped bottles as if he were looking at the new lineup of a hockey or baseball team on TV. He was stunned.

"Let's make some potions," he blurted excitedly. "We could make something that foamed and smoked, maybe even something that exploded— that'd be fun."

"Okay, but we need to put back what we pour out. I think they actually drink this stuff and might get mad if too much is missing."

We found some empty jars and started with the most grisly-looking liquid we could find. "Jack Daniels," read the label. It smelled like diesel fuel to us, a perfect start.

"Let's add some of this clear Russian stuff, that must be like nitroglycerine, what they put in race cars," J.T. said.

"Here's some red sour-grape-smelling stuff—toss that in, and some of this minty schnapps stuff that smells like liquid candy canes."

We added some Tab diet cola, and then some tonic water, crushed in a couple of olives, and shook vigorously. It fizzed and swirled and bubbled and then just sat there looking dark brown and scary. We took our concoction outside to a remote part of the driveway, shook it up vigorously, and then hurled it to the pavement to see if it would explode. It just shattered across the asphalt and sprayed a little bit. We were devastated. We thought maybe with different ingredients we might get different results. In the meantime, we would hide our experiments around the house in secret locations where no one would find them. They would be our secret potions for the future, in the event that we ever needed to escape.

The day came, though, when I wanted to drink our newest concoction. I held it to my nose as I'd seen my mother and father do, and then moved it toward my mouth. J.T. watched me in horror. "What are you doing? Don't drink that crap." I slowly and shamefully put the glass down.

* * *

Chris Barrenton became my best friend in fifth grade after J.T. was downgraded and we had moved from the Clock Tower to Crystal Street. It was the same town, but it might as well have been another country, given the dramatic shift from upper-crust country club suburb to working-class neighborhood. Chris helped me see alcohol not as a toxic potion but as a magical elixir that helped me shine. Chris lived a couple of streets over from Crystal Street. He was a tough, stout kid who loved adventure and getting into trouble. He had pale Irish skin, freckles, and teeth spaced slightly too far apart. He lived with his mother (divorced), their dog Sadie, two older brothers, and an older sister. It was these siblings, who were all in high school or college, who took us to our first Grateful Dead concert a couple of years later in the fall of ninth grade. This was the first of dozens of Grateful Dead concerts I would attend every year for a decade or so, until Jerry Garcia died in 1995. I loved the creativity, the comraderie, the unpredictable movement of the music—how each show was always a completely new experience. I loved the social connectivity, the way we were all united in a common language of music, fun, drugs, and thumbing our noses at mainstream society. The concerts and the culture around them became a new form of family for me.

I think my friends and I were trying to grab a piece of that 1960s anti-establishment vibe, and ditch a bit of our 1980s "yuppie" commercialism and suburban privilege. I remember a bumper sticker from the time that read "Die Yuppie Scum." I always thought that a bit harsh, but it did reflect the general anti-Reaganomics sentiment. There were also the larger causes the Grateful Dead were playing for: the Seva Foundation, Amnesty International, and Greenpeace. Most Deadheads I knew were tied to environmental or peace groups. Dad was a supporter of both, though definitely not of the Grateful Dead. Like most things, he chose to ignore my growing obsession. My little white Toyota would soon be stuck together, not only with Grateful Dead stickers, but slogans such as "Arms Are for Hugging" and "Nuclear Weapons: May They Rust in Peace."

Another thing that drew me to the Grateful Dead was the ecstatic energy at the concerts. It was the only time I felt wildly alive and uncontained, free to express myself through ridiculously spastic dancing and wild singing. Who had a worse voice than Jerry Garcia by the 1980s? I felt comfortable singing along, whereas normally, I was terrified to sing out loud. Mom was always quick to remind me I was tone deaf. By high school I would be memorizing Grateful Dead lyrics written by poet/songwriters Robert Hunter and John Barlow, which I now see as an early influence in my poetry and writing. I was drawn to many of their lyrics, but these in particular from a song called "Estimated Prophet," seem, well, almost prophetic:

*My time coming any day, don't worry 'bout me, no*
*Been so long I felt this way, I'm in no hurry no*
*Rainbows end down that highway where ocean breezes blow*
*My time coming, voices saying, they tell me where to go*
*Don't you worry 'bout me--oh no no, don't worry 'bout me, no*
*And I'm in no hurry--oh no no no, I know just where to go*


*California, preaching on the burning shore*
*California, I'll be knocking on the golden door*
*Like an angel, standing in a shaft of light*
*Rising up to paradise, I know I'm gonna shine. . .*


One night we all piled into Chris's older brother's VW microbus and off we went into a haze of malt liquor and pot, the song "Aiko Aiko" embedding itself in my brain. The next day at school, I barely made it through first period before winding up in the nurse's office, where the vice principal, Mr. Gaeman (pronounced "gay-man"—you can imagine the fun we had with that one!) came in and asked, "How's our little Deadhead doing?" How did he know?

Chris had been influenced by his brothers and sister for some time, drinking since the fourth grade and smoking pot since fifth, and one day during the summer after fifth grade, he asked me if I had ever smoked pot. This was around the time Nancy Reagan advised us to "Just Say No," and I had an almost healthy fear of marijuana at the time, and shyly did as Nancy instructed.

Attached to the Barrenton's garage was a ramshackle structure—a kind of hangout hut, the inside walls of which were draped in funky tapestries and black velvet Grateful Dead, Led Zepplin, and Jimi Hendrix posters. It had a beat-up couch with several burn holes in it, an ancient bent space heater, and one of those brown dorm fridges usually stocked with beer. Chris's brother and his friends called it the Derelict Den, for good reason, as for years they had partied continuously in this space.

Within a couple of months, Chris and I were smoking cigarettes in the Derelict Den after school. A few months after that, I tried pot for the first time. I was immediately excited by the shiny weirdness I felt, the wiggy detachment. Chris's brothers would leave beer in the fridge, usually tall bottles of Haffenreffer malt liquor, the ones with those fun picture puzzles in the bottle cap—perfect for kids age twelve and up. Chris had a pragmatic, balanced side to him, and after teaching me the ways of the cigarette and bottle, he always seemed to be the one maintaining enough sobriety to drag *me* home across the dewy Waveny Park fields, and then talk through the whole drama with my parents while I moaned in the other room.

Soon, Chris's brothers were onto us stealing their beer, and more often than not the fridge sat empty. That's when Chris and I would walk up to the high school looking for unopened cans or bottles of beer along the road. Often we would find *something*. We tried to stay away from the ones with faded labels and ants crawling all over them, but we weren't *too* picky. One time, we found an intact six-pack of Coors in the woods behind the high school. We were psyched. Nothing was more exciting to us than finding (or stealing) beer and cigarettes. Back to the Derelict Den we went to savor our find. Sometimes, one of Chris's brothers would catch us drinking beer and ask us where the hell we got it. We'd tell him and he'd ask for a sip, and then immediately spit it out and berate us for drinking "skunked" beer. Sometimes, he felt sorry enough for us that he bought us a fresh six-pack. Holy holy! This was the big score.

One night, Chris and I and our friend Giang, or "Oingo-Boingo" as we used to call him, found ourselves in possession of a half gallon of vodka. I can't remember if someone found it on the side of the road, stole it from their parents, or what, but off we went to a neutral place to drink it—a construction site near the Little League ballfield. We hovered around the bottle staring at it as if at a crystal ball, or as if we were bowing before some kind of sacred oracle. The excitement was akin to hooking up with a girl and actually getting somewhere, like up her shirt or down her pants, but this was even better because the bottle couldn't reject you. Or could it? There was that nervous anticipation mixed with confusion, kind of like trying to figure out how to pin down the neck of a poisonous thrashing snake. Now what do we do?

"Crack it open already!" shouted Giang with glee. Giang was a preppy, smart Vietnamese immigrant, edgy and quick-witted, who loved to chain smoke. He lived with eighty-seven cousins and his parents, who didn't speak English, in a small house down the road from Crystal Street. Giang's face always turned bright red when he drank.

We sat on stacks of two-by-fours for what seemed like hours wondering what to do with our drunken selves. I could practically see Giang's face glowing red in the dark, competing for brightness with the bottle itself. Giang expected me to come to his house; Chris suggested the Derelict Den. I felt neurotic and uncomfortable about either one and couldn't decide. Our exquisitely articulate conversation went something like this:

Giang: "Al, just come to my house, we'll crash there."

Al (sputtering between cannonballs, smoke billowing from nostrils and mouth): "Whoa, fuck . . . do you think so, I mean with all your family and relatives and stuff, I don't know, what if we just went back to the Den?"

Giang (annoyed): "Fine, whatever."

Chris: "I'm not sure we can go back to my house—my mom thinks I'm staying at Giang's."

Al: "What if we just stay out? We could go throw rocks at Pietro's window and see if he wants to come and sit around on some piles of nails and lumber. I'm sure he'll jump at the opportunity."

Giang: "I'm having a fucking blast" (tripping over a piece of ductwork and heading for the plywood side door).

We finished off the bottle and stumbled out of the half-framed condo following Giang. He wanted a decision, I was drunk and torn, and Chris didn't give a shit.

"I don't care what you do, dumb ass," Giang shouted.

"Sounds a little like you do . . . beeeitch," I said, stringing out the word *bitch*. "What if we just went back to the den?"

"You said that, ass face," barked Giang. "Just fucking decide."

"Why do I have to decide? We could maybe go and see if Lynn is around."

"If you don't make a decision now," spit Giang, "I'm gonna fuckin' hit you."

I jumped at the opportunity to taunt him, blind to my own fear and nervous confusion. I shuffled into his personal space, tapping clumsily at my chin. "Go ahead, big tough Mrs. Brucey Lee Lee, hit me," I said.

Giang shifted slightly toward me and then swung hard and quick, hitting me square on the jaw and lower lip. I went down with a thud on the asphalt and curled into the fetal position like a salted slug. Everything went dark for a moment, and I thought I was dead, then I found myself being shaken back to the moment by Chris.

"You fucking gook fuck cocksucker ass fucker cock bitch motherfucker . . ." I sputtered drunkenly, trying to assess whether I had lost any teeth. Pink saliva-diluted blood smeared upon the back of my hand when I wiped my lip.

"He's long gone," said Chris. "Now get up."

Giang was halfway down the sidewalk, remorse-free. Chris was hovering over me, telling me to shut the fuck up, trying to get me to stand. I was crying and sputtering, slowly feeling waves of remorse pooling in my belly like molten lead. I was beginning to realize that I'd managed to piss off and alienate my two best friends, two from my tribe, the only two who seemed to remotely understand and even accept me. Eventually, we stumbled back to the Derelict Den, where I passed out alone on the ratty couch beneath the Jimi Hendrix poster.

# 6

# Camp Pummelton

For many years, Chris had been attending a rustic summer camp on Vinalhaven Island, in the Penobscot Bay of northern Maine. In the summer of 1981, I was twelve, and Chris convinced me this would be a fun summer excursion. My parents, knowing nothing about the camp, were delighted to have me occupied for the summer. After hearing Chris's descriptions of its remote location, some mysterious initiation rite, his past harrowing adventures, and the spare accommodations, I nervously agreed to go. Initially, I was enchanted by the idea of an adventure, and by my first sight of Vinalhaven, with its rocky, pine-studded shores, blueberry scrub meadows, hidden bogs, and calm inlet bays with lobster boats floating in the glistening water.

The camp, however, was a bit more rustic than I had imagined. Located out on the far, most remote end of the island, it consisted of two flimsy A-frame structures and an outhouse, all with buckling floors and plenty of mice and flies. I loathed the shower, a cold water hose draped over a tree limb and through a rusty Chock Full o'Nuts coffee can. This was our bathing station every morning before dawn. It was like being shot with a spray of ice crystals, right after the soup-pot banging roused us out of bed in the dark. Numerous tilting sheds on the property were being reclaimed by bramble and weed, one of which housed a washbasin and an old hand-crank wringer we fed our clothes through before hanging them out on the line to dry. The place was devoid of "mod cons" as Mom liked to say, and that seemed to be the point. The only thing we didn't do was hunt and forage for our own food.

The camp was directed by a mysterious father figure we never saw except for a few minutes the first day, and so was entirely run by Dave, a twenty-four-year-old recent graduate of Dartmouth College. He seemed to only slightly know what he was doing. Fortunately, he got "help" from Chris's stoner brother, Jules, and his sidekick, Mattie, both seventeen. There were only five other campers besides Chris and me: Rick, the tall, righteous know-it-all from Pennsylvania; Nigel, the uncircumcised kid with a slight British accent from New York City; the spacey redneck, Boon, from rural New Hampshire; Kit, the geeky Dungeons & Dragons aficionado from Providence; and Reggie, the plump, shy black kid from New Jersey.

I'll never forget Reggie, first of all because he was black, and as Mom would say, "We didn't know from black" growing up in New Canaan—and second of all because he seemed to be the only one besides me to have such a hard time with the obligatory early-morning jog. One morning, he was struggling to finish the run, and actually puked as I stumbled wearily past him on the road. I didn't even stop to see if he was okay, not only because I was too delirious, but also because I had heard rumors that kids had been paddled for stopping in the past.

Reggie got teased and beat on constantly by the other boys. They taught me how. There was no one else to dominate. Most of the other kids were either bigger than me, too unpredictable, or too confident and sturdy. Reggie was the perfect victim.

Reggie was squat and dumpy, and waddled slightly when he walked. He was visibly uncomfortable in his skin, whereas I was *in*visibly uncomfortable in my skin. He had almost a mousy disposition, practically squeaking when he spoke. He didn't have what I imagined to be a "black kid" accent, which is to say an urban black accent. I guess he was from the suburbs too. I didn't know how to be or act around Reggie; he was as much an oddity to me as I was to myself. I took cues from the other boys, whose default approach was to dominate and make fun of him. I just mimicked their style of cruelty in order to fit in. This gave me a new sense of power. I had never felt such illusory control. I somehow knew that no matter how mean or physically brutish I became, I wasn't scared of the consequences, or at least of ever losing a fight with him.

I approached Reggie one night after dinner in the meadow next to the line of bent oil drums being swallowed by high grass, just off the driveway. He was half-reading, half-talking with Kit. Reggie was wearing a pair of blue shorts hiked up too high on his waist and a white sleeveless T-shirt. A chocolate roll of skin was sticking out from his T-shirt, and he was thumbing through his sci-fi novel when Rick approached from the outhouse.

"What's up, Reginaaaald?" said Rick.

"Yeah, what's up, Reginaaaaald?" I echoed.

"Nothing," said Reggie, sounding a little meek.

"I see you're reading a book, what's it about, Reginaaaaaald?"

"Nothing," he said anticipating some uncomfortable confrontation.

"Don't you want to play?" Rick said, dancing around him punching the air near his head.

I walked up slowly and made light contact with Reggie's upper arm with a fake to his belly. "Yeah, let's duke it out for fun, Reggie," I said.

"Go away, you guys, I'm reading," he said, swatting at us with his paperback as if waving away a swarm of flies.

Rick danced over and punched *me* solidly in the arm.

"I heard that, fart head." It was camp protocol to punch each other in the upper arm when you farted and failed to report it with the proper code word and rush of numbers, trying to make it to the count of ten before your fellow camper did. If they smelled it and you didn't report it, you got punched.

"What?—owww, you fuck," I said, jumping over to Reggie.

"I remember smelling something nasty back in the kitchen, Reg."

"It wasn't me, I swear," he replied.

"Sure smelled like it was coming from you," I said.

"Yeah, it smelled chocolatey," added Rick, laughing.

I chimed in on the laughter and punched Reggie nice and hard in the upper arm, hearing the smack and feeling the solid contact of knuckles on broad flesh. I noticed in the instant a flash of purple staining his dark skin, and a pang of remorse slid through my belly so fast I couldn't even catch it.

"Ow, Al, that fucking hurt," Reggie said, tearing up.

"What comes around goes around, right, Rick?" I said.

"Yeah, like some pages from my own little book of digestion—wanna read 'em Reg? It's actually a good read, tells the history of my last three meals," he said, lunging toward Reggie with a fistful of dirty toilet paper he'd been hiding under his shirt, and then pressing it into his face as Reggie lazily swatted at him again with his book.

Rick grabbed the book with his free hand and flung it into the meadow. Reggie immediately collapsed on the ground in a tight ball and started screaming in his squeaky high voice.

"Get away from me, you mean fucker!"

"Mean fucker? Who you calling 'mean fucker'?" said Rick, now straddling Reggie's side. "How's this for a mean fucker?" *Smack.* He started punching Reggie's already bruised upper arm. I could hear the slap of fist on meaty upper arm flesh, echoing again in my guilty head. It was the sound of intercepting a high-velocity jellyfish in the center of your palm, as it was thrown at your head by a fellow camper.

"Leave me alone," sobbed Reggie.

"Yeah, back off," yelled Chris, running over and butting in to pull Rick off Reggie.

"Oh yeah, tough guy Chris," said Rick.

"Get over yourself, Rick," Chris interrupted, clearly not afraid of Rick's almost six-foot height.

"You don't have to be such a hero, Chris. Let Reggie take care of himself. And this is none of your fuckin' beeswax! What the hell are *you* going to do about it, anyway?"

"Nothing, asshole, except invite you to pick on someone your own size, like me!"

Just then, Dave yelled from the kitchen. "Rick, get over here and finish scrubbing the pots!" There was a pause. *"Now!"* Rick peeled himself reluctantly off Reggie, giving him a frustrated final kick to the thigh.

"Watch yourself, mister hero boy," he said, towering over Chris poking at his throat. And then he walked off.

I just stood there taking it all in, trying to figure out whose side to align with. I craved the power of dominance, and yet Chris was quite the hero, sticking up for Reggie and being so brave. But there was something about his butting in and trying to save everyone that didn't sit right with me either. I couldn't make sense of it all or clarify yet what was actually the right thing to do. Reflecting back on it now, I'm appalled by our behavior—the callousness and blatant racism—and yet, this wasn't the kind of camp where we could explore our feelings and discuss issues of bullying and bigotry. You just toughened up a notch, kept quiet, and moved on.

Sometimes at night, I could hear Reggie crying into his pillow, and tinges of remorse and guilt would float through my heart. Funny thing was, I too, cried into my pillow, if only for slightly different reasons. I was homesick, and having second thoughts about the whole Island Camp routine. The day after I got to camp, with orientation over and Mom and Dad leaving, the *idea* of Island Camp wisped quickly away into a cold, solid reality. I became terrified. As Mom and Dad's weathered Mercedes backed down the rugged drive, crunching in slow motion along the gravel, I fought back tears and slowly followed their car out to the main road until it disappeared around a bend of overgrown blueberry scrub. I cried and cried for two days straight and called Mom, begging her to come fetch me. "I'm going to have to shit in a bucket, shower under a cold hose, and do my laundry by hand," I complained. I had never been away from home without my family, let alone on such a remote island off remotest northern Maine. To Mom's credit, she did promise to come pick me up if I still couldn't stand it after another three or four days. "Just try and stick it out, sweetheart," she said, as I sniffled and burbled into the phone. "And if you still absolutely hate it, I will drive up there myself next weekend and come get you!" The next time she called, I was too busy to talk. I think I was chopping wood.

We rotated "KP" for cooking and cleanup. Hot water had to be boiled on the stove to do the dishes after a meal. We constantly did chores just to keep the place running. When we weren't fixing something or doing chores, we had a bit of adventure time. We'd row old dories out through the uninhabited tiny islands off the north shore and engage in epic jellyfish fights. We'd hike up to Crow Rock and watch the sunset after dinner. One rainy afternoon, we went into town and caught a matinee of *Annie Hall* at the tiny movie theater on Main Street. A couple of times a week, we'd all pile in the back of the old pickup and drive out to the clothing-optional quarry for swims, Dave gunning it though the gigantic mud puddles along the dirt road, while we screamed through the muddy drenching.

Then there was the official "secret initiation" that I had been nervously anticipating for weeks. Chris refused to tell me what it was. He was sworn to secrecy, as was everyone else who had been to camp in previous years. I would beg them to tell me, and they would simply pretend they didn't hear me and ignore the request. If I pressed the issue, I would get punched in the arm, just like Reggie. I was surprised by their honor. And then scared that it might be something truly frightening. The day of the initiation, we were simply told to pack a bag for the day, because we were going out on a "little adventure."

We were taken out in a boat into the middle of Penobscot Bay. I was never a fan of boats, being prone to seasickness like Mom, and I got more and more nervous the farther from shore we went. And we went on and on, farther and farther out, the shore reduced to a gauzy sliver on the horizon. Finally, they cut the engine and I was told to strip down naked. I looked down, alarmed to notice my balls had shriveled into nothingness.

"Jump in, *now*!" commanded Dave.

"Wwwwhaaa . . ." I was shivering, freaked to the bone, staring into the black choppy water. Memories of the movie *Jaws* were streaming through my mind, and that lagoon scene, or was it a bay? Sharks love cold water, don't they? Finally, with a mean case of sewing-machine leg, I lifted one foot to the gunwales. Dave took a step toward me. "Now!" he said again.

I jumped, screaming, and hit the water with a smack. It felt as if I had in fact hit a thin layer of choppy ice. The smack was the air being knocked out of me by the shocking cold. I gasped, feeling as if my lungs had collapsed. My throat was frozen shut. I tried to yell, but my voice had turned to a plate of ice. I was flailing madly, trying to stay afloat and tread water for what seemed an eternity, but which was probably all of three minutes. Finally, they tossed me the inflatable ring, which I could barely lift my arms through, and they reeled me in like a giant hunk of dead cod.

Dave, Chris, and Rick fished me out and threw me into an open wool blanket on deck. Everyone was cheering and whistling. For a moment, I felt a surge of pride and accomplishment, as if I had just swum the English Channel and was being greeted on the English shore. I learned later the water temperature was somewhere in the upper thirties to low forties.

A few days after the initiation, when my teeth had stopped chattering from the chill, we got to work on our big project of the summer, building a plywood camper for our road trip to Nova Scotia. We spent more than a week constructing a space that was to house nine of us for two weeks on the road, and we ended up practically duct-taping it to the back of our trusty '57 Ford pickup truck. I forget exactly how we attached it, but it was a sketchy operation all around. I was convinced that at some random juncture we would just slip off the back of the pickup and shatter into a thousand pieces on the highway.

We somehow made it up to the border and throughout Nova Scotia for a two-week tour of the entire peninsula without an incident. We were all of twelve or thirteen that summer, when we visited the Labbat brewery in Halifax and shared our supposed first beers on a nearby beach. We swam the dramatic tidal lagoon at sunset, fighting the swift current as it tried to suck us out to sea.

One morning while we were on an overnight trip to Bar Harbor, Dave came by my tent to say the director wanted to see me. I couldn't imagine why, until I remembered that I had walked a short section of the previous day's run. My stomach lurched. Dave led me to a rusted-out bus on the far end of a meadow. Once a school bus, the stop sign had been ripped off, the lights painted over, and the yellow paint had been covered with army green in a camouflage pattern.

"We'll make this quick and simple," said the director, whom I only barely recognized from the first day of camp. He ordered me halfway down to where there was space between the seats next to the emergency exit. The bus creaked like an old ship as our footsteps thumped across the cold metal floor in tune to my heartbeat. I felt as if I were walking the plank. He pulled a wooden paddle out of a dark purple velvet case (the color reminding me of the bruises on Reggie's arm), the kind you might carry a rare musical instrument or trophy in. The paddle was old and faded, with the words "Island Camp" cheerfully written on it in Kelly green paint.

I pulled down my pants as instructed and prepared for the blow. I grimaced. Nothing. An eternity unfolded. I imagined the sting—like sitting on a porcupine, or on a bed of nails, or on a pile of Pick-Up Sticks. *Thwap.* The jolt rattled the sticky marrow *within* my bones, and sent me recoiling inward into some dark sub-muscular dungeon of the body. *Thwap.*

There was the sting, a dozen angry bees per cheek. *Thwap.* I turned my head to catch the director's face in the little round convex mirror sticking off the back corner of the bus. His sweating, bald head echoed the roundness of the mirror. "Objects are closer than they appear," was a phrase printed in bold white lettering on the rearview mirror of Chris's mom's Oldsmobile. This object appeared overwhelmingly close. I could see his mouth, the corners turned up with spittle gathering. Was he enjoying this? *Thwap.*

"Fuck," I whispered into the cold rusted metal frame of the seat in front of me, which I was clutching for dear life. The brassy smell of worn metal that had met too many hands stung my nose. Four down. How many more to go? *Thwap.* Beads of sweat were forming on Mr. Director's upper lip. He was getting a workout. I saw mirrors in each bead of sweat, more spittle, and perverted smiles multiplying in the mini hall of mirrors surrounding me. *Thwap.* I was losing count. Was that seven, lucky seven, the end? *Thwap.* I imagined my ass, red on red, Red Sox red, red like the sun at dusk slipping behind Crow Rock. *Thwap.* The tears bloomed like small glass cages and fell to watery pieces across my face. I was at my limit of "grinning and bearing it," as Dad used to instruct.

I fell to my knees as I finally heard "Okay, get outta here." And "No more stopping on the morning run."

I pulled up my pants and wiped my face. As I slinked by, he smiled, lightly patted my head and ruffled my hair, as you might a well-behaved retriever.

"Atta boy," he said, as I heard him suck in the spittle that had gathered to a dense foam at the corners of his mouth.

I had been hit before, but this was different. I suddenly thought of Reggie, and I never hit him again. I wish I could say that in that moment, I decided to take my rage, my capacity for violence, and turn it more and more exculsively inward on myself. But that was only partly true. All it would take was a little alcohol, the right timing, and a perfect trigger for me to impulsively lash out at someone else.

7

# East Jesus Junior High

Crystal Street was the big transition as I went into sixth grade, my sister Serena into eighth, and Margaret into tenth. I've read that it's a bad idea to move adolescents and teenagers into a new environment. I attended the first half of sixth grade at John Jay Junior High in New York, commuting from Connecticut, where I had been at the South School solidifying my new friendships with Chris and Giang. Margaret had just got her driver's license, so she could drive us. It was about an hour's drive.

We had an old, blue, wood-paneled Datsun 810 station wagon. My sister drove in silence, staring intently through the windshield as washes of reflected light from the trees and sky poured over her blank face. She steered with her two index fingers resting along the bottom of the wheel, pointing as if to reaffirm her direction and perhaps disguising her hidden prayer with a half-gesture. My anxiety grew as we drove over the border into New York State, things getting less and less familiar, less and less likable. I didn't like the orange and blue New York license plates, or the state trooper patrol cars with their dark blue and yellow striping. They depressed me and gave me a wrenching stomach ache. I didn't even like the trees and stone walls in New York, even though they looked pretty much the same as the ones in Connecticut. Everything Connecticut pleased and relieved me; everything

New York State made me despondent. I was leaving new friendships, old friendships, and a familiar and somewhat predictable affluent town for an unpredictable chaotic mess of kids at a big school in different state.

I hated John Jay Junior High from the get-go. I didn't understand why all the boys wore dress shirts that were too big for them, droopy drawers, and high-top sneakers with the laces bunched out like dead weeds, and which were untied so that your heels bounced and shuffled along. To fit in, I borrowed old shirts of my Dad's, but they smelled musty and of old cologne, were too big, and made me look as if I were wearing a smock and gearing up for finger-painting class. In the school bathroom, I was perplexed by the Dead Kennedys, Ramones, the Clash, and Sex Pistols graffiti. This was alien music. My friends Chris and Giang back in Connecticut listened to Yes, Led Zeppelin, Foreigner, the Cars, Van Halen, and Bad Company. They were my old tribe, the ones I wanted to be hanging out with all the time. Without them, I felt as if at John Jay I was permanently in Bad Company.

My sister would drop me at the back of the high school parking lot by the gigantic forest-green Dumpster with its eternally dark mouth open ready to engulf me. It had a bright orange WARNING sticker on the front that said: "DO NOT PLAY ON OR AROUND," which I thought meant the entire school. My sister just looked at me helplessly as if she were surrounded by armed guards and was forced to let me go. As she walked off to class, telling me unconvincingly that I would be all right, I was left with this bleak abandonment as if I were being sent to my death.

There was a little loading dock at the back of the junior high school with a thick, black flap in the brick. I felt as if at any moment one of the hall guards would appear and force me down on the conveyor belt that led through to the inside. Then I would be fed directly into a giant wood chipper housed deep in the bowels of the school building.

\* \* \*

At John Jay Junior High I basically shut down, went on strike emotionally, and refused to adjust. I made little effort to meet people, or to participate in any school activities, both of which would have probably made me feel better. I chose to stay locked in my thinking of good versus evil, Connecticut versus New York. All my energy went into the future, planning and preparing mentally to be with J.T. and my other Connecticut friends.

At school, I often fell into overwhelming bouts of depression where I would cry uncontrollably. Many times during class I would be overtaken and ask to see the nurse, who had no idea what to do with me because I wasn't bleeding. She'd send me to Mister Lustig's office, where I would have to repeat over and over, "I don't know." Poor Mr. Lustig, dressed in his short-sleeved rayon button-down with odd flecked patterns and his cheap dark slacks, would sit there with his half-bald head of receding black curls shaking from side to side, thoroughly perplexed. He looked pathetic, sputtering on with little clichéd anecdotes about "passing dark cloudy storms of sadness," all to try and make me feel better. And then he would quickly remind me that I couldn't stay in his office all day. Between him and my parents grilling me with questions I couldn't answer, I began to feel as if my tongue had been cut out. I was ashamed for even being depressed— there was no reason why that I could articulate— what, just because we moved? I became ashamed of being ashamed. Miss Hedy had taught me to do that as a kid. The most repeated phrase I recall from her was, "You should be ashamed of yourself." So I took her up on it, and whenever strong emotions emerged in me, I felt shame, almost as if to feel, or to express feeling, was a shameful act.

The waves of depression were so dark and foreboding that I felt physically ill at times. I started to notice what triggered these dark waves: certain places (John Jay), people (Mister Lustig), and objects (cars with New York plates). There were a few moments of reprieve. I did like the library at school. The light was soothing, and there was something about the mysterious possibility of books that made me curious. I could be alone in my head and become lost dreaming about brighter realities. And Mr. Grabowskie's science lab was okay. He was funny and odd, and we were always doing some unexpected experiment that kept me engaged. To this day, I still remember his name because the first day of class he said, "Hello, I'm Mr. Grabowski. You will never forget my name because if you do, I will grab your arm, you will scream "Oww," and then you will try and ski away to safety." Goofy, but effective.

I have a slight recollection of a story I wrote in English class about Stephanie, a monstrous fish with jagged teeth and fiery breath that lived in the North Sea. I remember the way my social studies teacher, Mr. Donaldson always put an "er" on the end of every country ending in an "a" — Russia became "Rusher," America became "Ameriker," China, "Chiner." And then there was our phys ed teacher, "Fill-in-the-Blank Frank," who always left a word out at the end of an instructional. "You run down the court and throw the ball in the . . . "

"Hoop," we would mumble, rolling our eyes, and then I would whisper to a classmate, "You open the can of beer and pour it down your . . . throat!"

These were my few distractions from the waves of depression and anxiety that plagued me daily. By this time, I was running off to New Canaan on the weekends to hang with Chris and Giang and my other Connecticut friends at the Derelict Den, drinking more and more, and smoking more and more pot.

I begged my parents for two years straight to let me transfer out of John Jay to a school in Connecticut. The only real option was a private day school, which was right down the street from our house at Sunny Hill. At the time, St. Luke's was where all the "slow learners," reprobates, and kids who got kicked out of prep schools went. At least that was the reputation. It was back in Connecticut, that's all I cared about. Finally in 1982, the autumn of ninth grade when I was fourteen, I made the transfer to

St. Luke's. For the first time in two years, I felt some sense of relief, and even a bit of curiosity about whom I might meet.

I fell into an exciting social circle after first meeting Pete, mega stoner and lacrosse athlete extraordinaire. He got me into pot and lacrosse. And then there was Pat, who loved to mock the vice principal, Mr. Gaeman. Pat did this thing with his throat where he'd compress the side of his trachea, making his voice sound like a sick and demented bullfrog. With his voice full throttle, he would say things like "Yo DeSilver, Mr. Gayyy-mannn is waiting for you, his *orifice* door is wide open for you to enter it." Pat was one of those kids who was constantly sending his friends into fits of uncontrollable hysterics, which often got them kicked out of class. When teachers asked for his homework, he would promptly compress his trachea and belch out that his bullfrog had eaten it.

As I entered high school at St. Luke's, my introduction to binge drinking, combined with the exciting discovery of girls and the crazed and confused surge of sexual energy, somehow helped numb my anxiety and yet would churn up a perfect storm of desperate and traumatic relationships. It was around this time, in eighth or ninth grade, that I earned the nickname "Al the Alkie," and in some ways I almost savored the identity. At least I was known for *something*. And Mom was so good at it (being a drinker). The more she drank, the more animated and funny she got, and the more popular she got. I thought I could do the same. I, too, desperately wanted to be popular.

# 8

# High School with Fathead

"Hey, Al, get in the car. We're going to a party at Mary Anne's!"

"What . . . who *is* that?" I said squinting into the windows of a dark green Ford Escort that had pulled up abruptly right in front of me on the sidewalk. I'd been standing alone in front of Baskin-Robbins for twenty minutes, feeling awkward and exposed, waiting for Chris and Giang to show up. That's where we always met on Friday or Saturday nights in high school to see if anything was "going on." As in a party: alcohol, pot, cigarettes, girls. In that order.

A bit blinded by the street lamp, I was trying to make out who the girl was sticking her head out the window and calling my name. I leaned in a little closer, and suddenly the back door swung open, and the girl grabed my arm and pulled me in the car. The driver floored it and we took off. I was delightedly shocked to be kidnapped by a car full of girls, before I even slowly recognized Mary Anne as the office manager for Dr. Shelkin, my orthodontist.

Mary Anne was probably in her late thirties, not quite obese, but getting there. She was smoking a Newport Red cigarette, which had turned her chubby face and light brown eyes hazy. Erika was in the front seat. She was the cute, skinny, blonde receptionist who I'd sort of noticed, but not really; I think she was a junior at New Canaan High. And in the back seat, my official abductor, Megan, probably nineteen or twenty, said she knew my sister, whom she graduated with last year. I guess Megan also used to work for Dr. Shelkin. We called him Dr. Scale-King because he had serious skin problems. Huge plates of skin would fall off his face and neck as he wired and rewired your mouth. They would make a racket as they clattered down your plastic bib like dried leaves scraping along a sidewalk.

The "girls" were giddy and amped up, obviously a little drunk. Each had a Coors Light either tucked between her legs or clutched tightly in her small, delicate hand. I was whisked away to Mary Anne's condo a mile or so from town, where I was greeted by a half-full bowl of alarmingly red, spiked Hawaiian Punch on the kitchen table. A case of Coors Light was packed into open blue coolers on the floor. They plopped me down in front of the TV and put on Dr. Ruth.

I was a bit embarrassed at first to be sitting with three women I didn't know, listening to Dr. Ruth get graphic. But it was nothing that a little punch and several beers couldn't assuage. Dr. Ruth was in the midst of listening to a woman explain how she had recently taken the good doctor's advice about how to spice up her predictable and routine sex life by bringing food into the bedroom. She described how she had invented a ring-toss game with her husband using onion rings ("fresh out of the oven" she giggled), which she would proceed to eat off of him as her (and his) special prize.

We howled with laughter at this image, and then the room fell silent and awkward. Mary Anne and Megan kept foisting beers on me until I was scary inebriated. At one point, Erika disappeared up the carpeted stairs and stayed there. Suddenly, Mary Anne whispered excitedly, "Erika is looking for you," as if we were playing a game of hide-and-seek. Immediately, a nervous flood of energy rushed through me, as if someone had just poured sizzling bacon grease straight into my bloodstream.

"Scrawny, nervous, awkward me?" I half-thought. The other half couldn't think. I guzzled down the rest of my eighty-seventh or so Coors Light, hoping to temper the bacon grease sensations. "Huh?" I said, dumbfounded, and then, "Oh, I dunno—I should probably go."

"Seriously, Erika is looking for you. She wants you upstairs." Mary Anne insisted, and then Megan chimed in.

"Let's go, Al, you don't want to leave a woman waiting."

I gulped. The thought "this is getting weird" was sloshing vaguely around in the half of my drunken brain that was left to actual thinking. The next thing I knew, they've pulled me up off the couch and pushed me up the stairs. I stumbled blindly into a dark bedroom to find Erika dressed in just a T-shirt. I got the idea, but was baffled by the fact I'd hardly ever spoken to this girl and could barely make out her form, though she was soon lying right next to me. I have only slight recollections of rustling around together: the banging of faces, the abrupt rubbing of bodies, and the blurry excitement sparked with numbing fear. I remember being blinded by dizziness and queasiness, and finally passing out after some sloppy attempts at intercourse. What a Romeo.

I woke up mortified, guilty, and confused in the morning and demanded that Mary Anne drive me home immediately. A week later, I was out when my mom said a girl named Erika had come by, and I couldn't for the life of me think of who it could have been. I never saw or talked to her again.

There were many similar "romantic" encounters throughout high school. There was Donna, a remotely cute, skinny metal-head who drove a recently converted Ford LTD cop car. Donna supposedly had a "slutty" reputation, which I drunkenly took advantage of one night after a party as I uncharacteristically offered to walk her to her car. She was mad at her boyfriend, or they were broken up for the week, or "whatever," I told myself as I kissed her goodnight, pressing her probably way too hard against the rear door panel. The next thing we knew, we were in the back seat ravaging each other.

There was Sarah Akers, and the blow jobs late on school nights out on the golf course. Carrie, at fifteen with incredible boobs, who wore tons of makeup and looked as if she was nineteen, willing to go for it on the floor of Chris's garage. Shelly, the banker's daughter, who dressed preppy, but was actually dark and mysterious and obsessed with Jim Morrison. A terrible kisser, but insistent about having sex in her father's office while he was nodding off in front of a Yankees game in the other room. Who was I to argue?

And then there was my high school sweetheart, Etoile Mayette (hippie French, I can only guess). She lived up to her gorgeous French name and self in a house just down the street from me, and was "the first." I mean the first everything: sex, intimacy, secrecy, "love" (if that's what you can call a high school relationship that lasts a couple of years). I was crazy for Etoile; I absolutely adored her. She was funny, kind, generous, and beautiful. Racing-green eyes, long amber-blond hair, a soft round face, and a perfectly sensuous curvy body—she was voluptuous and expressive, not nervous and skinny like a lot of the girls in my class. Our relationship was turbulent from the get-go. Her open sexuality and willingness was both exciting and unnerving.

She told me she couldn't get pregnant, so we didn't need to worry about birth control. A seventeen-year-old's dream. Or was I sixteen? After months of pressing her on why, she told me. A seventeen-year-old's nightmare. She had been sexually abused by her uncle when she was eleven, and told me that was why she couldn't get pregnant, even if she wanted to. I had no clue what to do with that information, or how to be understanding or supportive. She used to sneak over to my house after hours and spend the night—one of the few benefits of having oblivious parents. When she'd leave in the morning, she would just tell my dad that she'd come by to pick up a homework assignment for class. "Oh, okay," Dad would chortle, a little baffled.

One Friday night after a party, we were back at my house in the secret loft above my bedroom. To get there, you had to climb a set of steep stairs and enter through a black square in the ceiling. I kept my stereo and records up there, and there was a bookshelf and a small, dark blue fold-out couch. One minute we were making out on the couch, and the next thing I knew, Etoile pulled away and started whimpering and apologizing.

"I'm sorry . . . I'm sorry . . . Al . . . I'm really, really sorry . . ." she said.

"I slept with Ken."

I pictured stoner Ken with his bad posture, chronically torn Grateful Dead T-shirts, dour personality, and yet rather large size, thinking for a second how I might bash the shit out of someone that big, perhaps with my lacrosse stick.

"You what?" I said as I turned away and grimaced, feeling the wind knocked out of me as if I had been sucker punched in the gut. Then I turned back and said slowly, and with a slight slur, "You . . . fucking . . . bitch." I smacked her not once, but twice, and then a third time.

Etoile was bawling now, curled in the fetal position and pleading, begging me to stop. "Al, stop, please stop, you're hurting me!"

"You should just fucking leave. Get out!"

"I can't go home now, my parents think I'm at Allison's."

"That's not my fucking problem," I said, leaning against the wall, clutching one of Mom's Heinekens I had stolen from the fridge on my way upstairs.

"Please, Al, it's over between Ken and me."

"Bullshit, just go."

"Don't make me walk home in the dark, you know how scared I am of this walk . . ."

"Tough shit. Leave," I demanded. And with that, she slowly peeled herself from the couch and snuck downstairs past my father, who had nodded off in front of *Jeopardy.* She slipped out the kitchen door and walked the mile and a half back to her house in the dark.

I had never hit a girl before, except my own sisters, which is bad enough, but this was different and new, hitting a girl, a wounded, innocent girl. I cried for a minute or two, finished off the Heineken, and then passed out on the blue couch. Thinking back on it, there was something familiar in the way I hit it her, a kind of enraged swatting. It was all too reminiscent of the way Miss Hedy would swat at me when I talked back or refused to clean my room.

Etoile had the good sense to stop talking to me. And though I was still madly in love with her, after weeks of begging for forgiveness, I finally just gave up, and moved on.

With all these girls, there was always alcohol involved. Nothing was initiated without a minimum blood-alcohol content of at least 0.2 percent. There was something about the vulnerability, the raw exposure, the intimacy that I just couldn't handle. The body, my body, was somehow shameful or dirty. The whole sexual experience was somehow goofy and embarrassing. There were no men in my life or my friends' lives who were open and strong enough to initiate conversations about sexuality—no one who actually knew anything, or told us what to do, how to treat a girl with dignity and respect. We were always just winging it based on what we saw in the movies and magazines or on TV. When guys talked about sex, it was always joking and boasting, or ragging on one another for hooking up with so and so: "I can't believe you did Jenny Forini," or whoever—"I'd never do that shit!" Blah blah blah.

In my circle, there was this chronic nasty shit-talk and disrespect about girls; it was mean and disgraceful. There was never any talk about technique or how to give, just always how to *get* some." We were so lost and ignorant that we could only dismiss each other and jabber nastily in order to hide our true vulnerabilities. The primary feelings that I experienced and would never admit to were extreme nervousness and paralyzing fear. I was prone to great shyness, insecurity, and an awkwardness verging on paranoia.

At the same time, there was the animal lust, the primal craving for sexual expression, and ultimately, beneath that, I suppose, a longing for some kind of connection, of nurturing and acceptance. An acceptance that I never would have been able to recognize no matter how often it appeared in the sometimes sweet, gentle, and caring girls I ended up with. Girls, I might add, who were often as lost as I was, just in a different way. Girls, who were often struggling with absent or alcoholic fathers, or who, like Etoile, had been sexually abused. It felt safer to be numb, to blank out the deeper realities, to avoid the vulnerabilities and thereby remain blind to any acceptance and true attention I might have gotten.

\* \* \*

I'll never forget mid-spring senior year of high school, the night after a party at my friend Mike's house, and I was "hung as the dickens," as usual. We had a big banquet at school in the cafeteria. I was sitting on the radiator by the window next to Mr. Arrund, who had massive horse teeth, legendary halitosis, a Shakespearean-era beard, and a high-pitched wheezing laugh. We used to call him Mr. Airhead. He could have been the dad to our class president, Rich Goldletter: same beard, same big teeth. And they were both wearing paisley vests. Are they starting a movement? I thought to myself, as Rich stood up to give his predictions for what each of us would be doing in twenty years. I was excited, imagining what he might say about me: Division I lacrosse coach? Tennis pro? Movie director? I was wishing he *wouldn't* say something like "hopeless lush."

Mostly, it was hilarious. He was rattling on with exaggerated characterizations about each person in our small class of about sixty, clearly trying to be funny. Etoile, for example, was to own a lingerie shop. Pat was going to be an opera star; Jojo was going to be a physicist; Roger, a rock and roll producer; Mary, a scuba instructor in the Bahamas. When he got to me, I stood and perked up my ears like an attentive dog. He said, "In twenty years, ladies and gentleman, Al DeSilver is going to be . . . a really nice guy!" A couple of people chuckled, someone moaned. There was a brief uncomfortable silence, and then he launched into the next kid. I was crushed, devastated, deflated—everyone had a character and vocation except me. I would have settled for fireman, janitor, prison guard, serial killer for fuck's sake, but nice guy, that was pretty much like not existing.

We had nicknamed our history teacher Fathead because we couldn't take him seriously to teach us anything. He did, in fact, have a huge, fat head and a thinning comb-over, and tiny, delusional brown eyes. We used to steal and throw his Blucher moccasins out the window of the portables when he got all casual on us and took them off, crossing his legs on the desk exposing his chubby feet wrapped in expensive blue socks. He bought us booze and drugs and hung out with us on weekends. It's embarrassing to admit now, but he was a kind of party god to me at the time.

Fathead was slick and fun, and a fast talker. He was kind, generous, and forgiving to a fault, especially when it came to us *not* handing in our homework. He listened to our music, drove a new red BMW with spoilers (it turns out he was an heir to an aviation fortune), and was always joking with us, never being authoritative, mean, or controlling. This was huge for me, as I was suspicious of most adults, and Fathead was more like one of us. He ran all the outside-school adventure trips, ski trips in the winter (with never a shortage of cocaine), and a trip to Russia every year.

Then my friend Mike and I, and two other kids we didn't know that well, signed up for the five-week European tour in the summer of 1986. We were supposed to go to the Jazz Festival at Montreux, boating in Interlaken, and the beer gardens in Munich. Fathead rarely showed, or he showed up late. Otherwise, we were guided around by Kenneth, an athletic, brainy stoner guy just out of college. We spent much of our time sampling the many bars throughout France, Switzerland, Austria, Germany, and finally Amsterdam (God help us). The son of a certain secretary of state was on that trip, and we had him crawling around on his hands and knees stoned out of his head in a small hotel room outside of Innsbruck, looking for a chunk of hash that had been snarfed out of the bowl we had just been smoking.

Back home, word got out that we could stop by Fathead's house to say hi on certain Saturday nights. And so we did. He was often found sitting around with a few twenty- and thirty-somethings, drinking and doing lines of coke. This became a regular scene, and soon we were constantly hitting Fathead up for dope and beer. My friend, Leslie, at seventeen, was always there before I got there, and stayed after I left. She was a skinny, feisty, and rebellious redhead, permanently adorned in tie-dye threads, who lived, even more so than I, for the Grateful Dead. She loved to do acid, which skewed her judgment just a wee bit. It soon became obvious she was sleeping with our thirty-eight-year-old Fathead.

One night, we ran out of beer while at a party at Fathead's house. Fathead stood up and said "Beer run anyone?" No one volunteered, so I jumped at the chance to hang one-on-one with my "mentor." We took his M-Series BMW and blasted up to the New York State line where we could buy beer after hours. We bought a couple of cases and sped back down Route 123 toward the house. We must have been doing about eighty when Fathead busted out the lines right there on the dashboard and started cutting them up with a beer between his legs and one hand on the wheel. He leaned into the black abyss of the dashboard and snorted away as we veered into the other lane. I was simultaneously terrified and excited, in awe that Fathead could pull off such craziness and that I had been chosen to come along for the ride.

Fathead reportedly had connections on Nantucket Island for work and places to stay in the summer. So one year, Mike and Schmitty—my two best friends from St. Luke's at the time—and I went out early for the weekend—I think it was late April of 1987. He said he'd meet us out there and hook us up with a restaurant-owner friend of his for jobs and rooms to rent for the summer. Off we went with a car full of beer and about twenty dollars to our name, assuming Fathead would take care of us once we were on the island.

"We'll getcha squared away," he always used to say with a goofy smile, which exposed tiny teeth spaced way too far apart for such a fat head. Whenever he said he'd get us squared away, he always had a twisted glint in his beady little eyes, and we never actually ended up getting "squared away."

"Grab me another beer," I said to Mike once we were on the ferry.

"That's the last one," he said defensively.

"I've only had eight," I replied, swaying.

"Wow, that's all? I've had six, you fuck," said Mike. "God love ya, your generosity is a spiritual gift."

"Hey, check them out," sang out Schmitty, eyeing a group of thirty-something women.

"Sea scrag," giggled Mike. One of them peeled off the group and headed toward us. "Oh shit, now look what you've done," he whispered under his breath.

"Go, Schmitty, go!" I chided, way too loud, as the woman approached.

"What are you guys up to?"

"Oh, just having a few cocktails and checking out the beautiful scenery," I said, even though it was pitch black and we were inside the cabin drinking cheap beer.

"Where you headed?" she asked.

"I don't know," offered Schmitty, "the island is our oyster." He paused. "Actually, we're meeting a friend at The Wharf Bar or . . . and . . . Restaurant," he managed to add, trying not to sound too stupid and drunk.

"Oh, I know that place," she said. "A friend of mine works there."

"Oh, cool," said Schmitty awkwardly.

There was a pause, and then she waved her friends over. They looked like big people to me, as in older women, like close to our moms' ages. I felt immediately like the self-conscious eighteen year old I was.

"This is Melissa and Candace," she said. "Oh, and I'm Brandy."

They said hello with scrutiny and an obvious lack of enthusiasm as Schmitty pumped his chest up and I took another nervous swig from my beer. "Hey, girls," crooned Schmitty.

Melissa and Candace replied with a deflated "Hey" while rolling their eyes.

"Want a beer?" said Brandy, eye-balling Schmitty.

"Sure," chimed Schmitty. "I think Al here is finishing off the last one of ours—thanks, Al."

And then Mike said abruptly, "Hurry up, you fucking wuss! Drink up, bitch!" I was completely blasted already and having a hard time staying on my feet, especially given that the boat was rocking in the early-spring waves.

It wasn't as if we didn't shit-talk each other into oblivion on a daily basis, but somehow this time I'd hit my limit. Just as my "Fuck you" rebuttal was escaping my lips, I turned, feeling the lightning-fast guttural vomit impulse take over, and found myself retching into the standing ashtray to my right. It was one of those silver ones with the split top that opens onto a small tray of sand.

I'm one of those alarmingly loud retchers. Like you think my guts are being torn out by a Rototiller. Melissa—or was it Brandy?—or whoever was standing next to me smoking in a dingy blue dress the color of bleak waves, shot sideways as if she was being electrocuted. Then she threw her cigarette at me in disgust, like I *was* the ashtray. Everyone turned to stare. I felt pinned to the wall by a sheet of eyeballs that read, "What a pathetic kid! He can't even hold his liquor." This was written in bloodshot red ink in the whites of glaring eyes, when in reality, they all had probably turned away in horror and resumed their drunken banter. I was just another casualty of the late-night ferry to Nantucket.

As I slid down the wall, gathering up my shame in a tidy heap for proper storage, I realized that I was in sketchy company. Familiar, but sketchy. There was a cutting depth and meanness to Mike's comment about me being a wuss that hurt, even though it happened all the time. He got me this time at the perfect moment of vulnerability in front of women. I became quietly ashamed. I couldn't hold my liquor and couldn't keep up with the boys, or anyone on the boat, or in my life at the time!

We had no real contacts, no money, no place to stay, and no way of connecting with Fathead. We didn't even have any more beer. So we glommed on to these women and they, tentatively, to us. We arrived on the island around 11 P.M., drunk as hell and without a clue in the world as to where we were. I remember hanging around a sparsely populated bar for a while after getting separated from our women friends, feeling uncomfortable and then wandering out into the cold, salty Nantucket night.

We sat on a fog-coated bench and contemplated our fate for what seemed like an eternity, when out of the night, headlights slowly appeared. The car pulled up, the window rolled down. It was Brandy, demanding that we get in. Behind the wheel was an obese salty dog of a man who seemed to be driving with his distended belly. She introduced him as Bluefin Bob and said he had a little song to sing to us. And then after some awkward silence followed by deafening wheezing, Bluefin Bob proceeded to mutter under his belabored breath something like "Don't complain, do cocaine, go insane." He would chuckle, take an excessively long drag on his cigarette, and then repeat the lyrics to his "song." This went on for what seemed like an hour as we drove farther into the Nantucket night.

I didn't think the island was that big. Was Bluefin Bob driving us in circles? Brandy was looking for a place we could all sleep. Finally, we arrived at a place that was being remodeled. There was plaster and plywood strewn about, buckets of nails, exposed walls, stacks of Sheetrock, and beer bottles and cigarette butts everywhere. There were a couple of mattresses leaned up against a wall, and a piano. Bluefin Bob came in and played a tune on the piano. It was three in the morning. We were drunk and exhausted.

I woke up a few hours later in an ominous haze with Mike snoring loudly next to me on a ratty mattress. I felt immediately disoriented and then depressed, sensing a scary energy in the room. I looked up toward the wall behind me and noticed a huge black cross above the mattress. Brandy came by in the morning to give us a ride back to town, and when we asked her what was with the black cross, she said nonchalantly, "Oh yeah, Jakey died in that room a few weeks back from a heroin overdose."

Fathead never showed. No jobs, no connections, no fucking blow! In town, we sat on a bench near the ferry terminal nursing a warm Michelob she had found under the seat of her car, wondering how the hell we would be getting back to Hyannisport.

9

# Chuck

Though we did make it back from Hyannisport (hungover and depressed as usual), I ended up barely making it out of high school, or into college, alive, let alone with decent grades. Good grades were about as high on my list of priorities as joining the debate team, learning to sew, or becoming an altar boy (though a friend of mine who came from a devout Catholic family and went to church most Sundays told me that the blood of Christ he got to taste at communion was actually red wine, and I thought, shit, I'll drink to that). Needless to say, I didn't get into any of my first choice colleges. Throughout high school, my grades went from Ds and Cs to Cs, and then a couple of Bs appeared. Some saw this as an "improvement." But just as Mom dreaded, I wound up at "East Jesus U." This was Mom's name for an obscure college "no one ever heard of," like Hartwick in upstate New York (which was on my list), or like the College of Wooster in Ohio, where I ended up for a year. Mom wanted me to go to Yale, Harvard, or Princeton with the upper classes. Sorry, Mom.

Right after high school, I spent eight miserable months in north central Ohio, which is enough to drive anyone to drink. My dorm room was a gray concrete block jail cell, complete with opposing bunk beds extending out from matching built-in desks. The windows even had wire mesh in them so we couldn't escape. To say it was a bit cramped is to say the Pacific Ocean is a bit big. It was disgusting, and then on top of it, I got paired with a super-geek named Keener. The first day, I spotted a fellow Deadhead kid down the hall paired with a preppy soccer player. I knew there had been a mistake with the pairings on our hall, and set about to reconfigure the entire social order.

I soon wound up rooming with Tommy, the Deadhead from Buffalo. He was a perfect influence, a hard-edged intellectual drug addict. His parents were city politicians, and we had a civics class together that I went to all the time and failed, and Tommy never went to and got an A. Tommy drank like a fish and did tons of acid and even heroin. This seemed to help his grades. When our literature professor asked him to be his teaching assistant, I was convinced he was a genius. *Maybe I just need to do more hard drugs*, I thought briefly to myself. He introduced me to Cody and Rick, also Deadheads and drug addicts, but definitely not geniuses. It turned out they grew up a couple towns over from me in Connecticut.

We all hit it off "like gangbusters," as Mom used to say. We got right to smoking pot more often than we breathed air, and immediately discovered and began frequenting the drive-through liquor store five times a day, which was three more times than we went to the Hardee's or KFC. Tommy and I went to class some of the time, Cody and Rick, never. They lived in a notoriously shady dorm, where there was a party pretty much every night of the week in their hall. These guys were severe stoners and completely twisted. I mean super twisted, like look who's talking. They practically wore hash pipes around their necks. Their primary piece of furniture was a legendary gigantic glass bong that you had to stand up to use. It was perpetually packed with weed, and God knows what else. They called it Chuck.

Chuck had a terrifying picture of Charles Manson Scotch-taped to its side. "Come here, my children, and smoke with Chuck," Cody and Rick giggled and slurred with crazed bloodshot eyes whenever we showed up in the doorway. On numerous occasions, we would get so drunk and stoned at their place, we would just crawl out of their room after finishing our twelfth or thirteenth Milwaukee's Best ($3.99 a case!) and toss our bottles down to the far end of the hall, shattering them against the concrete. There was a perpetual pile of broken glass at the end of the hall. When we got tired of that, we would hurl our bottles out into the courtyard or the back parking lot, reveling in the sound. This shattering of glass was a kind of music to our ears, the visceral music of explosions, the mindlessly seductive music of self-destruction.

Sometimes, when we were done with the shattering of things, we would wander campus with a half-eaten box of pizza, looking for an open third-story window to throw our leftover slices into. A loud and alarmed "What the fuck?" sent us into joyous fits of laughter as we stumbled across the gloomy campus green at 3 A.M.

One night, I was driving back to my dorm from a party off campus completely hammered when I veered into the other lane and back again one too many times. A cop pulled me over right in front of Delta Tau's front door. He hauled me out of the car to perform all the classic sobriety tests (except for a Breathalyzer, by some miracle of grace, which I would have instantly failed): fingers to nose, reciting the alphabet backward, etc. I promptly poked myself in the eye and forgot the letters V, S, P, and H in between long pauses and saying, "Wait, wait, I got it this time."

Meanwhile, a rowdy collection of Delta Tau guys had assembled on the front lawn and were yelling, "Throw him in the fucking can!" "Haul his ass off to jail!" "Cuff him and stuff him!"

As if that wasn't inspiration enough, I didn't have my license on me, because I had altered it to make me twenty-six when I was actually only nineteen. I didn't carry it on me for this specific reason. I thought I was thinking that one through. However, it quickly came to my attention that the police like you to have an ID on you at all times, and they especially like you to have your license on you when operating heavy machinery, like a motor vehicle. So I begged and pleaded with the cop and told him my license was right around the corner at my dorm. He hesitated, and then said, "Okay, kid, I'll follow you around the corner to your dorm. Drive nice and slow and steady."

Off we drove around the block to my dorm room, stepping through piles of broken glass in the parking lot and in the stairwells, and when I opened the door to my room, there were, surprise surprise, dozens of empty beer cans strewn about and a large bong sitting on the window sill. "Oh, that's my roommate's stuff," I said, rummaging through the top drawer of my dresser pretending to look for my license and saying loudly, "Geez, you know I had it this afternoon, and I swear I put it in here before I went to the pool . . . it's got to be around here somewhere," and just as I was about to give up and surrender, I found the receipt for my license that New York state used to issue before they sent the actual license in the mail.

So I said, "Oh, wow, will this work? It's the receipt they gave me when I renewed my license last year."

Officer Softy looked at it suspiciously and then called in some numbers on his walkie-talkie. He paced around the room and then after some muffled static came back through, turned to me and said, "You lucked out, kid. Just promise me you won't get back behind the wheel tonight, yes? And have a good night." With that, he turned and left, and I breathed the longest sigh of relief ever. With the fear and adrenaline still churning through my veins, I mindlessly took a huge slug off one of the half-drunk warm Milwaukee's Best cans sitting on Tommy's dresser. And then in a panicked fit of quick disgust, spit out the cigarette butt that had been floating silently within, right onto Tommy's pillow.

\* \* \*

"There's no way I'm staying trapped in this shit-hole, surrounded by such dumb-ass vermin—and neither are you!" Tommy had said as he dropped my mail from a couple of days before on the bed next to me. I was sitting on the bed in my cellblock at Wooster one morning in October nursing a warm beer and a hideous hangover. At the top of the pile was the CU Boulder spring catalogue. I had forgotten I sent away for it. On the cover was a full-page aerial view of campus, with the famous "Flatiron" rock formations contrasted against the towering snow-capped peaks of the Rocky Mountain front range. I was mesmerized. Ever since Etoile had gone off to the University of Denver straight out of high school, I had idolized Colorado, or was it her *in* Colorado? If she had decided to go to Detroit Tech, I probably would have idolized Detroit.

Growing up skiing the frustratingly small hills of Connecticut and Massachusetts, I had always dreamed of skiing the glorious slopes of Vail, Breckenridge, and Copper Mountain. In that moment, I decided I would go to the University of Colorado at Boulder. I wasn't sure how, given my shitty grades and commitment to cheap beer, but I somehow became instantly determined. I started dragging my generally resistant ass to the library after class, and conducting research on the school. Tommy and I actually set time aside to write our papers, and to read for our literature, archeology, and geology classes. We put in a little effort to get our grades up. I took my first photography class, and people liked my pictures. From then on, I started carrying a camera around with me wherever I went. Someone had mentioned that you could actually major in art, in taking pictures. What a concept. That was my in.

We sent in our applications, mine to Boulder, Tommy's to NYU. We supported each other's dreams of escape between drunken binges, with Tommy constantly declaring, "I'm done with this shit-hole, and free of these dumb-assed vermin!" For spring break I went to visit CU and stayed with some high school friends in Boulder and in Ft. Collins at CSU. I had the ultimate blast of a time partying with my friend's older brother at his fraternity and skiing at Vail and Copper Mountain. I became further obsessed with everything Colorado. The University of Eternal Bliss and Fun! On my return from spring break, I received a conditional acceptance from CU. I needed to attend summer school. Surrrrre. No problem.

Summertime in Boulder—heaven on earth! But first, I would have to get through a depressingly cold, rainy season or two in Ohio.

\* \* \*

Toward the end of my first semester at Wooster, I called Mom a few weeks before Christmas just to check in on everyone's plans for the holidays. I imagined her sitting on the couch by the window, mindlessly combing her eyebrows with her perfect fingernails, reading an Agatha Christie novel, a glass of white wine placed on a coaster with an image of an Italian piazza on it, and a Benson & Hedges 100 burning in the ashtray.

"Hello my treasure. Oh, oh, listen, I have a terrific joke for you—what's Irish and stays outside all year round?"

"I don't know Mom, what?" was my drowsy I'm-sure-I've-heard-this-one-a-thousand-times reply.

"Patty O'Furniture," she said, laughing hysterically and so loudly that I had to hold the phone away from my ear.

"Isn't that heaven?" she said. "Oh, guess who I had dinner with last night?"

"I don't know Mom, Vaclav Havel?"

"Good guess, but no. Alan Alda."

"You're kidding," I said genuinely excited. "What's he like in real life?"

"Well, I'm not sure honestly. I mean, he was at the next table over, but isn't that marvelous!"

"Yes, marvelous—" I said with a slightly disappointed sigh. There was an empty pause.

"So, how are you, my angel? What's new? How is O-Hi-O? Is it still terrible, rainy, and cold, and fantastically miserable?"

"Yes, still miserable, though I'm not so sure about the fantastically part," I said. "I'm planning to transfer to Colorado."

"Colorado, why the hell would you want to go there? Your father dragged me to Colorado Springs one time. Ugh, such a leper colony!"

"I'm planning on Boulder, which I think is pretty much leper-free. But they do have this thing called sun, plus Etoile is at the University of Denver. Boulder has a decent art department, and I could ski a lot."

"Is that what we're paying for, an extended ski vacation? I thought you and Etoile were finished. Why don't you just go to Yale, like your father?"

"Because I could never get into Yale like my father. And yes, Etoile and I are finished, but I'm still mad for her."

"Don't we know someone who could help you get in the door?"

"No, Mom, I don't want to go to Yale, all right? I just want to go to Colorado."

"All right then, never mind . . ." She paused for a second and then continued with a more serious tone. "There actually *is* some big news I should to tell you." I held my breath trying to imagine what it could be. So uncharacteristic of Mom to reveal "big news."

"Miss Hedy corked it last month."

"Oh," I said going blank and numb. "Wow, that is something. How did she die?" I asked, incurious.

"A heart attack, I think," said Mom, "That seems appropriate, don't ya think?"

"Sure," I said quietly.

"You kids couldn't stand her, could you? She was kind of a shit, really."

"That would be an understatement—are they having some kind of service?" I interrupted myself so as to not go off on a manic accusatory rant.

"Oh, I suppose her sister will." In classic Mom style she abruptly changed the subject, which was a relief. I wasn't sure how much of that news I wanted to get into.

"So when are you coming? Your father and I can't wait to see you for Christmas! I think your sister, Margaret, is coming; you know she's run off to Ireland and has cooped herself up in some religious cult. She's even shaved her head and looks like fucking Sinead O'Connor—and Christ knows what they feed her over there. You know we're having a lovely roast beef for Christmas dinner—God help me if she's gone vegetarian on us. Tell me you're not one of *those*."

"Okay, I'm not one of *those*," I said, "but I'm still a vegetarian. Remember, Mom? We went through all of this at Thanksgiving."

"Oh for fuck's sake. Well, then, you kids are on your own. You and your sister can fight over the canned beets, mashed potatoes, and pureed broccoli—promise me you'll bring some decent clothes. Last time your sister came to visit I took her to a very smart restaurant in New York and she showed up in monk's attire. I was so embarrassed I didn't know where to look. I said to Joannie the other day at lunch, for Christ's sake, my kids are such hoods. I mean, really, you don't wear your fucking Buddhist robes to see Bobby Short at the Carlyle."

* * *

I met Amy that first semester at Wooster. She was from Rochester or Syracuse, one of those Greco Roman up-state New York cities that seemed so remote and exotic to me. I decided Amy was the one to help me get over Etoile. We met in the art building. She was taking drawing and painting, and we ended up in a photography class together. She was a talented illustrator and artist, and she said something nice about one of my pictures and that was it. No one had said anything nice to or about me since I'd been there. Plus, she had blond straight hair, a cute smile, was athletic and healthy looking, and didn't wear makeup. She was super friendly and sweet in that innocent Midwestern kind of way. She was the opposite of Etoile, in that she was a bit prudish, not much of a partier, emotionally reserved, and fairly conservative, whereas Etoile was curvy and voluptuous and sexually easy, would experiment with drugs, and was silly and dramatic.

I'm not sure how Amy and I even hooked up (though I'm certain I was drunk at the time) or what she possibly could have seen in miserable little me. We were pretty much opposites. Even though it took us forever by freshman-college-boy standards to sleep together, we finally did, and it was a big deal for her, like her second time or something, and then we ended up getting pretty attached to each other.

As spring turned to summer and I was leaving Ohio for Colorado, our relationship began to come apart. We had one last glorious early-summer week together in the Thousand Islands of the Saint Lawrence Seaway, where her parents owned an island. We snuggled and made love under the stars, swam and picked blueberries, and explored the tiny uninhabited islands by canoe.

As I was leaving, Amy said, "We have to talk."

I said, "About what?"

And she said, "About you going to Colorado."

And I said, "What about it?"

And she said, "I don't think we can keep this going," and I said, "What do you mean? We're having this amazing time, and I love you, and . . ." And she said, "I can't do this anymore from a distance. . ."

I was torn, and yet some silent part of me knew there was no way I wasn't going to Colorado. I had built up such a hatred of Ohio, and after my spring break adventures, I knew Colorado was my place. Getting out of Ohio was simply more important to me than staying with Amy, which didn't make me any less emotionally attached to her. And so we separated, with me feeling pretty much dumped after an epic week in the Seaway being "in love."

Part II

# 10

# Rocky Mountain Low

"Is it true you passed out in the Daley's driveway?" Mom asked, leaning over the hospital bed and gripping the shiny metal rails violently, as if she were holding the safety bar of the roller coaster that was me.

I could tell she was disappointed. No matter how much she drank, she *never* passed out.

"What were you thinking, son?" said Dad. Both parents staring at me, their eyes simultaneously narrowing as if they were listening to an inscrutable physics lecture at the Smithsonian. And for all of what they might have said, what stuck was the disappointment.

I thought about saying, "Well, Mom and Dad, you see, I was contemplating Descarte's reflections on existence, and was feeling that since Amy bailed on me, I didn't even exist, and since I was feeling like I didn't exist, well then maybe I didn't, so what's the point? I mean nobody gives a shit anyway (clearly you don't), so let's fucking party to the point of annihilation."

But instead I said what I always said, "I don't know . . . I don't know," I repeated softly into the void of the hospital ceiling tiles.

The silence could have sawed the hospital room in half. They stared and stared at me and shook their heads in disbelief. I turned my head toward the crumpled blinds and noticed a rectangle of uncovered window that suddenly appeared as both a gigantic glass tower leaning ominously over me, and a sliver of light I might one day escape through. The top part of the window housed a faded blue sky with a single cloud that looked like a half-eaten powdered doughnut that had collapsed in on itself. The lower part held a cement truck backing into a ditch on the other side of the freeway. I imagined myself crushed in that ditch pinned under the cement truck. A shiver ran through my body. I thought I could hear the repetitive beeping of its backing up. But, then I realized it was a nearby cardio machine keeping track of somebody's slowing heartbeat. Was that mine? It seemed an awful long time between beats. There was a grave darkness pooling inside me as Mom and Dad stood over the hospital bed, their eyes glazed in befuddlement.

By all accounts, I was lucky to be alive. Mike Castelton's car had mangled my left leg with severe lacerations, not to mention the fact that my blood-alcohol level was almost .4%, fatal for most people. Somehow Mike had heard me screaming or felt something over the blasting CSN tape, his lust for Deirdre, and his own drunkenness. He stopped the car in time, he and Deirdre dragged me bleeding into the back seat and rushed me to the hospital.

Being so close to death didn't faze me in the least, probably because I felt so far away from life. The mysterious force that sent me staggering back to the keg again and again, and finally blacking out within an inch of certain death, turned out to be same force that would eventually begin to offer me increasing glimpses of light that I would slowly open to. Eventually, I would see beauty and purpose. I would start to see that my presence, even my words, and the silences between, could matter to the world. As a small child I know, however diaphanously, that I felt bursts of enchantment, and even an appreciation for the beauty of the world. I saw it in the peonies in my parents' garden at the Clock Tower, the buds peppered with tiny ants, buds the size of an adult fist, their fuchsia explosions of color and light, petals slightly lifting, wanting, wanting more light, aching to unfold, all the while glowing against my curious face. And yet, somehow I also felt a grave distance between me and that beauty, a distance that would lengthen over time, and eventually contract back into oneness.

\* \* \*

After the "accident" the summer before, I quit drinking for a couple of months. However, by the time I moved to Colorado in the fall, the social pressure and temptation were too great. I still just didn't get it. I was so nervous and socially insecure, and so familiar with drinking as antidote, as social lubricant, that I started to feel good about how animated and at ease I was around people when drunk. It became an identity. I saw myself as such a bore when sober, nervous and reserved, but when drunk, look out, I could spin a fabulous yarn, just like Mom, and in that increasingly important social context, I could beam.

I started slowly, with a few beers here and there, then a few more. Then some bargaining in the form of telling myself I would drink only fine micro brews and imported beers in limited amounts. This didn't last, yet didn't register much as I rationalized that I hadn't been completely out-of-control drunk in months, so "what's the big deal?"

I grew my hair long to be a proper deadhead, to fit in, to make a statement for I didn't know what, and to create a kind of emo-hedge I could hide behind. I fell in with the wrong crowd, led by my roommate, Ted, stud long-hair partier extraordinaire. It wasn't but a couple weeks into fall semester, after we moved off campus, that we had our first party. There was plenty of Ecstasy, cocaine, and endless amounts of beer. We started at some frat house across from campus, and I was so high on X that I couldn't talk. And I was thirsty, like chronically dragging-my-wounded-ass- across-the-desert thirsty, and so I just stood by the keg to rehydrate, practicing my role as "keg barnacle." Little did I know this was one of the "side effects" of X—dehydration. In no time, I was close to blind drunk and was offered some mushrooms, which I promptly ate, and then wound up back at our apartment only to find a pile of naked people in my bed completely strung out on coke and Ecstasy. They were writhing around like a pit of paisley snakes, drooling and slurring, bubbling into an amoebic mass, all the while massaging each other with sweaty tentacled limbs, moaning loudly, and smacking their lips. It sounded like having my head forced inside a washing machine just after the soap had been dispensed.

I stood there in mounting horror and then screamed at the top of my lungs. At first just sound came out, a kind of mortified I'm-about-to-get-hit-by-a-truck terror scream, and then the words "GET THE FUCK OUT OF MY ROOM!" fell out of my mouth like a bucket of lead hammers—"OUT, OUT, OUT, NOW!!" There was a lot of "Whoa, dude, chill out, buzz clamp, mannnnn—we're all just having a loving time here . . ." and some reaching out to hug me, and I just responded, "Don't fucking touch me, LEAVE NOW!!"

"Okay, okay, man, we're going, don't be such a Nazi freak . . ."

They left and then I left, and proceeded to wander around with some lusty blurred memory of trying to hook up with my friend Kaitlin. I guess Ted saw me panic and storm off into the night. I made it a couple blocks down the road before I blacked out for real.

Apparently Ted found me a few blocks from the apartment, stumbling around with a broomstick smashing mailboxes, outdoor sidewalk lamps, headlights—anything that would make a shattering noise.

The next morning, I woke up in Ted's bed, naked, nauseous, nerve-rattled—with more than just a hangover. I felt psychotically depressed, as in, scary dis-regulated. Ted brought me my glasses, which he found under the couch and which looked like they had been run over by a steamroller. Both lenses were missing, and the frames were pretzeled. One look at my face, and Ted could tell I wasn't right. Even he was concerned, though relieved I had made it through the night alive (still breathing and not behind bars), and eventually we kind of laughed about how I, in a hallucinatory rage, shouted the orgy ensemble out of my room, naked and dragging their clothes behind them.

The psychotic, depressed feeling wouldn't go away. This was no ordinary hangover. I felt as if I had been held underwater too long, and in the absence of oxygen I had lost some of my brain. I was trapped in a sticky, dank concrete cell that turned out to be the thick, deadening weight of my own skin. I moped around the apartment for the next week, confused, bagging class after class. Finally, I phoned my parents and told them I needed to come home for a long weekend. "Things are moving too fast for me out here" is how I phrased it.

They were a bit baffled. "Sure, come on home. We'd love to see you."

Back in New York one night, Dad and I were sitting at the round wooden kitchen table while Mom was making dinner. She asked me to open the wine that now stood glowing on the table before us. The sun had just gone down, and I was staring out the big solarium window at the giant tulip tree that was spared when they built this new house. The leaves looked exactly like the profile shape of a tulip flower, if flattened.

"How's my beamish boy?" said Dad, putting his hand on my shoulder, and clearly *trying* to be affectionate. It was sweet, but forced.

"Not that great, actually," I said quietly.

"Oh Harrison, tell Albert your lovely new rhyming thingy," said Mom.

"That would be called a Limerick, dear. Ah, yes, let's see." Dad was ruminating. I was bracing myself.

"Okay, I've got it.
*There once was a fellow from Sparta*
*a truly magnificent farter.*
*On the strength of the bean,*
*He'd fart 'God Save the Queen'*

*And Beethoven's Moonlight Sonata."*

"Would you like a bit of wine, darling?" Mom said, interrupting our giggles. She had a Benson & Hedges hanging out of her mouth. She was dressed in a stained Zabar's apron over her faded green cashmere sweater, a large gold brooch sloppily dangling just below her left clavicle. She had a Kleenex stuffed in the sleeve of her left arm.

"No, thanks," I said with visible agitation. "That's why I'm here, Mom."

"It's not like you're an alcoholic or something," Dad said.

"Oh no?" I said.

"Aren't you just having perhaps a bit too much fun right now, son? I mean, we used to drink quite a bit when I was in college."

"And get run over by cars and wind up in the hospital?" I said.

"Well, I did get sick a couple of times."

"Yeah, well, I've been smoking a lot of pot, too," I blurted out. I guess I was trying to alarm them. I had never mentioned pot to them, never talked about drugs of any kind.

"Oh, Albert," Mom gasped, as if I had told her I'd shot someone. A puff of smoke she was holding in her mouth funneled quickly between her pursed lips.

"Marijuana's not soooo bad," Dad said. "I tried it once at the University of Chicago. It made me dizzy and weird feeling, like the whole room was going to tip over on top of me."

Mom's tone changed, almost to excitement, her voice raised an octave.

"Remember that time Deesie served hash pudding at her dinner party in London, Harrison?"

Dad looked caught off guard, and then said, "Sort of, though I don't remember it having much of an effect."

"Well, of course it was after we all had eighty-seven glasses of sherry," Mom reminded him. "Harry, you went on about this cubicle and that cubicle, and angles of repository, and some other infinitely incomprehensible diatribe about the architecture of Outer Mongolia."

"I don't remember that, Collette," Dad said defensively, though cracking a smile.

"How would you after your eighty-seventh glass of sherry—I had to interrupt you with a fabulous story about the Duchess of Windsor," Mom said.

"I never drink eighty-whatever glasses of sherry; I don't even like sherry."

"That night you did, dear," said Mom, and then with pride, "I can't smoke dope because I don't inhale . . . Thank God Deesie had the genius and forethought to swirl it into our dessert, so we could eat it," as she crushed the end of her fourth cigarette in an hour on the edge of the sink.

"That's bullshit, Mom. How can you not inhale?"

"Honest, I don't," she said. "One time your brother, David, came over with Dolores, and they lit up right in the living room and offered us some, and I just blew it out like I do with my ciggies. They told me I had to inhale for it to work. I told them I didn't, I couldn't, and they said, oh goodie then, all the more for us."

"Well, *we* all inhale, Coco," Dad said, waving his hand through the cloud of smoke gathered in the kitchen.

"Dinner's ready!" Mom announced, happily ignoring Dad's comment.

\* \* \*

After this episode I resolved to quit drinking. . .again—for "a while," anyway. Which lasted, as you can imagine, for a little while, an itsy bitsy while. I was spooked enough to know that I didn't want to hang out with such committed drug addicts—I mean, some of my friends were doing X *every* night of the week. So when I got back to Boulder I distanced myself. I just knew I needed to get as far away from Boulder and the Ted clan as possible, and I slowly prepared myself to find a kinder, gentler drinking environment overseas.

I had the opportunity to do a semester abroad in my junior year, and though tempted by the "Semester at Sea," which Amy and several other friends had done, I started thinking about something more exotic and different. I thought of Mom's mysterious trips to Africa in the seventies, and her stories of being on safari with the Hemingways in the fifties, about her adventures in South Africa with a man named Johnny Whitehouse, the wooden animal sculptures she had brought back, and how in the summertime she would often wear a khanga (a traditional African woman's wrap) around the house.

I remembered "reading" (skimming is more like it) "The Snows of Kilimanjaro" in high school, and though at the time it seemed more of a vague dramatic pastoral, it did give me some fleeting dreamy visions of the reflective artist or "wannabe" artist traveling in mysterious African lands. Only recently did the symbolic parallels and coincidences make me think twice. The main character, named Harry, is found reflecting about how little he accomplished in his life as a writer, and experiences an on-going inner conflict between his compassion for the common "interesting" natives, and the upper classes he'd found himself surrounded by. I wish I could say that I was dramatically influenced by the fact that Hemingway hung out at my grandmother's house in Brooklyn with Jon Dos Passos, Dawn Powell and others, and I voraciously devoured all his books, etc. etc., but it was more subtle than that. I was a slow absorber. And still talk of Africa came up around the dinner table, I found myself slowly drawn to more lit classes at Boulder, and seeing Mom's photo's around the house, all helped inspire the decision. She kept one photo in particular that I loved perched in a small wicker basket on the kitchen counter. It was of her at twenty-five in Tanganyika in her tilted pith helmet, plaid shorts and sleeveless white blouse, standing behind a pointing sign that read "USA," as in "ooo-sa" not the United States of America. This made me imagine what was outside the frame: a giraffe nibbling the tops of the trees nearby, a heard of startled zebras galloping across the savannah, a family of elephants lumbering into the sunset, a writer leaning against a Boabab tree, notebook in his lap, camera around his neck, writing forth his adventures in brilliant prose, documenting his unique vision of the world. Her talk of Hemingways and Johnny Whitehouses made me believe that shiny, cultured people went to Africa. Maybe I would meet them or even become one of them. Maybe I would even begin to write.

# 11

# A Balcony in Africa

My first few days in Nairobi were a mix of jangly nerves and bleak depression. I'm pretty sure I cried myself to sleep the first two or three nights. It was early September in 1990, and I was at the YMCA with the rest of our crew from the School for International Training on a four-month program in East Africa. Even though it had been a year or more since we broke up, I couldn't stop thinking about Amy or resist writing her endless sappy love letters on that beautiful light-blue Kenyan airmail stationary with the elegant elephant graphic gracing the top fold.

Amy was my tether to the familiar, and letters to her were the only things I could write the first few days, though I was soon swept into the magical caress of the Kenyan experience, which begged for reflection and documentation. Cindy, our charmingly tall, skinny leader from Tennessee, with her gigantic, umber eyes, short-cropped midnight hair, and spacey disposition, instructed us to keep a daily journal of our experiences, both written and photographic. At first, I was extremely shy and self-conscious, generally uncomfortable with my pen and camera, not to mention meeting and getting to know the other participants (mostly women) in our group. Until, of course, we finally went out drinking together, and then I was fine! I had traveled in Europe, and thought I was pretty sophisticated and worldly. That is, until I stepped off the plane in Nairobi. The physical and emotional vulnerability I felt was jolting, and yet, it was mixed with a nagging sense of mystique and insatiable wonder.

Not long after our arrival, I found myself getting rides around Nairobi repeatedly from the same cab drivers, Johnny and Dumo, who introduced me to a woman named Bibi Makena and some of the other locals, which started to help me feel a bit more integrated and connected to a place that, just a few days before, had felt so alien and remote and, at times, even terrifying.

*"Napendi nyeli yako, lakini sipendi wewe!"* said Bibi Makena, self-proclaimed prostitute, on the balcony of the YMCA in downtown Nairobi, as she combed her beautiful, dark fingers through my long, stringy hair: Swahili for "I love your hair, but I don't love you." I knew enough Swahili at that point to get most of it. This was a couple of months later at the end of October, and we were back up-country from the coast for some more classes at the University of Nairobi. We laughed, and then took another drag on a gargantuan joint she and her friends were passing around.

I had originally met Bibi Makena with Dumo and Johnny during an introductory cab ride around Nairobi, about a week into the trip. I ran into them again with Sarah and a couple other women from my group who loved to go out drinking. On this occasion, we met them at the Hollywood Bar & Nightclub and then bribed a security guard in order to sneak them all up to our room at the Y with armfuls of Tusker beer late one night. Bibi Makena and I drifted away from the group, pressed ourselves up against the balcony railing, and stared out over the lights of Nairobi glittering magically in the night.

"Why are you here in my country, Bwana Al?" she asked almost accusingly, her accent emphasizing *Al*, making it sound like *all*.

"I wanted to travel, have an adventure, escape the scene I was trapped in back in America. I'm getting pretty sick of my story. I want to invent a new one, maybe. Plus, I wanted to learn about a new culture, a new language, new stories."

She looked at me intently, her brown eyes the color of acacia trees in shadow, catching an orange glint off a street lamp from the parking lot below.

"And what does hearing new stories do for you, huh? I am not the stories I tell, and you, Bwana Al, you are not your story from America. We, as people, are much more than our stories, are we not?" She paused for a moment, while I drank in her curious insight. I stared at her compact, efficient body, how she held herself with a strength and sturdiness as she leaned into me, gesticulating with fingertips to thumb as if drawing on air.

"Does that mean we're lying to each other?" I asked.

"More like to ourselves," she replied. "Now, you could have gone to England, Paris, or Italy, no?"

"I've actually been there already," I said, following the flow of her braids across her collared red blouse opening to a flimsy V.

"Oh, I see, you get around," she said, smiling. She had a beautiful and seductive smile. She was clearly flirting, and I guess so was I. I was nervous, but intrigued. There was something bold and sophisticated and honest about Bibi Makena. She was displaying an almost mesmerizing self-confidence that sparked within me envy and a growing urge to ask myself, "How do people do that?"

We students were constantly being warned about the locals, how they were always mugging and stealing from tourists, couldn't be trusted, blah blah blah. But like Dumo and Johnny, Bibi Makena was so kind and fun, totally harmless. We had spent hours driving the city with them smoking joints and getting the "locals' tour." I felt somehow safe with Bibi Makena too—she was edgy (after all I was stoned out of my head and flirting with a prostitute I had just met at a nightclub and snuck back up to a room at the Y) but trusting. We were having fun.

"Tell me about your life in America," she said.

"Well, I live in Colorado, in the mountains, sort of like Mount Kenya, but . . ." I trailed off. "Wait, my life in America is not that interesting, I'm here to learn about you and Nairobi."

She jumped right in, ready to share excitedly, like a little girl. "Okay, well, I am Kikuyu. I grew up in a small village in what they called the White Highlands, Kikuyuland, because it is the best, most fertile land, which the colonialists took when they came in the 1800s. My family worked a local tea plantation."

I couldn't help thinking about the brief stories Mom had told me about her time in Kenya in the fifties, hanging out at the Mathega Club, staying on extravagant plantations, probably being waited on by Bibi Makena's family. A pang of white guilt rushed my belly.

"You've learned about the Mau Mau rebellion, yes?"

I nodded, engrossed, as we had studied about the rebellion a few weeks earlier with a professor at the university. I remembered so clearly how he had locked the door to the classroom and told us we were not to speak about what we learned in his class to anyone outside our group. The current regime of Daniel arap Moi forbade the discussion of any populist movements, even if they were anticolonialist. University professors were under periodic surveillance and constant scrutiny for any perceived antigovernment discourse. Bibi was whispering now.

"My father was a freedom fighter; he helped the underground movements and kept the fighters supplied with plenty of ganja."

"I came to Nairobi, to the big city, as a teenager to get an education on the street. And boy, did I ever. I grew up fast and dangerous, wandering River Road at night, and then fell in with a crew who hung out at the Hollywood, and soon I got a job there, first as a waitress, and then I started entertaining tourists, so to speak." She smiled, her gorgeous white teeth catching a glint of light from that same streetlamp.

"It's hard to make a living in the bush. Now, I can help my family, take classes at the university, and maybe someday come to America. Or maybe you take me to America now. I'll be your bride! Come on, Bwana Al, you and me together forever!"

She started laughing, and I did, too, though a bit nervously at first, as I could tell she was only slightly kidding. The African men we met were constantly asking the girls in our group to marry them and take them back to America. This, after no more than two words had been spoken between them. This was a first from an African woman, but at least Bibi Makena and I were deep in conversation.

"So what are you doing here in my country, besides drinking, smoking ganja, and flirting with prostitutes?"

"Well," I began, leaning my hips against the railing, turning to face the sea of lights that was Nairobi at night, tripping out on the colors, the vastness, the distance from any sense of familiarity, and then noticing how, facing toward Kibera, the lights dimmed and faded into uneven patches, and farther out into the savanna at night, blackness.

I started telling her about our language study at the university, and some of our experiences down at the coast.

"Speak to me in Swahili," she said.

"Okay, um," I paused, feeling a rush of affectionate excitement, and almost blurted out *"Napenda wewe"* ("I like you" or "I love you," depending on the context). But I caught myself and said excitedly, *"Una taka machungwa gani?"* Which was the only phrase I could remember at the moment. It means, "Which orange would you like?"

Bibi Makena threw her head back and started cackling, then said, "That one," pointing to my crotch. We were hysterical now.

Then I yelled, *"Usi kubali kushindwa!"* ("I will not agree to be defeated!"), quoting a phrase printed on a khanga I had purchased recently at a local market. She was in tears, doubled over in laughter, listening to this white guy spew random Swahili phrases. *"Watu kwa amani!"* ("People for peace!") I shouted, quoting from another khanga.

107

\* \* \*

After a couple of weeks in Nairobi, we headed for the coast, to Lamu, a UNESCO World Heritage Site, a truly timeless and magical place—a kind of heaven, with its swaying palms, whitewashed coral brick houses, quaint narrow streets, and exclusive travel by foot or donkey. There are no motorized vehicles on Lamu. We had intensive language classes and were taken on tours of the town to some of the oldest mosques and historic sites. We participated in a sublime overnight dhow (an ancient Arab fishing boat) trip to Pate Island with a band of traditional Swahili fisherman who sailed us even farther out one day to a small archipelago just south of the Somali border. There, we swam with a pod of dolphins just off shore, and ate coconut rice and cardamom-spiced fish around a bonfire on the beach.

Of course, Lamu had its bleak and scary side: the open sewers, the piles of garbage burning in the streets, the ever-nagging fear of malaria, the suffering feral cats and donkeys screaming in agony throughout the night blurred with the chronic haunting call to early-morning prayer. Just as in Nairobi, we had family stays in Lamu, where we spent more than three weeks. Lamu inspired more committed journal writing and a growing boldness in photographing.

Lamu, Kenya, September 21, 1990

Ahminah sleeps softly while Ali and Sophia pray. Very serious is Sophia, whispering Arabic sayings and hymns, says them over and over again to herself. Ali blesses himself from a water bowl and kneels down beside us. Ahminah is so peaceful, so serene sleeping nearby. Then the radio is turned on rather abruptly to get the latest "football" score from Dar Es Salaam. Sophia continues her prayers and recitations from the Quran. A brief sprinkle of rain settles the dust out in the streets. Ali chews his merah. The Arabic writing on the walls glows as Sophia continues to chant. Aminah shuffles a bit, irked by a bad dream. The bedroom is harshly lit, the shadow my pen casts could hide thugs. There is one lone light bulb. Ali sprays my feet for bugs, I stare at my feet camouflaged in the chewed merah sprinkling the floor. The bars above the doorway remind me of an ancient European prison. The radio crackles and fizzles. Ali tells me that a woman's mind is like a river, one direction. A man's mind is like an ocean . . .

I snapped a beautiful photograph of three of Ali's kids standing in their front yard, adorned in diamond-patterned dresses of bright purple and blue and standing next to a palm tree and behind a pile of garbage that had just been set afire. The flames were reaching up toward their laughing faces and alarmingly close to the frayed bark at the base of the tree. No one was the least bit concerned.

One of the things that initially inspired me to write more consistently was reading Ngugi and Meja Mwangi novels while up-country in Nairobi. These books revealed a powerful indigenous perspective, immediate in-your-face accounts of the reality of life on the streets of Nairobi as well as in small villages—and the heartbreaking clashes that arose between colonial and traditional East African cultures. There was also the string of magnificent landscapes streaming before our eyes daily, which kept pen to paper and camera to eye.

One such string of landscapes appeared along our journey to Makamini, a remote village southeast of Mombasa near the Tanzanian border. A couple of weeks after we left Lamu, we were scheduled to work at a water-catchment site helping to prevent erosion. We drove for miles past red dirt, dry brush, and thorn trees, with the occasional palm tree signaling a lone mud-hut or a decrepit ranch with a mangy goat stumbling about.

Our truck got stuck in the mud for two days in the middle of this exotic nowhere after driving literally through the bush for miles—no roads, no direction, just forward. And after three days, we finally arrived at sunset in the midst of a funeral, which we respectfully viewed from afar. I'll never forget the woman with the bright red headscarf who peeled off from the circle of dancing women, stumbled toward us, and fell at our feet, vomiting with grief and despair. We were in Makomini for about two weeks, and the drumming never stopped. There was a hunt for dik dik, feasts of the stewed antelope, always plenty of palm wine, and the telling of endless African stories around the fire.

October 17, 1990, Makomimi, Kenya

It's afternoon and the flies are at me again swarming around my feet and head. Oh yes and one of those thick red slimy centipedes has just crawled out from under Cree's sleeping bag. Last night I woke up with one on my neck and ran screaming bloody murder into the African night. *Wadodo*, as they're called in Swahili. *Dodo, wadodo.* Singular, plural. And the cement. All sixteen of us sleep on a cement slab draped in mosquito netting praying not to get bit. Hard to sleep at night with Rubin, Okeo, and Abdella, who stay up late every night listening to Bob Marley (great), Tracy Chapman (fabulous), and assorted country/pop (ackkk). They insist on slaughtering an animal after our regular "American" dinner. Last night it was a chicken, the night before dik dik (antelope). A local guy came by to sell Bwana O a live chicken. He paid maybe 40 ks, and then brought it around behind the water- catchment tank to beat and de-feather. Then he came over to where we were all hanging out talking and proceeded to clean and cut the ragged flesh to pieces. He proceeded to scrap the innards, keep the edible part and then rammed a stick through the carcass to roast on the bonfire. No question where our food comes from around here . . .

The common communicative force among us Americans with each other as well as with our African friends was primarily beer—Tusker and Guinness Extra Stout. Those were our options—oh, and occasionally palm wine. We went out drinking with our language teachers, Bwana O and Rubin, constantly, often after taking our malaria meds, a gruesome combo. On waking, I experienced either mild psychosis, a temporary borderline personality disorder, or manic depression. This would last for a couple of days and then eventually disappear.

Somehow, I managed to stay generally in control when out drinking in Africa. Part of it was fear—of being attacked, or mugged, or of getting taken into custody. I did not want to have a run-in with the law in Kenya. They had machine guns and could take your passport and not give it back. We heard stories. But part of it was also the stimulation and engagement I felt there, wanting to be as awake as possible for the next incredible experience.

One cornerstone of the program was our independent study project. I chose to study the funerary art of the Giriama people. I had started taking some art history classes at Boulder the previous semester, and these same funerary sculptures were mentioned in a lecture when we first arrived in Kenya. Cindy mentioned she had a contact named Abdella in Malindi who knew some sculptors. I was fascinated by the architectural aspects of these artworks (an influence of Dad's, perhaps?), the integration of ancient Arab design patterns, and the social order of the artists who made them. Vigango were made from Mkone, and other coastal hardwoods and carved into tall narrow posts between three and five feet high. Sometimes the top was rounded into the shape of a head, sometimes it was kept square. They were almost always adorned with various triangular patterns, sometimes painted, sometimes left as raw wood. They were not made so much as traditional grave markers, but more as contact points for the spirits of the deceased.

I met Abdella one classically scorching late-November day back on the coast, at his office in the sparse and humble Malindi Museum. It was a charming old double-story structure, with walls of white plaster laid over lumps of coral set in lime mortar, a colonnade of rounded pillars, Swahili carved doors, and a roof terrace stacked with Portuguese roof tiles.

Abdella was a stout, tough-looking fellow dressed in conservative Western garb: a light blue collared button-down and dark brown trousers, and those simple black sandals made from tires that all the locals wore. You could get pair on the street for the equivalent of a quarter. He had a set of classic bug-eyed seventies gold-rimmed sunglasses permanently affixed to his face.

"Are you ready, Ali?" he said, shortly after I arrived for the introduction to my independent study project. (No one in coastal Kenya could get with "Al"; there was no such name in their culture, so almost everyone I met called me "Ali.")

"The festivities are underway. I'll take you to a funeral, and perhaps we meet a Giriama sculptor. We can walk from here."

After walking for a couple of miles into the bush, we arrived at a clearing in the forest, the site of a small remote village that was in the throes of a dramatic funerary festival. Abdella approached an old man who looked forlorn and a bit drunk, slumped at the base of a baobab tree. His cloudy eyes were sunken. He was wearing a dark green and black Swahili-patterned wrap, tied at the waist, no shirt, and a necklace of concentric ivory rings. He had long, droopy earlobes with a black plug in the left one. He wore a dirty, doily-patterned Muslim cap and was holding shakily to a wooden staff. He kept thumping it half-heartedly on the ground, maybe to emphasize a thought, but it would then repeatedly fall over again at his feet. His friend kept picking it up and placing it back in his hand, helping him delicately wrap his fingers around it.

"*Pole sana, pole sana, sana,*" Abdella said. ("I'm very, very sorry.") Abdella nodded toward me and introduced me in Swahili. I bowed, offered my condolences in English, and held out my hand. The old man reached out his hand, got halfway to mine, and then dropped it. His milky eyes drifted upward as his head swayed back and forth, searching for a distant light through the canopy of trees.

"He's blind," Abdella whispered into my ear. "It was one of his wives that has died. But he has four more."

Wow, at the same time? I thought to myself. Sounds complicated, but not unlike Dad, though he paced himself over time.

"*Kaa kitako!*" ("Sit down!") yelled the old man, pounding his staff on the ground and then dropping it again. We sat.

It turned out our blind chief was a sculptor from a secret society called Gohu. I sat with him for a long time asking question after question as Abdella translated. My first question had to do with how exactly one sculpts such beautifully intricate patterns when blind?

"I go by memory and touch, feel my way through, in my mind—slowly, a little bit every day," was the translation.

Soon, he said he was tired and it was time to eat. A couple of women were hunched over a massive cauldron of *ugali* (a cornmeal mush), and nearby piles of dried fish shimmered in the cup of a large waxy leaf. A goat had been sacrificed and the blood placed at the grave of the woman who had died. The rest of the goat went into another pot, and the head hung lazily from a nearby tree branch.

"*Kula, kula!*" ("Eat, eat!") shouted the old man, as I stared skeptically into a pot of boiled goat parts, each nugget smelling more rancid than the next. I did the polite WASP thing, and ate. Abdella, the old man, and his friends laughed at the panicked look on my face and offered me dried fish, which tasted even worse.

Then the frenetic drumming and dancing began. A group of women formed a circle, linked arms, and bowed their heads in rhythmic measure to the drums. They simultaneously flung their arms up to the sky and began wailing blindly. Then they came back together, linking arms and bowing heads, and brought their voices lower as they leaned into to the earth and moaned. The ceremony, drumming, and dancing went on for hours. Darkness fell, and soon the old man and his friends were passing around a coconut full of palm wine. Known back in America as "hootch," this was mighty strong stuff.

Abdella smiled at the concerned look on my face and said, *"Kunywa! Kunywa!"* ("Drink! Drink!").

I was somehow hoping this might be an antidote for my growing stomach pains. No such luck. I got instantly drunk and disoriented, and progressively felt worse. I finally asked Abdella to take me back to town, grabbing his arm as I doubled over in pain and drunkenness.

I barely made it to the guesthouse, where I passed out immediately upon my return. It couldn't have been more than a couple of hours before I awoke to even more severe pains shooting through my gut, followed by serious chills. I was violently ill, losing it from both ends. I'd stumble back to bed, only to have to return to the toilet the second I lay back down. The chills turned to sweats, then chills again. The pain increased. I screamed and moaned in agony.

Finally, Habib, my guesthouse host, became worried he'd have a dead American in his house, and after repeated whimperings, offered to take me to the local clinic. I had to have the taxi pull over every two minutes to heave out the door. It was grim. I was hallucinating and could barely talk. It was a classic violent case of dysentery that soon overlapped into malaria. The clinic, which they referred to as a "hospital," was no more than a squat coral-rock house with a couple of extra rooms.

I was hooked up to an IV, given random shots, and lay there hour after hour ravaged by fever and hallucinations. Abdella never came by the clinic to see me. I had no access to a phone. The rest of my student group was either in Lamu or in Mombasa, and I knew I wouldn't see Cindy, our trip leader, for at least another week.

I cried and cried and went batty staring at the patterns of jaundiced-colored paint peeling in messy patterns on the ceiling, and the wobbling ceiling fan with a couple screws missing, that I was sure at any minute would drop from its fragile tethers and crush me. At times I was convinced

I was dying. I would drift in and out in a panic scared I would never wake up. Visions of Etoile, and Amy, Mom and Dad, my sisters, friends from high school and Boulder, Cindy and my language teachers—all swirled chaotically through my mind, folding across the pale walls and through the fan blades, like film strips or ghostly torn bits of thinly colored gauze. I thought of Johnny and Dumo, and especially of Bibi Makena, wondering: If I were in a clinic in Nairobi, would she come visit me? The weight of the loneliness was severe, and yet something eventually turned in me, a kind of survival instinct, a strength, an alliance with my deeper self that was determined to push through the drag and heft of emotion and keep me moving on, no matter how grim the circumstances appeared. I couldn't eat for more than a week. I was depressed, exhausted, and desperately homesick, but somehow still alive.

November 30, 1990, Malindi, Kenya

After three days in the hospital and five since I've done any work—I feel like shit. Can't sleep, read, or eat much, and am so out of touch with Giriama funerary art, I can't even tell you. I'm weak, disenchanted, lost, and I'm ready to leave. Counting the days to get back on that night train headed for cool Nairobi. The sun has come up again as a raging fire, scaring people and inhibiting the wind. The palm trees won't move, and as usual the streets are as hot and dusty as can be, which is extremely hot and dusty. I usually dart from shady overhang to shady overhang on my way to town. At this point, there is no money for taxis and I'm so worn down I can barely walk the stretch through town—god—through blinding thick dust and screaming Muslims, reckless busses, and skinny old men dragging food carts. I'm weak and battered by time, and distraught, the thought of groveling across town choking and spitting dust, sweating beyond recognition just makes me more ill. I just want mountains, cold snowy peaks, pizza, some After 8 mints . . . oh how I crave a cool roll in the snows of Colorado, a frigid walk through Chautauqua Park, a coffee ice cream milkshake at Ben & Jerry's.

It was always a bit sketchy walking the roads into Malindi town, as the only thing worse than an African driver is perhaps an Indian one. And on the coast of East Africa, it's practically a contest between the two cultures— who can be more manic and dangerous behind the wheel. I was stumbling along the road two or three days after my release from the clinic, when a Matatu, one of the colorful twenty-seater taxis complete with psychedelic paint job, dangling bodies, and pop music blasting, came screaming around the bend at a familiarly unreasonable speed. I stepped to the edge of the road. He was hauling ass, this guy, and closing in fast toward me.

I stepped farther off the road to be safe, but there was a deep ditch at the road's edge filled with sludge (one can only imagine sewage, as it hadn't rained in weeks), and sure enough, it was either get creamed by the Matatu or take one more step back. I swear I contemplated for a split second happily meeting the front grill of the Matatu, but God took over in the last second, and the next thing I knew, I was up to my chest in sludge, spitting and swearing screaming, "Help, help, help!"

A couple of guys across the road were laughing hysterically, something about "Mzungu, muzungu, ha haa ha . . ." basically, "Check out whitey in the ditch, ha haa ha." Finally, a woman with a ten-gallon water bucket on her head stopped mid-stride, laid down her sixty pounds of water, and reached out her hand. I reached up to her with both my soft western hands and was met with crusty leather, a rugged landscape of touch—as she easily hauled my horrified white ass out of the ditch with a loud slurping sound.

I was mortified, embarrassed, and then began to panic. I imagined leaches eating at my privates, bacteria wiggling their way into my pores, worms instantly entering any available opening. The smell was excruciating. I barely thanked the woman and shuffled off looking like a wiry version of

Pizza the Hut from that Mel Brooks movie *Spaceballs,* dripping sewage from each limb. Back at the guesthouse I showered maniacally, scrubbing myself so hard and close to the bone that I reminded myself of Miss Hedy. My skin was raw for days. Here I was, ten thousand miles from home, still haunted by memories of Miss Hedy, still unable to scrub away my story, still unable to be truly free.

That same evening, Abdella finally came by my guesthouse, barely asked how I was doing, and then said, "Hey, want to go out for *pombe* [beer]?"

"No thanks," I groaned, surprising myself. This was one of the first times I can remember ever declining an invitation to go out drinking. It felt a bit out of character, a slight blurring to the always-up-for-a-beer-party-dude view I had of myself. But I still felt so sick, or otherwise I would have been right there, ordering up a fresh Guinness.

This trip to Kenya was the first time I kept a consistent journal, the first time I seriously wrote. The more I wrote, the more I began to sense a glimmer of value to my own experience, forming the idea that somehow maybe my perceptions, feelings, and ideas might matter to the world. My African journals, however embarrassing now, were my gateway to writing.

After our independent study projects were over and we were back up-country in Nairobi again, Carol Beckwith and Angela Fisher were in town for a slide show, talk, and book signing for *African Ark,* their extraordinary book on the Horn of Africa, which was published in September 1990. I was completely stunned by their work. And not only the amazing images that they were now famous for, shot for this book throughout Kenya, Ethiopia, Eritrea, Djibouti, and Somalia, but their amazing courage and commitment to their craft. Two women traveling alone to some of the most remote and dangerous areas of the world, and returning with such startlingly beautiful photographs of humanity engaged in unbelievably magical displays of adornment and ritual. This set my imagination afire, inspiring a powerful sense of possibility in terms of what photography and writing could do in the world, how it could communicate across cultures and across continents.

After seeing this show, I became certainly more inspired, but also a bit more confident in my picture taking. Instead of being my typical shy self, I found myself stepping up and asking people if I could take their portraits. I would spend more time with each shot, considering the light, the frame, and the overall compositional elements and how they could come together to further illuminate an instant.

One of my favorite pictures is a landscape I took from the top of a hill overlooking Lamu. It was sunset, and two or three men were standing out in a series of shallow fishing ponds outlined in black rocks right at the ocean's edge. These pools created an incredible honeycomb pattern from a distance. As each man in shadow walked along the black rock edges, his image was mirrored in the sea. Meanwhile, the sun was setting behind the men, sparkling the surface of the Indian Ocean and extending to the horizon while lighting up a dazzling pattern of streaked clouds.

Keeping a photographic and written journal helped me place these extraordinary events within the arc of my life, so my experience wouldn't become just another case of cultural consumption, but rather a kind of spiritual integration. The beautiful thing was that I wasn't trying to make art (this is baggage I would pick up a little later); rather, I was just being as real and immediate as possible. The photographing and writing helped me metabolize and absorb the intensity of my African experience, while my alcohol consumption kept it somehow manageable. But not for long.

## 12

# Raine, Like the Weather

Back in Colorado a few months later, I was sitting at a café with my Ben & Jerry's coffee ice cream milkshake, which just wasn't cutting it—it was simply not taking enough of the edge off! I was desperately trying to digest, to integrate, to somehow make sense of the incredible experience I'd just had in Africa. I was in reverse culture shock. Nobody understood what I'd just experienced. I'd been transformed. I was alone again in my experiences. I felt somehow that I simply didn't exist anymore. Life in America was fucked up! I needed a beer.

After quitting drinking for five minutes and distancing myself from the Ted clan before I left for Africa, I had moved in with my new buddy, Mike, over on Sixth Street in west Boulder. When I returned the following summer, I met Raine.

One day, I came back to our apartment, which smelled uncharacteristically like a bakery. Normally, it smelled like sweat, beer, or at best, laundry detergent. No Mike, no Doug, but instead a short, full-figured sexy girl with a sweet face was puttering about in the kitchen. She was pigeon-toed and teetered slightly when she walked, as if she had tennis balls taped permanently to the bottom of her feet. She had a bright yellow, striped dishtowel draped over her left shoulder. She stared right into me with stunning, green eyes.

"Hey, I'm Raine . . . like the weather. Sorry my hands are wet," she said, snorting awkwardly and frantically shaking her hands and then wiping them repeatedly on her thighs. She was wearing cut-off jeans and a tight pink tank top that had the word *Love* written in small, red cursive script across the exquisite shelf of her breasts. She gave me a tender half-handshake just around the fingers, with a penetrating, almost seductive look in her eyes. All of this came together around a smile that just about made my legs collapse.

"Al, I'm Al," I said, taking a deep, grounding breath and trying not to stare into the word *Love* laid out across her chest. "This is unit three, right? Are Doug and Mike around?"

"They'll be right back; they just went to grab some beer at . . . Liquor Smart, is it?" her voice crescendoing into question.

"Ahh, yes, Liver Smart, home away from home! I think it's technically called Liquor Mart, but whatever."

"I just got off the trip with Doug, and he said it would be all right to stay here for a night or two."

"Absolutely, make yourself at home."

"You want a cookie? I just baked you guys some cookies."

* * *

Raine was generous to a fault. She was a fun-loving person who went out of her way to please you. Raine was the kind of person who would give you a corny card on an obscure holiday like Palm Sunday. She was constantly making us cookies or brownies, and then dinner, and always offering to pay for us. Her bright, goofy smile with its sly hint of "Let's get into some trouble together" just crushed me. It ended with parentheses at the corners of her mouth. The parenthetical in her smile was her cunning desperation to be seen—truly seen. And I could relate.

She had met my friend Doug on a National Outdoor Leadership School trip in Wyoming, and had moved to Boulder to be near him. Doug stayed with Mike and me in our apartment on Sixth Street for six months until he found his own place. Often, Raine stayed with him. She wanted him, but he was noncommittal. Raine, Mike, and I became good friends. She became "one of the guys," and we hung out all the time together for a few months—tubing down Boulder Creek, hiking up at Sugarloaf, taking in a Michael Hedges concert at Chautauqua Park, and of course, bar-hopping.

Raine was cute and dramatic and super clingy, which kept the guys sexually attracted and emotionally distant. I was no exception. As Doug pulled away, I pulled in. First, she was with Doug, then Mike, and then she and I hooked up. She fell in with whoever would have her. The first time we fooled around was late one night during summer break back in Connecticut, in the sand trap at the seventh hole of the New Canaan Country Club golf course. Turns out she grew up in New Canaan, but somehow we had never met as kids. Technically, she was still with Mike. I never told him.

Back in Boulder, I used to wander over drunk to her house at two in the morning. It wasn't pretty. She had this way of sucking me in with her charming drama, and then expecting marathon pal-around sessions to follow. I wasn't in it for the relationship. I was in it for the attention and sex. I was conflicted. Her neediness and clinging left me repulsed, yet her beauty and sensuality kept me magnetized. I liked her, and craved the attention, and needed her, in many ways just as much as she needed me. She was so kind and generous to me, and yet I was afraid to reciprocate, scared she would lock onto me even more, and somehow suffocate me. My drinking inspired primal sexual drives while nullifying emotional sensitivities or insight.

Raine had an overzealous pride in self-sacrifice and would go along with just about anything anyone proposed. She was out to please and fit in, no matter the cost to herself. I knew that on some level she was in love with me, and the truth is, I shamefully took advantage.

One night, we were out drinking together on Cinco de Mayo—good old tequila, or "ta kill ya" as we used to call it. And at one point late in the night, Raine wanted to leave the bar and I didn't. I was itching to stay behind with Andrea (yet another friend I had a crush on, who also happened to be a friend of Raine's) and some other friends. Raine decided she would walk home alone. I was hesitant. Even though it was just a few blocks, I didn't want to go with her, and yet some part of me didn't think it was the best idea for her to walk home alone.

"I'm fine, I'm fine," she insisted. I could hear the clinging and doubt in the quick high-pitch of her voice, and chose to ignore it.

"Are you sure? I'm happy to walk you home," I said, shuffling my feet uneasily on the sidewalk, lying through my clenched teeth.

"No, I'm fine," she said with a forced smile as she stared me down with her puppy-dog eyes. Off she walked west toward Sixth and Arapahoe. I stayed behind with Andrea. I had a slightly nagging feeling I shouldn't have left her. Nothing a couple more beers couldn't assuage.

Early the next morning, I was curled in the all-too-familiar fetal position at the edge of Andrea's bed, feeling awkward and embarrassed because I couldn't remember how I got there or what had actually happened. Plus, I was still feeling guilty about bailing on Raine. I was barely awake, contemplating a suave exit strategy when the phone rang. There was a piercing thread of sunlight stabbing at my eyes, and a fermented metallic taste coiled in my parched mouth. Andrea rolled over and grabbed it.

"What?—You're fucking kidding! Oh my God. Is she all right? Oh, Jesus, of course she is, oh Jesus. How the fuck . . . I'll come right now."

I was staring blankly though the thick gauze of her lavender curtains, counting the thumping pulsations against my agonized head, trying to ignore the alarm in Andrea's voice. It took a while to register that something serious had happened to someone. Andrea hung up the phone with a frightened and despondent look in her eyes.

"What's up?" I moaned groggily.

"It's Raine. She was raped last night under the Sixth Street bridge."

I felt my stomach collapse and all the air within me get sucked out to the point that when I tried to speak, nothing came out. I just mouthed a horrified "Oh God, no."

"I need to go see her at the hospital, right now." Andrea said nodding her head toward the door. "You should leave. Now."

"C-c-c-can I . . . sh-sh-sh-should I . . . g-go with you?" I was stuttering. Then began shaking.

"No, no, I think she's with counselors and stuff. Just go home. Don't say anything to anyone."

Her voice was sharp and full of regret. It almost sounded accusatory. My mind began racing madly. What I heard in her voice was disgust. With me. It matched the sickening feeling I now had for myself. A renewed and further embedded identity was taking shape. After all, I was the last person to see her safe. The "shoulds" and "shouldn'ts" began to flood my head. *I shouldn't have left her. I should have walked her home. I shouldn't have drunk so much. I shouldn't have had those feelings for Andrea.* This was all in addition to the rejection I felt from Andrea. As I left her apartment, there were no warm words of affection spoken between us. Just shock and regret piled on regret.

I felt like screaming in Andrea's face, "I should have been with her instead of staying at the bar and then coming home with *you!*" I remained silent. The self-blame and guilt was overwhelming and crushing. I was so consumed with it that I had a hard time drumming up any immediate compassion for Raine. I had no idea how to respond. It was almost as if *I* was responsible, I was an accomplice, a rapist myself.

A couple of nights later, I went out drinking with the boys. The situation with Raine, compounded with the culture shock of my return from Africa, was more than I could handle. She was a mess, calling me all the time crying, wanting to get back "together" again, as if we were ever together to begin with. I was lost.

Already buzzed from drinking a couple of beers at the house, I rode my bike to a keg party up Four Mile Canyon with a couple of friends, and after eight or nine cups of beer, we hauled ass down the canyon on our bikes. We came flying into town on Canyon Boulevard and skidded to a flailing halt at the intersection of Ninth Street, not wiping out per se, but just collapsing from laughing so hard in our drunken silliness. We peeled ourselves from the pavement and proceeded across the street to the brewery for shots of Jaegermeister and pints of stout. A perfect combination.

I slightly recollect getting kicked out of the bar, losing my friends, blacking out for a while, and then winding up twenty blocks away in a heap at Raine's doorstep. I was found wailing and screaming uncontrollably, *"Get it out, get . . . it . . . out!"* One of the neighbors who was awakened by all the commotion reportedly said, "That boy has the devil inside of him."

And I did, and she was dressed up as a German governess, and I was trying to expel her. I obviously still hadn't processed the fact that Miss Hedy was dead, and how I truly felt about her when she was alive, and the disconnect from my own mother, and the fact that no conscious feelings whatsoever about any of this registered at the time. Finally, the emotional repression became too great, and a violent, explosive release was imminent. It was as if she was haunting me from the grave.

Not knowing what to do with me, Raine and her roommate, rushed me to the Emergency Room. It was 3:30 A.M. The ER was not the best place for me, as I was in an uncontrollable alcoholic rage and was unable to even sit upright in a chair. As Raine told me later, the ER attendant kept trying to get me to sit upright and I kept resisting, falling to the floor in a heap, screaming. He kept pushing and I kept resisting and that's when I started swinging and spitting at him. Next, there was a blurry scuffle with washes of badges and blue uniforms as I was violently restrained by four huge policemen. Next, I was dragged down the hall, put in restraints, and handcuffed to the bed, where I woke up a few hours later tangled in tubes, smeared in my own shit, and arrested for assault and battery. Raine had to clean me up, as the ER staff refused to get near me. That was September 1, 1991, and the last time I ever drank alcohol. I was twenty-three years old.

\* \* \*

I never told my parents about any of this. I still felt as if I couldn't talk to them, that they simply wouldn't understand yet another one of my forays into self-annihilation. I did what I had to do to get my record clean and get the assault and battery charges dismissed.

A few weeks later, I approached the Boulder County Courthouse with great dread, as if I were approaching Mordor. I stared up at the blocky structure, which was bathed in a bleak gray shadow, and immediately noticed the clock at the top, which inspired freakish flashbacks to my childhood. I thought for a second that I might be attacked by a swarm of bats. I shuddered and then felt as if one of those huge blocks might slip loose and crush me like an ant underfoot. No such luck. I shook my head clear for the third time and stumbled up the cement stairs to the assistant DA's office. After filling out some paperwork, I was led down a long, dreary pasty-yellow hallway.

"You're lucky to be alive, son . . ." the woman said, as I sat down in a creaky, wooden chair opposite her. My eyes caught a photo on the wall behind her left shoulder of a man at the top of a snowy peak in a hooded blue down parka with one arm around a burly woman in a red down parka. They were both wearing reflective goggles filled with snowy peaks. They looked inflated, like they might float off into the fake-looking dark purple sky behind them. They both had their free arm in the air presumably held in a fist, but the frame cut their arms off at the wrist.

She spoke with a seriousness that spooked me. "Since you made it out alive, they seriously considered pressing charges, and could have sentenced you to some time in jail."

I stared at her blurry hazel eyes and then out the window to my left, which was crowded with dark gray clouds. I squirmed a little in the chair.

"You know, not everyone's so lucky."

"I know." I said, swallowing heavily, even though I didn't.

"Do you know? I mean, really, do you have *any fucking idea?*" She was raising her voice now and tightening her throat, getting choked up, it appeared. I couldn't believe she said "fucking." She took a deep breath and then said, "You know, I lost my uncle to alcoholism. It's ugly." She took another, much slower breath. "It's a terrible, *terrible* way to go, and it's not just you, it tears up the whole family." She paused, after thoroughly emphasizing the second *terrible.* Her eyes were tearing up.

I looked back to the picture behind her. Was that her uncle at the top of K2, a famous climber downed by his addiction to alcohol?

"Promise me you'll get help. You'll need to go to AA for ninety days, and the county has a great program, and it's only $35 a session. These people have *been there*, they understand what you're going through! Plus, this is a court order. I need you to promise me you'll attend this program . . . every session?"

"I promise," I said quietly. And I meant it. The way she said *terrible* twice and seemed to be sincerely *begging* me to get help had a chilling and profound effect.

A couple of days later I went to see Butch down at the county in a grey cubicle boxed in by massive beige file cabinets. Butch was a recovering addict Vietnam vet. Wirey, high strung, cement-colored eyes, six four. His arms were like heavy branches swirling over me in large sweeping gesticulations generating a small breeze when he spoke. Butch had a physical presence, an internal sturdiness and strength I got from just sitting there. I could tell he was one of those people who had *Lived*, with a capital L. Butch had seen things that I would hopefully never see. He had done things I would hopefully never do. Trying to kill myself seemed plausible, killing other people, impossible. Butch wore a mustache and faded courderoys, and a plaid shirt. He looked like Paul Bunyan with scars.

"Can I tell you a story, kid?"

"No," I said. Not wanting to hear some dramatic near-death story from the battlefields of Nam. "Okay then." He took a deep breath. "It's like this. Ya got two critters inside of you, kid." *Why was he calling me kid? I felt like replying to him with "pops."* "Albert, the rational, one, gets up in the morning, does what he needs to do, deals with what needs to be dealt with, is cordial, kind, figures out the world. Then ya got Sebastian, yer evil twin, who loves to go out and get blasted and cause trouble." *Sebastian? Spare me. Couldn't he have come up with a better name than that?* "He's against Albert, wants to ruin his life, basically fuck him up. Comes around offering drinks and girls, and a good time. Sebastian is always up for a party. We're going to dump Sebastian, we're gonna relegate him to the background, to the nether reaches of your mind and experience so he can't take over, so that he has no pull on you, no matter how you are feeling in the moment." He paused, then leaned in close. "We're gonna vaporize the cocksucker. Am I clear?"

"Umm, I guess. . .kind of," I said. *I need to get out of here. This guy is freaking me out.*

"What the fuck is that? Um kind of?" he said, raising his voice and tightening his jaw, trying not to scream. "Listen kid, do you want help or not? I got a list of fifty of you motherfuckers, and the reality is I'm gonna lose probably 50%, because they're not invested, they're too far gone. Their Sebastian has taken their soul. Do you want to die, kid? Cause that what's it come to, a matter of living and dying and I'll tell you right now, you keep on this path of yours much longer and yer a dead man! Sebastian will drag you down. Sebastian will throw your ass under the bus, or in jail for good next time, and ain't no mommy and daddy in the world gonna be able to bail your sorry ass out! Do I make myself clear, now?"

"Yes, sir" I said quietly.

"I can't fucking hear you," he said glaring.

"Yes, sir, I'm in." I said, louder this time. *Jesus Christ, your scaring me now, pops.*

I left that first meeting rattled, slightly annoyed, and thoroughly frightened, trying to find this Sebastian critter in my head. All I saw was an angry fifth grader with bed-head trying to bash my face in with a Darth Vader lunch box. I was caught between thinking this was a stupid name for my evil twin, and trying to figure out the concept of an evil twin in the first place. Where was he now? This meeting with Butch gave new meaning to the term "scared to death." I was scared to death. In a good way, in a way that pretty much sealed the deal on ever drinking again. I tried over and over again to imagine drinking and a surge of fear so real and immediate, so terrifying and physically nauseating came up, that I started associating alcohol with a poison I simply could not touch. And yet life without alcohol, without partying, at first seemed vacant, boring, vacuous. But it slowly started to take on the shape of possibility. What Raine had said to me the morning after the hospital nightmare also kept ringing in my head. "If you ever, *ever* do that again, don't call me, I'll never speak to you again." No matter how conflicted I was about Raine, those words sank in. They seemed to merge with the DAs'and with Butch's words. There was a kind of absolute fact emerging.

And so I went to AA. To the poorly lit church basements and sat meekly in circles of broken humans, avoiding the cheap coffee and cigarettes, dragging my eyes over the other participants, marveling at what unique wrecks they had made of their lives, and initially thinking how different I was from all of them. There was the now homeless man who I recognized from the benches at Arapahoe park, who used to live in a fancy house on West Pearl Street, but had recently lost his family and his house. The other post-student, my age who was arrested for taunting the cops at Mall Crawl by dancing naked atop their patrol car high on several grams of mushrooms. There was the immaculately-dressed prim-and-proper-looking librarian who drank brandy in the stacks and started cutting herself after reading *Ethan Frome*. And then there was Kevin, the alcoholic sex-addict turned obsessive cyclist and network marketer.

I was stunned by those first meetings. Listening to these people's stories, people I would see at the supermarket or pass by in the street, who had done terrible things to themselves and their friends and family. I tried to convince myself I was different. I would never cut myself, or sleep with five different women in one week, or abandon my family. Ha. But the truth was there was no telling what I was capable of when drunk, and I wasn't that different after all. And here they were now making a commitment to a new life. Some of them were beaten down and withered, others seemed to be reclaiming a kind of confidence, a post-apocalyptic resurgence. Kevin was one of those. He was assigned to me as an initial sponsor. And for all of what he said, what I remembered was his manic enthusiasm for AA and his new life beyond drinking.

He was hawking something called "Liqua-K," some mysterious energy drink. He was downright zealous about the stuff, saying he drank it by the case. And it was only $59.00 for an eighteen ounce bottle. He tried to rope me into "the program," asking me to buy a couple cases and try it out. I tried to imagine foisting the stuff on my friends and family and my mind went blank. At the time I didn't have the courage or confidence to sell Girl Scout cookies, let alone $59.00-a-bottle energy drinks.

I did my ninety days and was changed by them. Changed by the stories, by the possibilities of life beyond alcohol. Kevin wore me out at the same time he gave me hope, and then he moved to Oregon around the time I started feeling strong on my own. I kept clear of my drinking friends, saw Butch weekly, and stayed on the path. Things got better. I got a job painting houses for a while, started tinkering with my camera again and dreaming of grad school. The temptation to drink faded. A month turned into three and then a year. I collected my chips, quietly celebrated and took on a bit of pride and identity around being a sober person. At a certain point I knew I would never drink again. I convinced myself I was done with my addictions. And then, I met Maya.

# 13

# Pictures of Maya

*Poetry, almost blind like a camera*
*Is alive in sight only for a second. Click,*
*Snap goes the eyelid of the eye before movement*
*Almost as the word happens . . .*


*. . . The temporary tempts poetry*
*Tempts photographs, tempts eyes.*


—Jack Spicer, from "Imaginary Elegies"

"Fuck you!" he bellowed loudly, emphasizing each word while stumbling toward me, his voice echoing through the gigantic studio. He continued; "Hey, fuck you . . . [pause, voice rising to a yell] no, FUCK YOU, I MEANNNNN, FUUUUCK YOUUUUU!" He was beginning to sound like Steve Martin. Was he drunk? Come to think of it, his nose did appear shinier than normal.

I just stuttered in grave disbelief, "I . . . I . . . I . . . Hey, Arlan, it's me, Albert. We have a two o'clock?"

"Yeah? Fuuuuuck you, buddy!"

"Should I come back later, I mean I can . . ."

He was standing right over me now, leaning in uncomfortably close. I could smell the sting of alcohol on his breath. It smelled oddly good, as breath goes, and almost made me want a beer.

"A photograph is like a woman," he said, whispering. "The glimmer of silver, the surface highlights of her curves, her bones, the flow of her body, her beauty and seduction, searing. The shadows are the shadows, watch out for those, don't get fucking lost in the shadows, son, in the murky midnight of them. Her story is often hidden, shielded by what you don't see just outside the frame. A woman tends to her darkness, nurtures her shadows, and then unleashes them upon unsuspecting men. Live in the mid-tones, my son, gather her there, gather yourself there in the expansive zones of gray. This is the only place you can see straight. The highlights will blind you, the shadows consume yooou . . . Oooo, ooo, ooo." And then in a louder high-pitched voice,

"Didja bring any pictures? Let's take a peek."

It was the spring of 1991 or 1992, and I had been in Colorado for four years, finishing up an undergraduate degree in photography and fine arts with the unpredictable and wacky photo-historian Arlan Silverman. He looked like a living, breathing Richard Avedon portrait, or like some kind of weathered Russian rock star: tall and slim, bright red face, large bulbous sloping nose, wavy greasy gray hair. He was loud, cocky and smart, confident and sometimes brutally direct.

Fine arts seemed the easiest route through college I could imagine. I was not an A student by any stretch of the imagination and was always looking for a way out of doing traditional schoolwork. Taking pictures seemed easy enough. I actually liked it. My dad had given me my first camera the summer of my junior year in high school for the trip to Europe with Fathead. Photography quickly became a way for me to solidify or secure memory and simultaneously invent it. Or at least reinvent it. This became a realization for me, a growing power. Add to that the fact that I wasn't completely terrible at it.

This is the first thing I remember being remotely acknowledged for, besides drinking. I distinctly remember Arlan storming around the photo classroom hurling harsh critiques at most everyone's work, often making the sorority girls cry. I was quietly terrified of him, but enjoyed the slide shows and looking at other students' pictures, so I stayed. When he came to my pictures in critique, he got quiet, seemed somewhat interested, and then passed the critiquing onto the other students.

An emotional impulse began to stir within me as I looked at great photographs: Cartier-Bresson's man leaping off a fallen ladder, held aloft above the water, his reflection hovering like a specter; Dorothea Lang's portrait of a Dust Bowl mother—an hourglass of time imprinted in the creases of her face—weathered like the dusty Oklahoma landscape itself. I saw symbolic power in these pictures, and something mystical began to shift inside me. It must have been the searing imprint of the moment, captured and held as a monument to presence.

The still points of beauty and mystery, of moments frozen in time, further charged my imagination. They helped me dream of other realities, of mysterious places I could travel to, or people I might meet or, even some day, be—they gave me a sense of possibility, and inspired within me a capacity to visualize. I participated actively enough in assignments to earn a bit less harassment from Arlan, and his interest in my work grew.

As a photo-historian, Arlan had a great knowledge of photography and spoke with such passion and certitude about these photographers that I slowly became more and more intrigued. I started to notice some of the photo books Arlan had mentioned on the shelves at Mom and Dad's house: *Eadweard Muybridge: The Father of the Motion Picture;* Robert Frank's *The Americans; The Photographs of Edward Weston; Changing New York* by Berenice Abbott; and many others. This further implanted the seeds of creativity.

In my senior year of high school, Miss Toth had taken us to a show of David Hockney's photo-collages in New York at the International Center of Photography. There was a Garry Winogrand retrospective at MOMA my first year of college, and the catalogue was ever-present on my parents' coffee table. When I went to visit them, I would flip through it for hours as if I were reading maps.

That same summer after my first year of college, I was back in New York dropping a friend off at Grand Central when I happened upon the annual Puerto Rican Parade outside the station. For some reason, I happened to take my camera along. It must have been after a session of flipping through the Winogrand catalogue. I was instantly mesmerized, and spent hours in the city that day shooting dozens of rolls of film.

When I look back at these pictures, I can't believe how uncharacteristically bold I was to approach people at such close range. My favorite of these pictures is of a couple that I shot from the hip as they were passing by particularly close. Their faces are blurred, a bit grainy, and they appear zealous, almost religiously so. Right above their heads in the store window beaming out of the bright reflection from my flash is the word *Eternity*. Arlan liked these pictures, and told me to keep going. I did.

Right around this time, I showed Arlan a rough portfolio of my favorite pictures from my trip to Africa, and he seemed impressed. I finally decided to put together a portfolio of my favorite color slides, which I felt more accurately told the story of my experiences there. Somehow, the images weren't enough, so I had them printed 4x6 on 8x10 paper, with a spacious black background so I could illuminate the visual narrative with notes from my journal. I wrote, in silver marker, words that spoke to the experience of the photographs and the imagined situations beyond them. Arlan loved the pictures and suggested I apply for graduate school in photography. I sent my portfolio to the San Francisco Art Institute after researching their staff and deciding it was the only urban area I was willing to move to. Arlan gave me stellar references, and they loved the Africa pictures and offered me a place in their Masters of Photography program beginning in the fall of 1993. I was ecstatic.

* * *

Garp the dog and I arrived in San Francisco on the Fourth of July, 1993, and sat on U-Haul boxes in the living room watching fireworks through the fog from our apartment in Ashbury Heights. The show was just a series of murky glows through the low clouds. Every once in a while, a distant spark would emerge from the sea of dark gray like a limp flare.

Garp was originally Raine's idea. One day back in Boulder, she had dragged me over to the house of a friend whose dog had just had puppies. I wasn't a dog person, nor was I in the market for a dog, as I was barely able to take care of myself. That was until I saw Garp and picked him up. He was a Quaalude puppy, so to speak. He melted in my arms, a pool of unconditional love and adoration. He immediately became my soulmate and greatest companion. He was a Newfoundland/retriever mix and looked like a giant, black golden retriever. Garp and I were always together, and when I left Boulder in 1993, though Raine and I originally got Garp "together," between the rape and emotional turmoil and confusion that followed, we agreed he should move with me to San Francisco.

Garp and I would go on to travel throughout the West, skiing and hiking thirteen-thousand foot peaks in winter and summer. He would be there through my sobriety, my major relationships, and every other major life drama, and when he died in 2006, I cried for weeks straight, far more for the loss of him than for my own father.

A couple months after arriving in San Francisco, I ran into a friend from high school while walking with Garp to Golden Gate Park. Karen had also just moved to San Francisco. She was walking with her friend Maya just off Stanyan Street in the Upper Haight.

"Oh my God, look at him," Maya said, with a voice of iris petals and ash. She was smiling and pressing her face into Garp's. "He's so beautiful, is he yours?"

"Yup, the world's greatest pooch."

"How old is he?" Maya said, scratching Garp's ears and making cooing and slurping noises in his face.

"About 2 1/2 . . . hi, I'm Albert," I said extending my hand.

"Oh, hey, sorry, I'm Maya," she said, still staring at Garp, but eventually offering me a quick, sweet smile.

"Maya as in 'Sweet Virginia' Maya? I've heard about your band. Karen here raves about you guys." Maya got shy and silent.

"You know, they're playing at the Paradise this weekend. You should come," Karen chimed in.

"Would that be okay?" I asked nervously.

"Of course, definitely come. We're playing with Dieselhead, they're awesome. I wonder if you could bring Mr. Garp here." She was focused on scratching Garp's ears and staring into his face. "What's your story?" she said, still facing Garp.

"My story, well, I'm covered in fur, I'm a really good boy, I love to fetch sticks at that gnarly little pond in the park, and—"

"No . . . you . . . Al . . . I'm sorry. . . he's so friggin' cute."

"And what, I'm chopped liver over here?" I said, with a lame Bronx accent. Maya laughed politely, and looked at me again with a smile that made my heart sing. "It's a bit long and complicated, you got a minute?"

"No, I mean why are you here?"

"Here, like right here, standing before you?"

"No, like San Francisco, what brings you here?"

"Oh, I'm at the Art Institute, in their MFA program, studying photography."

"So you're a photographer?"

"Well, kind of, not yet anyway." I said, dismissively.

"What do you take pictures of?"

"Things . . . you know . . ."

"Can you be more specific?"

"Street scenes, and landscapes and stuff, like us standing here talking might be a terrific picture. And I love Marin, I've been spending a lot of time out in Point Reyes photographing the landscapes out there."

"Oh my God, I friggin' love Point Reyes!" Her face lit up and she stood up from her crouched position with Garp. "I was just out there last week hiking the Palo Marin Trail, and coincidentally enough, I recently went to a great photo show downtown with a friend who goes to State," she said, staring at me. I felt that immediate pang of affection for someone you've just met, whom you have an instant passionate commonality with, and whom you could easily imagine scooping affectionately up in your arms.

We stared at each other smiling for a long time in silence until finally Karen broke in and said loudly, "Okay then, we need to get over to Flax before they close. Great to see you Al, and Garpie, you be a good boy!"

Snapping out of my trance, I managed to say, "Hey, great to meet you, Maya, I'd love to hear about that show downtown sometime."

"It was at the Mary Smither . . . something, or Margo Smarth . . . or . . . I can't remember, but yeah . . . great to meet you, *Al*," she said, emphasizing the "Al" and then in a silly voice as if talking to a toddler, "And you too, Garp, you are soooo beautiful." She turned to look at me again and smiled. And then the two of them walked off toward Haight Street.

"I'll see you Saturday night at the Paradise," I called out after them. As they turned around the block and out of sight, I said out loud, "Wowwwww, friggin' A!" and felt a huge rush of excitement pool into my belly.

I fell instantly for Maya, and she fell instantly for Garp. One way to a woman's heart is through your dog. Maya was vivacious, luscious, and totally uninhibited. She had enormous crinkly eyelids, sweet, innocent, greenish eyes, and was compact and sexy, with lightly freckled skin and an enchanting smile. She was a singer in a local band, and she was from Southern California. She was trouble. Perfectly delicious trouble. A cute Southern California woman with guitar. She had *drama* written all over her. Hers *and* mine.

I fell hard and fast, especially after going to one of Maya's shows. She was a successful artist (or what I thought of as successful artist at the time), warming up for Counting Crows and Dieselhead at the Fillmore. To me, she was like Tori Amos or Joni Mitchell. She was brilliant, beautiful, and passionate with a capital, gyrating "P." She had within her body and being, the ethereal bright curvature of a calla lily, one I could fall so easily into the glowing white cup of, and be instantly blinded by, as if deliciously lost in the whiteness of a perfect blizzard. Being a struggling artist myself at the time, I was instantly dazzled by her successes. She had come to life right before my eyes and was actually interested in *me*. Or at least in the *idea* of me, which was good enough at the time. Not only was she interested, but she celebrated me in a way that made me feel important, as if my struggling creativity somehow mattered. Sign me up for that kind of attention! Goodbye alcohol, hello Maya.

Within a few days, I was invited to a show, and then a party at her house after a show, and then another, and before I knew it, Garp and I were part of the entourage. It was one of those late nights on her sofa after a show at the Hotel Utah or the Great American Music Hall, when the rest of the crew had left, and we were together alone. Sitting there beside her, I started shaking and burning from the inside out as if eighty-seven sparklers had just been simultaneously lit and placed haphazardly between my ribs, instantly torching up my sternum like a hotplate. I was having my own internal Fourth of July celebration. I thought for a second Maya might burn her hand when she touched my face. I gulped. Maya gulped back.

And then we devoured each other like two impatient crocodiles. There was thrashing and clamoring, scales grating, teeth gnashing, and basically a mad feverish crocodile passion ensued. We stumbled into the bedroom together, still embracing, and fell onto the bed. I fell into her body completely with full abandon until I *was* no longer. I melted, merged, and disappeared into the void of her. It was pure ecstasy, and it was intoxicating and overwhelming. It was more thorough and complete, more distant and divine, than any drug or epic night of drinking. The emotional enmeshment and surrender were instantaneous. One night in bed together on a jasmine-scented side street in San Francisco, and I was smitten so blindly I could barely remember my own name.

In the hormonal haze of our first few weeks together, the fact that Maya was allergic to dogs didn't faze us. She loved dogs, and particularly Garp. And yet her allergies would affect her singing voice dramatically. Her face and throat would become red and inflamed, and she would turn itchy and congested. She had a habit of grabbing her whole nose when she had even the slightest itch, as if she were about to slip underwater, and then report a nasally, "Don't worry I'm fine, I'm fine." And I would worry and say in my own nasally imitation, "You're not fine, you're not fine," and feel slightly guilty, and eventually convince myself she was subconsciously allergic to *me*.

On one of our first dates, we went to an Ethiopian restaurant in the Fillmore. We ordered a gigantic, messy chicken platter. There were no forks or knives, and when the food came, there was an awkward moment where I just paused and stared blankly into the steaming miasma, not wanting be rude by eating with my hands. Maya dove right in, pulling apart the flesh as if she were out there in the bush hovering over a fire pit of freshly killed antelope. I immediately thought of Bibi Makena and my culinary adventures in Africa. I was impressed and awed by Maya's primal approach. She seemed to spend extra time gnawing on the bones and passionately relishing each bite.

For the next few months, we ate our way through San Francisco, stopping at every hip ethnic and otherwise eatery from North Beach to the Outer Sunset, from the Embarcadero to the Inner Richmond. We became serious foodies, devouring the *SF Zagat* guide like a book of great poetry (which of course it is), or perhaps a Joni Mitchell songbook. From Cha Cha Cha's Spanish/Caribbean tapas in the Haight to the House of Nanking in North Beach for their scallops and sweet potatoes in garlic sauce, to Marnee

Thai in the Sunset for spicy barbecued chicken wings and Minh's Garden in the Richmond for perfect pho, maxing out our credit cards along the way. Our hours were so manic and weird; we'd get up at eleven and eat lunch late in the afternoon and then freak out around 10 P.M., starving. We would drive around, oversexed and moody, looking for a place we'd never been and that was actually still open, often winding up at the Baghdad Café, Sparky's, or another one of the marginal late-night diners.

Though I was no longer referred to as a "keg barnacle," I was now behaving like a Maya barnacle. She was the ultimate narcotic. I want to say that she was my muse for all the great poetry and art I would make, but the truth is, she was more like my emotional art project, and I spent more time fawning and obsessing over her than actually making any decent art. I was sick "in love" with her. "In love," because I was in infatuation, which for me was being in addiction. I had no idea at the time, but this relationship and my addiction to it were just as potentially fatal as my addiction to alcohol. The relationship and its impending loss would drive me further into the dark abyss of unconscious shame, guilt, and abandonment, and push me to the farthest edges of myself.

It wasn't that I didn't love Maya; it was just an immature love. I was in love with the *idea* of Maya, the image and the projection. The true grit and human detail were lost to the dream. I mean, I could barely do anything else except obsess about and hang around with Maya. Every time I went to see her sing, I would cry. It was both sweet and pathetic at the same time. The truth is I wanted to beam like I saw her beaming on stage. I wanted that kind of passion, that kind of attention. I wanted an audience!

Besides obsessing on Maya, I didn't have much else going on. I was in a Masters of Fine Arts program at the San Francisco Art Institute and not working, just floating around San Francisco making bad art. I was a lost, floating art boy—sensitive, creative, and emotional—a great catch. A complete teetering emotional wreck was more like it—especially once I got triggered.

When I wasn't in class at the Art Institute, I was busy making random, tangential works of bad art that had no focus or continuity. I had given up on photography as I got exposed to film, performance, video, and installation art. I felt compelled to experiment. All of my friends were doing important, fascinating, and deep works that were redefining art history. Or so I thought. My friend Zane, for example, filled a gallery with a giant square of turmeric. At the opening, people kept walking in it, thinking it was a piece of cloth. Zane flew into fits of rage and anguish. He refused to put up some kind of barrier, because he said it would ruin the piece. He moved on to paprika. People tracked that up as well. I thought it looked kind of interesting with the footprints. We all thought he was an inscrutable genius.

Most of my friends had the habit of renting studios in the worst possible neighborhoods. They always said it was an economic decision, but I knew that they were secretly suffering from white guilt and felt like "integrating" themselves and broadening their cultural horizons. I noticed that all my ethnic friends always had their studios in Ashbury Heights or the Richmond, not somewhere there was a high likelihood of being ripped off, shot, or run over, like in the Tenderloin. Zane insisted on Sixth Street. One night, a pimp high on crack drove into the front window of his studio at 3 A.M., almost smashing the giant slate blackboard on which Zane was painting Einstein's calculations on the theory of relativity in pigeon shit.

One day, I got the irresistibly brilliant idea that I would make a giant ball of some kind. All the art stars at the time seemed to be making balls of one kind or another: Anne Hamilton and her ball of horsehair, David Ireland and his handmade balls of cement, Zane and his balls of spices and bird feces. I figured I'd make a giant ball of aluminum foil and roll it around San Francisco, place it in odd locations, and take pictures of it! Genius.

I went down to Costco and bought about a hundred rolls of aluminum foil. I started with one sheet and crumpled it up to the size of a golf ball. After a few days, the ball was so big I could sit on the thing. Then I began to worry about getting it out the front door of my apartment. We went everywhere together for a few weeks, me and my ball of aluminum foil. It became a character in the imaginary art movie of my life. I photographed it rolling through the grass in Golden Gate Park and perched it on the seawall at Ocean Beach, where it hovered on the horizon line above the ocean like a slowly rising metallic planet. I placed it on sidewalks with people watching it, and photographed them together sharing tentative space. For a second, I felt like a deep and profound artist—I was like John Malkovich in *Art School Confidential,* where he's at an opening on campus of his "new" triangle paintings, and he says with exquisite seriousness to a curious student, "You know, I invented triangles." I felt like I was part of the movement that had invented balls. Or art balls, anyway.

After a week, I convinced myself it was a stupid gag, not worthy of high art, and I donated my ball to the recycling center at Kezar Stadium. They were thrilled. "Whoa, dude, where'd you find that thing?" the recycling king asked when I showed up in his doorway with my ball.

"I made it," I said, full of half-baked pride.

After my first year at the Art Institute, I failed my year-end review, which I needed in order to graduate. The faculty committee wanted a portfolio or installation of photographs, and what I put up on the walls were all my recent experiments: a terrible painting made of color landscape photographs duct-taped to burlap and drowning in splatters of black acrylic paint; some documentation of my aluminum foil ball; and a couple of "visual poems" printed extra large on white butcher paper.

I was excited and proud to be entering new territory. My photo faculty committee was alarmed and distressed. Their faces twitched as they spoke, and they seemed to be almost offended. So I dropped out of the photography department and joined the New Genres department, where

I would be welcomed by all the other misfits experimenting their lives away. The New Genres faculty let me resubmit, and I passed, this time by doing a "performance installation," which consisted of placing a bag of ice on the thermostat on the outside of the main building, thereby making the boiler come on to rattle the pipes in the lower studio, which I amplified with microphones. Every time a pipe clanged loudly, I ran around the room with a huge stick of charcoal, drawing the sound waves on the walls. It was fucking profound. Somehow, the faculty committee thought it "worked," so I passed.

I did a lot of other odd, cheap, confused visual puns that had no meaning or power. Like the time I filled the lower studio with onion grass from my backyard and placed an umbrella in a huge terra-cotta pot filled with dirt. I thought it was going to put Magritte and Dalí to shame, make them somehow irrelevant, because my work was an *in-stal-lation*!! It was friggin' alive, man, not trapped in some two-dimensional bullshit façade. Someone in my critique seminar called it an unresolved Surrealist stunt. I was crushed. They just didn't get it, I mused.

But the reality was, I just didn't get it, and grew more despondent, convinced that I was a shitty artist. I eventually found my way back to photography for my final graduate show, and was quite pleased with much of the work. The show consisted of a 30-by-40-inch self-portrait of me caught in a shaft of sunlight while sprinting through the dark redwoods like a fleeting spirit; a five-foot collage of 125 images of water patterns that accounted for one second in the life of Lagunitas Creek; and a series of sand drawings I did with my toes at the edge of the ocean. These last photos were mounted low and perpendicular to the wall so one could better imagine the tide rising up around your feet and *drawing* the sand through your toes, leaving an elegant pattern in its wake. A couple of hours before the opening of my final show, one of the teachers from the photo department came by and quickly scanned my wall, thought about the work for a second and said, "I'd ditch that one to the left, doesn't go, maybe mount those three horizontally. Who the hell printed these?" And then, whispering, added, "I'd find a better frame for this one, sweetheart." She smiled and wandered off to inspire the suicidal tendencies of another fragile artist.

In the summer of 1994, Maya's band was on tour in Colorado, and I decided to meet them there after a solo backpacking trip in the Rockies. I dropped my scattered routine, including a job offer from the Art Institute to teach color photography, to revolve my time around their tour. I desperately needed the money, because at the time I was living on credit cards and handouts inspired by Dad's guilt. It felt shitty, but not as shitty as being apart from Maya. I more desperately "needed" to be with Maya. I bagged out on the job and hit the road. I remember the band playing a lot of empty bars in Colorado, but it was all stardom to me, albeit a tentative, fragile stardom on the verge of collapse.

One day after the tour we were sitting in Maya's garden room back in San Francisco, on the same couch where we first kissed, when the phone rang. It was her gynecologist. I took one look at her face, and some part of me already knew, given how much unprotected sex we had had. She had gone alone to the gynecologist a couple weeks before without telling me, apparently to confirm the in-home test. I was already in tears before she hung up the phone. She put her hands in her face and began sobbing. "I can't believe this. I can't believe I've done this to myself again. Oh, God." There was a long pause, and then she looked up with a penetrating rage in her eyes. "The appointment is the on the 17th! Why the fuck are *you* crying?" she said.

"Because I, I, I don't know, I should have . . ." I was flailing.

She stood up, wiping her face, and started pacing back and forth around the room. I tried to comfort her, but she squirmed out of the way and sobbed louder. I felt the guilt pouring into my bones like black cement.

"Don't touch me," she said.

"Oh, so this is my fault?"

"No, it's not your fucking fault. The appointment is the 17th," she repeated.

"I heard that." I said defensively. There was a long silence between us while my mind raced and searched for the right thing to say. "I don't know, Maya."

"What don't you know?" She looked at me like she might pick up the nearest object and hurl it at me.

"Nothing."

"What, Al, go ahead and say it!"

"I don't know if I can be in the room with...you, I mean, I . . ."

This was clearly the wrong thing to say. "Are you fucking kidding me?"

"No, I mean I'll come, but I might, I . . ." I was stuttering, and clamoring for clarity, back-pedaling—it felt as if I had just gotten socked unexpectedly by a huge, cold wave and was being pounded into the sand, sucked in by the undertow.

"What the fuck are you saying? Are you going to show up for me or not?—I can't believe this shit, I mean I'm the pregnant one, and we have to take care of your meltdown—get over yourself."

I slumped further into the couch. I was bawling now, completely overwhelmed by the impact of the situation.

"I didn't sign up for this shit. You're supposed to be taking care of me," she snarled.

"I know, I can't . . . I don't know if I can, I mean what if . . ."

"What if what?" She was screaming now. "What if they stuck the vacuum up your dick and tried to pull the baby out of you? I'm the goddamn one who gets violated here! All you have to do is hold my fucking hand, is that too much to ask?"

"I just don't want to . . ."

"Fuck you, then, I don't want you there anyway. I'll have Josh or Carrie come. I can't deal with this—you are being so pathetic."

We were both sobbing uncontrollably now, with no one to comfort us. Not only had I gotten her pregnant, but then I balked at showing up to the procedure for fear of passing out. I admit it, I'm one of those squeamish types who gets queasy around blood and guts and large spiders, even conversations about medical offices, let alone waiting around in one. One time I went to see my friend Anita at the hospital. I walked in the door, announced my name to the receptionist, and then promptly fell to the floor like a sack of potatoes.

"Get the fuck out. Just leave. I need to be alone," Maya said. The sadness in her voice included a devastating mix of disappointment and disgust. In me. She had never been so mean and so self-righteous, and I had never been so cowardly and so wounded. I didn't recognize her. I didn't recognize myself. This incident inspired the absolute worst in both of us.

A couple of weeks later, after Maya had written me off almost completely, I made it to the gray haze of the waiting room. I sat on a cold, black, plastic chair flipping nervously through magazines, as if through layers of my own flimsy skin. Maya was silent. Now, she had an exasperated look in her eyes, one of contempt mixed with fear and loathing.

"Why'd you come? I told you *not* to." She said, whispering fiercely through pursed lips.

"I wanted to be here for you . . . for us."

"Bullshit. Us is over. I told you I didn't want you here."

"Well, I'm here . . . Fine, I'll leave then."

"Oh great, you're going to abandon me again? Twice? That's supportive and manly."

"No, no, I mean, I just—I mean what the fuck, Maya, I'm just trying to . . ." I felt myself tearing up again.

"Trying to what? Trying to make up for bailing on me? Well, it's a little late for that, Al."

"Maya?" said an inquisitive voice through a cracked door. The doctor was a skinny, peppy Asian woman, who kept smiling as if we were actually keeping the baby. Didn't she get we were going through the wringer here?

She just smiled her fake doctorly smile and reassured us of the simplicity of the procedure. The procedure, she said, as if chewing on an orange rind and smiling. *Procedure*—I've always hated that word. It's too close to the word *injure* or *beleaguer.* It's clinical and cold, like the steel table they slipped Maya on as I left the room.

As "the procedure" wrapped up, the doctor felt obligated to say, "Oh, and by the way, it was twins."

"It," she said, as if talking about a wallet someone left in the waiting room. I paused, feeling as if someone had just dropped a concrete block on my head—make that two concrete blocks. This doubled the remorse and loss we both felt. A flash of memory stormed through my head, of a story Dad once told me about Dana, his first wife, and how, after she remarried, she had enchanting twin girls with her second husband, and how both were killed in a car accident one icy January night on a back road in Connecticut. They were just five years old.

Maya and I were clearly not suited to, or committed enough for child rearing. This was Maya's fourth unwanted pregnancy, and my third. After so many days of grief, tears, rage, and blame in which Maya had built up so much contempt for me, and was spewing so much venom, it became almost impossible to be around her. I was pretty convinced she had me nailed on all counts. But supposedly it takes two to tango.

I became filled with a debilitating self-loathing and an extreme sense of loss. All the sweetness and dreamy affection we had accumulated in our manic infatuation account was instantly withdrawn. I was insufficient. Insufficient in my person, insufficient in my actions, insufficient as a man. Afterward, there was a quiet desperation between us that just never left. We had only been together for about eight months, though it felt like eight years, when the relationship completely fell apart.

\* \* \*

In my bewilderment and grief, I moved to the country, to the solace, beauty, and stunning open spaces of Marin County. Somehow, I felt as if all that nature might be able to help me handle the debilitating grief, could perhaps cushion the blow. I saw myself wandering through those blindingly blond hills in midsummer, seeking shade in a small grove of madrone trees, listening to their thick, waxy leaves clack in a foggy breeze—getting lost in the majestic spiraling flight of a redtail hawk. I imagined riding one of those thermals myself, into a high, bright, more ethereal azure calm. I would hike the chalky cliffs above Drake's Beach at dawn, being soothed by the powerful roar of waves and sizzling wash of foam. And that distance to the horizon—I would stare into it with my mouth agape, absorbing an endless beckoning of light and color, beauty and hope. In the city, my grief seemed to ricochet off all the other wounded souls milling about lost in the streets, only to come flying back in my face.

I found a small attic room for rent in a bungalow on a side street in San Rafael with two roommates. One guy was a landscape architect I never saw, and the other a terrifyingly beautiful woman straight out of the Victoria's Secret catalogue named Shanti Z, or something to that effect. Like Maya, she was the lead singer in a local band. Imagine that. I stood good and clear of her. I was so depressed and despondent anyway, I barely noticed her sensuous brunette locks, her achingly perfect body, or how she used to run around the house in her lacey pink bra and underwear, singing commands to her two gigantic Bernese mountain dogs named Groucho and Puppet. When I wasn't working part time as an errand boy at a Landscape Architect firm in Berkeley, I could be found locked in my room, sniffling into Garp's fur. One day, my friend Theo came over with some groceries to make sure I was still alive.

"You need therapy, dude," he said, leaning over my deflated body, which was coiled into a little ball on the bed.

"Fuck therapy," I said, sniffling, and then bursting into tears again.

"Oh man, what am I going to do with you? You need to move on. Maya's a spaz, she's no good for you anyway."

I stared up at the monument that was Theo, a great obelisk, and into his chestnut eyes, and then at his gigantic crinkly eyelids that reminded me of Maya's. I felt a sharp pang shoot through my stomach, and the tears welled up again.

"You need—"

"Fuck that, I don't need shit," I interrupted.

"You're a mess, Al. Seriously, look at yourself, you haven't left this room in how many days? You should just check it out. I've been going for two months, and look at me, I'm a model of balance, self-awareness, and regularity." He smiled, only half-kidding.

"What the fuck, are they prescribing fiber pills or something?"

"I mean, like, I'm pulling my shit together. I'm more consistent with my appointments, and time, and whatnot."

"You mean like to your proctologist?"

"What are you, twelve? You should just check it out, is all I'm saying."

"What the hell are you doing in therapy, anyway? I mean, you have a girlfriend, and she's fucking hot."

"Hey, easy man . . . and there's more to life than a girlfriend, especially a hot one."

"Yeah, like what? Pot?"

"No, like art, and nature, and life. You need to get a life."

"Yeah, thanks, that's supportive . . . Whatever, Theo."

"You should just come check it out at least and try it— I see a woman in Oakland. She's cool. I just kind of babble at her for an hour, and she listens and helps me figure stuff out."

"Is she cute?"

"Oh man, you're friggin' chronic— I'm not going there. Here, I brought you some applesauce and ice cream."

"What is this, the tonsillitis ward? I feel like I've had my fucking heart ripped out with a chainsaw, stomped on with a pair of spur-laden cowboy boots, thrown into a wood chipper, and then flushed down the toilet, and even after all that, I'm still eating solid food!"

"Is that right? When was the last time you ate anything substantial, anyway?"

"Thursday . . . I had a piece of toast." (It was Saturday.)

"Okay, get up. We're going to Phyllis's Giant Burger right now."

*  *  *

Theo was my angel, and still is, for putting up with me and my infantile behavior at the time, for seeing me through such obsessive drama, and understanding the real pain behind it. I *was* acting like a twelve year old, because that's what I had regressed into. All I wanted was attention, sympathy, and validation of some kind.

Theo was one of the first people I met in art school, and we hit it off immediately. We would goof on the undergrad "PIBs" (People in Black), drowning in their charcoal eye makeup, bleak moods, and suicidal art (which I somehow avoided, though just barely). You know the stuff: the blurry photographs filled with raven shadows and hooded figures. The completely black canvasses with splatters of red. And all the while you're asking yourself, *is that real blood? Their own blood? Where did they get all that blood?* Don't forget the jars of preserved body parts. All displayed for your viewing (and discussing for hours on end) pleasure. They had piercings that made them look as if they had had face-sucking time with a barbed wire fence. We made endless fun of them and our professors' overly intellectualized and sometimes stony critiques. And of course, there was the gossip around who fucked who in darkroom No. 7.

Theo seemed to understand me and my crazy obsessions, my hypersensitivity to the world, and my irrational commitment to art and poetry. He, too, was hypersensitive, and seemed to have been batted around by the world quite a bit himself. We spent a lot of time together roaming the Point Reyes Peninsula, talking sauce about photography, art, the enigmatic nature of women and relationships, and of course, therapy.

\* \* \*

It's about two or three months after the abortion, and I'm echoing through the Waldo Tunnel in my little gold Toyota, heading south toward the Golden Gate Bridge. I'm white-knuckling the steering wheel; I can see the bone glowing beneath my tightened skin. Ten o'clock and two o'clock, just like in the DMV manual. I never drive with both hands on the steering wheel, let alone all ten fingers—I mean never. But I'm headed to therapy. I need two hands on the steering wheel.

Fog is billowing ominously over the hilltops to my right as if from the edges of a giant coffin. The wind is hissing at me through the slightly cracked window. Tears begin to bloom again from my eyes like small jellyfish being tossed from the tongue of an impatient wave. As I approach the bridge, the panic mounts. The grief is gnawing. I'm at the breaking point.

At mid-span I snap, and imagine suddenly swerving my car sharply right into and through the flimsy-looking low barrier of the bridge. I bust through this barrier as if it's merely wimpy aluminum, or a simple pattern of thick red ribbon. I've finally won the race. I've crossed the finish line, and here I am mid-air several hundred feet above the roiling frigid Pacific Ocean. There is a great silence, a thin breeze is washing through my skin, and the car is coming apart around me, the windows and doors peeling away like glass and metal leaves, the wheels floating up into the clouds—a suspended weightlessness has taken me, everything has slowed.

And then the light of the horizon where the sky meets the sea suddenly darkens like a blade and rushes toward me as the weight of what I've done sinks in. I'm immediately pulled full-force downward. The terror rushes in as if a molten steel has cooled and solidified around my organs. My body seizes up into a tiny compact black box the weight of a thousand lifetimes, like the black box they recover from a plane wreck, dense with the weight of last words. I realize there's no turning back: no more Garp the dog, no more sisters, no more Mom and Dad, no more Theo or Maya (even as a friend), no more coffee ice cream milkshakes. This is all woven in with the thrilling, choking feeling of the descent to the ocean. I'm amazed at the acceleration. What started as serene floating has turned ominous and loud, sharply black, and incredibly fast. I'm being pulled against my will now, in toward the churning cold emptiness of death . . .

. . . I slammed on the brakes and my little gold Toyota shook violently and rattled but somehow stayed in my lane, and miraculously there was no one behind me. I accelerated again and made it across the span, only to meet the toll collector with puffy crazed eyes and snot-glistened cheeks.

Nothing was left; there was no further escape. No Maya, no alcohol, nothing but my own inner trauma, surfacing like an angry god.

14

# When in Doubt, Join a Cult

Antoinette spoke in a soft French accent, her voice the sound of blowing snow streaming through dead grass. She came off as worldly and refined holding an air of confidence and determination. Her face was drawn with exotic clown-face features and a giant smile that pulled the skin around her mouth into deep folds. She had inky brown, mysterious eyes, and dark brown hair silvering at the roots. Supposedly, she was a licensed marriage and family therapist, but did no formal intake or assessment, no paperwork or chart to fill out. I had been to a therapist in seventh grade and I distinctly remember being pelted with endless questions and paperwork. This was different.

I settled into the giant green sofa piled with bulky pillows, held up by stubby teak legs, which could easily have accommodated six or seven good-sized adults. All alone on this thing I felt a little like a gull with oiled wings perched on the bow of the Titanic. The sofa itself, or maybe it was the choppy sea of grief surrounding me, that seemed to be pulling at me, as every time I tried to move to the front edge I got sucked back down into its leaden bottom. My eyes flashed around the sun lit room, landing on a mini zen sandbox in the corner with a small stone neatly placed in the center. There was a tiny rake laid on its wooden rim, rows of perfectly hoed sand. Just outside the sand box there was a pile of mini action figures, people of all shades and vocations, from firemen to nurses, school teachers to businesspeople. I was straining to find an unemployed slacker art-dude. The people were all tangled together in a messy heap like the site of a massacre or recent explosion. Were these her old clients? Death by therapy. I wasn't sure. I tried to convince myself they would come back to life shortly and resume their gleeful play in the sand box.

A papier mache mask painted black and collaged with random objects and photos hung oddly high on one lone wall staring down at me with an ominous expression—teeth like light bulbs, a nose of moonlight, ears of cauliflower, and hollow eyes made from purple buttons—one eye staring off in an opposite direction, and much smaller than the other. Running along the same wall was a sparse white shelf with an old milk bottle being used as a vase, cupping a single dried pale orange Chinese lantern flower. It was tilting uncomfortably to one side, as if it were trying to escape the confines of the bottle. Along the window hung ghostly white curtains that danced to the cadence of the floor heaters.

"As Theo told you, we use medicines in the opening process."

Medicines? The opening process? Was I a can of crushed tomatoes?

"We take you on journeys into the depth of your self," she continued. I was pretty certain I had hit bottom, and there was no more depth. "You can try it or not," she said, smiling, with a mysterious twinkle in her eye that said, "It's soooo incredible, and you've got to check this shit *out.*"

"It can be very powerful and revealing, and can open you to your true self." Hmm, my true self. What self was I dragging around now? I shifted uncomfortably on the sofa, hearing the springs send out a muffled twang like the tuning of a guitar under water. I felt the weight of the sofa as if its mass could at any moment suck me under. I sat there roiling in a soup of anticipatory excitement mixed with great dread. Dread at dredging up a dark and frightening past, and the slight excitement or relief of voicing long withheld stories. Similar to when you are holding a great secret and are sworn to secrecy, and then circumstances change, the cat's out of the bag and you're free to spill your guts.

I began by telling her a bit of the background on Hell Frau, my parents' unavailability, Maya, my alcoholism, etc. At the second session, I asked her about her group sessions with the "substances" Theo had briefly mentioned, and then insisted that I wasn't interested. It reminded me of when I was in sixth grade and my best friend, Chris, asked me if I smoked pot and I shyly said, "No, I'll *never* do that."

Antoinette went on to tell me how she and her husband, Zavad, used such substances, or "medicines," as she called them, to help people experience profound states of consciousness, connection, and emotion often repressed or left unconscious due to trauma or intense grief. I told her I wasn't interested in that. And for a couple months, anyway, I wasn't.

Soon, however, I became curious, as Theo would come back from a weekend session all pie-eyed with stories of journeying to distant dimensions, experiencing wild hallucinations, having profound emotional insights, and feelings of deep connection. I started to believe he was involved in some incredibly unique experiment in human consciousness and psychology, à la Ram Dass and Timothy Leary in the sixties. This was the 1990s, and yet, here I was searching for some profound transcendence *from* my experience—and from all reports, this was truly transcendent. I was three or four months in to my one-on-one therapy when I finally agreed to a solo "medicine session" with Antoinette.

Even though I was confronted with the taking of drugs, I somehow convinced myself (or they convinced me) that it was truly medicine, like extra-strength Tylenol or something. I was never concerned about "going off the wagon," as I assured myself that my main addiction was always alcohol, but honestly at the time, I was hurting for some kind of quick and immediate intervention, and in my grief and confusion, I simply neglected to fully consider any potential fallout from the use of such drugs.

It wouldn't be until much later that I witnessed the addictive nature of these "medicines" and to the whole group/cult dynamic itself.

The first session I participated in was a weekend day-long at Antoinette and Zavad's compound in Mendocino. I insisted that Theo be there to support me. As I hesitated, Antoinette asked me what I had to lose.

"How about my sanity, my own mind."

"Your grieving, depressed, suicidal mind?" she replied. "Perhaps you'd want to lose that, no?" She smiled, a bit like a psychotic clown.

Yikes, I thought for a second, and then, yeah, what *do* I have to lose, my life pretty much sucks. I swallowed thickly, as if I had a blob of cooling wax in my throat, and said quietly, "Okay."

The compound in Mendocino consisted of a single ranch-style adobe with a couple of outbuildings, one of which was devoted to group sessions. It was a hexagonal space with skylights, filled with pillows, soft carpeting, driftwood sculptures, sage, and various statues—Buddha, Hanuman, Tara, etc.

It was a foggy Saturday morning. I had taken mushrooms a few times in high school and college, so I thought I knew what I was in for. However, it was usually only a quarter gram here, a half gram there. I had experienced the requisite queasy nervousness, vast giggling, and groovy hallucinations, but it turned out, that was just child's play.

Antoinette left me alone in the round space with my prayers (whatever those were—I had never prayed for anything in my life) and then came back to smudge me with a sage wand. Her eyes were closed, and she was muttering under her breath. She left me with a polished wooden bowl of mushrooms and told me to go ahead and eat. Not just any bowl, but a six-inch bowl *filled* with mushrooms. She offered me a small piece of banana in case I had trouble getting them down.

"The whole thing?" I asked, gulping incredulously. She nodded, and handed me a blindfold. "What's this?"

"You will wear this to keep yourself focused inward." And she wandered out of the room.

"I'm completely fucked," was one of my last sane thoughts.

My mouth tightened as it filled with the taste of moldy twigs and dirt, just as foul as I remembered, and I savored each piece of banana to cushion the blow. Within twenty minutes, I started to feel the effects of the "medicine" coming on. I felt queasy, dizzy, and generally petrified. Soon, sharp twists erupted in my belly, tingling through my arms and legs.

Antoinette came back to adjust my blindfold and told me to relax and "go inside." This made me panic even more. She left the room again (more panic), and soon I heard music coming from the speakers I had noticed near the ceiling. At first, the music was soothing and generally quiet, a Windham Hill piano piece, but abruptly switched to some grating thumpy electronica that started to choreograph an increasingly alarming set of images which spiraled through my mind with bizarre force. Initially, I was interested and then just plain scared as they swirled around violently in fractal patterns and intricate washes of color. The knots in my stomach tightened, the nausea bloomed, the fear deepened. Aztec blanket patterns morphed into repetitive bulbous deep-sea creatures dipped in rainbow halos bleeding through boulevards of knives with wings.

Soon, a wall of golden sharks descended through purple clouds, devouring the winged blades flashing bared teeth that turned into pinwheels, then pinwheels into peonies, until I had a wave of nausea so strong I leaned over and heaved into an imagined lava pit. Nothing came up, except the gravelly echo of my own fears clanging around in my ribcage. I would lean back down, only to be impaled by zebra tortillas attached to the mutilated faces of multiple gorillas.

The music seemed to affect the quantity and quality of the images. How much I freaked out depended on whether or not I liked the music. At one point, I completely wigged, certain that I was going mad, and that I had been coerced into some weird experiment in a government laboratory. I pulled off my blindfold and was assaulted with such a wash of blinding white pixilated chaos that I instantly collapsed among the pillows and pulled the blindfold back over my eyes. I rolled around moaning in agony and screamed out for Antoinette, convinced that I was losing my mind.

I heard shuffling and then felt her at my side, her burbling, distorted voice mixing in with the chaos of the music and imagery.

"Surrender and look within; there you will find the heart of the world," she whispered intently.

The music turned ominous. Think Psycho during the shower scene, or Jaws during the first attack, and in turn, I was doubly haunted by a new set of images: inexplicable heaps of blood-clot trombones, dismembered featherless chickens, spears of rusty bones stabbing at my mind. I was hanging onto my sanity for dear life, screaming for some sense of familiar reality as I knew it. It was gone. I could find no heart of the world in this terror. This was utter and complete madness—I was in the process of going mad, and I wasn't coming back. I was ravaged by continuous forests of rat skulls, obsidian hatchets, and crimson clarinets, as the music folded chaotically around my ears.

I screamed for help, and an umbrella of bats flew out from between my teeth. I screamed louder, and my tongue turned into a foamy electric green anaconda. I kept screaming, no words, just foam, and snakes and then amoebas, and bubbles, softer bubbles, glass bubbles, bubbles with faces of coyotes, bears, ravens, dolphins.

As the music slipped back into a soft, gentle flute music, the images softened as well, turning more familiar. There were clouds, and castles of mossy cliffs and mist, like being dunked in a Roger Dean painting. Eventually, I became more curious, less anxious, willing to investigate as my mind was slowly "coming back" into view. I started just flowing with whatever showed up. The images were still blended with surreal paisley shapes, but they were less threatening—the knot in my stomach eased. I began to laugh a bit, especially when the rubberband people showed up, springing from the eyes of a blue tree frog. These morphed into the reflective beaks of crows, and then piano keys laid out in a hall of mirrors repeating endlessly.

I heard wind chimes from outside, and then slowly memories of Theo and my own life reemerged. My own personal memories and experiences had been eclipsed by this wash of psychedelic mind tricks and dark panic. I began remembering my first meetings with Maya, and with Raine, and instead of grief, felt some sense of perspective and gratitude that they had been in my life to guide me and teach me about myself. I started to think about Theo, and my parents and sisters, friends and relatives, anyone who ever meant anything to me. I was suddenly filled with an immense sense of gratitude and appreciation—emotions just spilled forth, emotions of happiness and joy.

Was this the heart of the world Antoinette was speaking of? Was this, too, buried deep within me? I was so grateful to have my mind back and have some sense of cognitive familiarity! At a certain point, I had absolutely and completely died psychically, I had literally lost my mind, and here it was back again, and yet filled with a renewed sense of appreciation—as I took off my blindfold, I was overwhelmed by the sheer beauty and radiance of the scene before and within me—Antoinette's face, her shiny eyes like polished Baltic Amber, her radiant love and compassion, Theo's friendship, and the fact that I was alive . . . I was alive. For now, anyway.

Back at Antoinette's office a couple days later, we went over the session. "What the fuck *was* that? I mean, seriously, what *was* that?"

"That was you, your mind, Al."

"Me? My mind? But, but, but . . ." I was sputtering. "What does it all mean?"

"It means you are not your story, Al . . . You are not your past or your memories, or your fantasies. You are something much more vast and mysterious. You are that which makes your story possible."

Something clicked inside my head and the skin on my neck began to tingle. An echo sounded, a repetition of the familiar, memories of Bibi

Makena saying the exact same thing. I smiled to myself. The heavy wooden door to my heart creaked open a bit wider, and spires of light began to stream in. "What about all that weird psychedelic shit streaming through my head?"

"It is just garbage, the junk of thought, the accumulated fear manifesting as chaotic imagery."

I sat silently, trying to digest what she was saying. I tried to think about what the thing was that made my story possible, and my mind went blank. I think that's the point. Blank. Empty. Silent. This was the silence of change, of transformation, of possibility. It was so alien and new to me and I was initially scared. This was simply the space between words. The space between thoughts, the space in a room, always present, usually ignored. The silence that makes sound and voice possible. Antoinette was encouraging me to turn my attention there. To the silence and emptiness, and there, she promised, was the gateway to self-understanding, acceptance, and ultimately love of the world as it is.

Six months later, I found myself in the central Nevada desert, having committed to a group medicine journey with ten other lost and insane men. The session was run by Zavad, who hosted periodic men's circles in remote wild places throughout Northern California and Nevada. I had never worked with Zavad.

Zavad was a sturdy, serious Egyptian, self-composed, rigorous and determined, kind and mysterious, seemingly wise. He was thick and burly, six feet tall, with short, wavy sand- and silver-colored hair. His piercing, green eyes spoke of Mideastern desert seas and a mysterious unresolved distance. He had a light beard, about two weeks' growth. He was an old soul with a new mission.

A select group of clients, Theo and myself included, assembled in the desert along the high rim of a vast basin surrounded by chalky blond mountains spilling into the distance. The landscape was strewn with blocks of mahogany and dark apricot rock, swales of reddish sand and blond dust sprinkled with pinyon and sage. All cupped by a penetrating azure sky, the color appearing to bleed right into you.

We began by fasting for a day and a half, and then at dawn were sent out for "solo time" in a remote place away from camp and anyone else, and told not to leave the five-foot circle drawn in the dust around our body. No food, a bit of water, no journal to write in— just me and the contents of my own mind.

At dusk, we were called back to camp and ordered to help finish construction on a stone maze. There was a fire sputtering in the center of our camp, and songs were sung, directions hailed, sage waved around, and then mushrooms handed out. Our sleeping bags were laid out in a circle around the fire like the petals of a great sunflower. After ingesting our medicine, we were instructed to walk the maze, which took a surprisingly long time. Of course, toward the end, the mushrooms were kicking in, and the stones began morphing into amoebic plaid fractals then butterfly paisley chunks of stew meat and dizziness.

I stumbled back to my sleeping bag, eager to lie down and brace myself for the hectic ride. Soon, Zavad's assistant came around and handed us our blindfolds so we could begin our journey inward. Then, Zavad himself came around to personally bless each one of us with a thick bundle of smoking sage. I felt him next to me, and then heard his voice and familiar accent whispering near me, as if coming from the branches of a piñon bush.

"Go inside, Owl." This was Zavad's term of endearment for me, after we established during a previous wilderness session that the owl was my totem animal. From then on, to Antoinette and Zavad, I was Owl. I loved having a nickname with them. It made me feel, not just acknowledged or important, but included as part of their clan.

"Trust the journey, and surrender. All of your power is in the present moment. The more awake you are in the present moment, the more power you have. This power is of a different order. It is not power *over*, it is power *with*. It is alignment with the power and energy of the universe. The only way to have true control is to absolutely let go of control. The only way to have true power is to surrender to your powerlessness. Touch the emptiness inside, and you will contact a fullness beyond your wildest dreams. You will be blessed in that moment by the light of the world, knowing that all light, and love, and joy, abundance, and happiness lie within you. You will cease to look outward into the world for fulfillment and happiness, and you will find joy and freedom blossoming in your own heart. Let go now, Owl, and be free . . ."

"I'm terrified; I feel sick to my stomach," I whined.

"Just try and relax into the medicine. The desert will hold you and guide you. Look inward beyond the fear."

"I'm freaking out," I complained.

I was being eaten by fear. I felt small and fragile, vulnerable beyond comprehension. It always seemed easier for the other men in the group; some of them even seemed to enjoy these journeys. I always met them with dread. Particularly in the beginning.

"Yes, it's okay to freak out. We are here for you, the desert is here for you, the stars are here for you."

*When you wish upon a star.* Mom's voice spilled in from when I was a kid falling asleep in her lap in the back seat of the Volvo. This freaked me out even more.

"Fuck the stars! I feel like I'm dying; I can't handle all the gah. . .gah. . . gagsfghuh." The mushrooms had taken my voice, had swiped my words.

"Throw up if you have to, and surrender to the medicine. Surrender to the moment, you are safe in this moment. The night sky has opened its heart to you."

Then down I went. The fire crackled and there was silence for a while, then the rustling of sleeping bags increased and someone let out a moan, someone else a grunt, and then a scream, then the chilling sound of retching. Was that me?

Soon, Theo started moaning like a wounded cow and rolled into the fire. He had to be stomped out and pulled from the flames as he went on moaning, oblivious of his burning sleeping bag.

Then Zavad's assistant, Ajax, brought out the didgeridoo and began to play around the fire. Eventually, he wound up playing into the top of my skull, which inspired fantastic hallucinations. He seemed to be egging me on to the beyond. And even though my stomach was in great knots and I was hallucinating madly, I was desperately holding onto some thin, slippery leaves of consciousness, to some familiar semblance of "reality"— whatever that was.

Meanwhile, across the circle, another member, Jeff, was completely losing it, ranting and raving about the insanity of it all and Zavad's incompetence as a therapist. Then he was spewing completely off-the-wall tangential insanity that started to make me nervous. He went on about how we were all burning in hell at this moment, subjects of Zavad's twisted little experiment.

And then the voices and sounds blended into babble, the hallucinations into a matrix of deepening blackness, and then everything I knew of as "me"—consciousness, thought, memory, dreaming, bodily sensation— disappeared. I simply ceased to exist. The only way to describe it is that I was sucked into a great void, a complete emptiness. It bears no further description because the experience was beyond words. *I cannot tell what I am, because words can describe only what I am not.* So said the great Vedantan teacher Nisargadatta.

I was dead, and I was fine with that. No fear, no struggle, no pain. Absolute freedom from embodiment, absolute bliss. And then before I knew it, I was back. Time was irrelevant. Had it been an hour? Ten hours? A lifetime? I had no idea and I didn't care, and I couldn't believe it. I was so astounded to reemerge back into consciousness and embodiment that I immediately began to cry. And again, I was flooded with an overwhelming sense of gratitude for mere consciousness, for the simple act of thinking and feeling, for memory and perception. What a profound mystery and joy it is, what an absolute miracle!

As I reentered, I found myself back in the fray of hallucinating men in the middle of the night on the edge of a great desert basin. I noticed that not everyone was having a terrible time. Eric was letting out ecstatic, almost orgasmic moans; he would then roll over and tell Jeff to shut the fuck up, that he was ruining his journey. Theo, meanwhile, was continuing to shuffle into the fire while fighting off demons, and yelling random epithets at the stars.

Zavad and his assistant had been chanting for what seemed like hours when things went relatively silent, the fire died down, and I felt the journey winding down. Soon, a dim light appeared from beneath my blindfold, and I got the sense that daylight was arriving. I tried to look into the fire and saw bundles of floating clown lips splitting into a shower of sparks and baboon underbellies. Not yet.

Theo was still moaning as if he'd been shot, and Jeff was shrieking again at Zavad, this time standing up, demanding to see his badge and then collapsing in the dust with a thud. I hung on tight while familiar scenes of my life, memories, and an expanding sense of gratitude and appreciation continued to wash over me as I felt my "regular" mind coming back. I became filled with a deep emotional sensibility and compassion for all my "brothers" around the fire who were suffering.

Soon, the sounds of sniffling and then weeping arose. The light began creeping more into the sides of my blindfold, and I felt ready to pull it back. I heard some muffled voices and then some giggling and then laughter. This turned into explosions of hysterics from a couple of sleeping bags, and now Zavad and his assistants chimed in. What could they possibly be laughing about? This was serious stuff! We'd all just been through a profound hell—there were men crying, for fuck's sake!

And when I actually arose and pulled back my blindfold to assess the scene, I saw a yard sale of bodies strewn around the fire covered in blonde dust. I, too, couldn't help but laugh; what else to do in the face of such madness? This was the madness of the world, the madness of repressed emotion, of ignored feelings. This was the madness of unexpressed rage, of childhood fears being released into the desert air.

As I cleared my eyes, some people were rocking back and forth mumbling to themselves, some were still buried in their bags, and there in Zavad's lap were Theo and Jeff, weeping like little boys. Zavad looked like a proud father, stroking their heads tenderly and laughing periodically as someone else awoke disheveled from the ashes, completely transformed.

* * *

The urge to be seen by Antoinette and Zavad, to be a chosen son, to sponge up their praises, to be held in the light of their hearts, was intoxicating, and it was the antidote to the experience of not truly knowing or feeling connected to my own parents. I ended up doing a few more of these sessions in wild places over the next two years, sometimes with different "medicines," other times free of medicine all together. And all the while a hollow echo of loss sounded deeper within me, as a repeating voice, a loss that my father must have felt all too viscerally (albeit, perhaps not consciously) as he watched his father fall off the moving train, his voice receding farther and farther into the distance of generational time: "My father, my father, my father . . ."

A few months later, I participated in a weekend workshop called "The Dark Side" on Mount Diablo. I wasn't sure what to expect. How could it be any more terrifying than a weekend medicine journey? The theme, as you can imagine, dealt with the dark side of human nature: the killing impulse, the hatred, the meanness, the rage and anger that we all embody to one degree or another, particularly as men.

We began the weekend by exploring our own inclinations to inflict and cause pain and suffering. At one point, we were instructed to gang up on someone and throw him down a hillside. I'm not sure what he was thinking, but our friend Jeff volunteered. We promptly gathered around him, one person grabbing a leg the other an arm, two more shoving at the hips, and hurled him over the edge of a steep embankment. He was so big it didn't faze him. We surrounded another guy and told him he was a worthless little punk—a wimpy little faggot. At first he just smirked uncomfortably and rolled his eyes as if to say "whatever," until he started getting pushed around more violently, and the incessant vicious shouts of "loser," "gay-boy," and "pussy" wore him down. He came at us swinging and kicking, trying to break out of the circle, and then broke down face first in the dust, crying.

*This is a bit twisted,* I started thinking to myself. I was instantly transported back to the Island Camp in Maine and filled with pangs of rusty old shame and regret at how I had treated Reggie. I reflected on the pain and humiliation I, too, had endured by getting paddled. I had a hard time participating fully in these initial exercises and sat a couple of them out. It became too disturbing to be a direct agent of suffering in this moment, as I began dredging up in my mind how much pain and suffering I had inflicted on others throughout my life. From throwing knives and bricks at my sisters to hitting Etoile and abandoning Raine and Maya, to being a constant source of worry and concern for my parents throughout high school and college.

The first night, we were taken to a remote part of the mountain. We were blindfolded and all twelve of us were roped together by the left leg. The first man was not blindfolded and was to follow an anonymous leader through the underbrush in the pitch black. When the head of the line moved, it had to be in synch with the back of the line or your leg would get horribly burned by the rope. People were tripping and getting hung up in the brush, cursing at the person in front of them and yelling to the head of the line. It was ugly. Throughout the whole weekend, we never knew what was next. We just knew it would get worse.

On the last night, we gathered around a fire and a kind of death ceremony was held. Zavad showed up all in black wearing a hood; he was flanked by two hooded beefy-looking guys we hadn't seen before. I was exhausted and nervous. We were in for some weird, spooky ritual, judging by the events of the day, the previous medicine journeys, and the dark, fearful energy floating around the circle.

There was an ominous silence, a dreaded anticipation, and then Zavad spoke with a seriousness and sobriety I hadn't heard before. He asked us to write down three of the most important elements of our current life, such as relationships, experiences, or possessions. We went around the circle and spoke to each element in turn. We then ritualistically had to let each one go into the fire. I was fine with that. Okay, no problem. But then, there was a long, extended silence as we let that experience sink in.

After another few minutes, Zavad abruptly shouted, "You!" and pointed directly at me. "Any last words?"

My head snapped up and I looked behind me, hoping to see someone standing there, but there was just the faded orange firelight and gloomy shadows shifting among the trees. "Me?" I said meekly.

"Yes, you. Any last words?" he said angrily.

"I, I, I, I dunno, I, what am I . . . should I, I'm not sure . . ." I stammered.

"Take him!!" commanded Zavad. And his two gnarly looking henchmen rushed over with a burlap sack and some rope. One tied my hands behind my back, while the other blindfolded me and then dropped the burlap sack over my head and quickly tied it around my waist. They led me swiftly away from camp and off into the night.

We stumbled and shuffled for several minutes deeper into the forest, and I thought, okay, joke over, let me go. But they rushed me forward. I started to panic. This was for real! Perhaps they were just going to dump me over a cliff or leave me out in the forest somewhere until the next day. My paranoia crept in and yet I tried to stay calm—I mean what could they do, really? They'd pushed the limit with the drugs and my psychic safety;

were they now going to push the limit with my physical safety? Apparently. I was freaking out and feeling claustrophobic. I stalled and stumbled along as they pushed and dragged me forward. The minutes dragged on—okay, this is far enough, I sang to myself. They kept dragging me farther into the dark forest.

Eventually, we stopped. How long had we been walking? Twenty minutes? A half-hour, an hour? I was completely disoriented and panicked. I became convinced, since I was the first, I must be the only one subject to such treatment. Zavad was picking "favorites."

They shifted me around a bit and then told me to lean back. They pushed and then held me against a tree. One tied my legs to the tree, the other my upper torso. And then they vanished.

I called out. "Hey, don't leave, what the fuck, okay, okay, I give up! Come back, come back!" I screamed.

Silence. More silence. Then the silence was broken by an alarming screeching from a nearby tree. My heart leapt. Next I heard a low growling. I knew there were mountain lions in the area that could easily tear me limb from limb, wild boars with jagged yellow tusks who could skewer me, owls with sharp talons with which to pluck out my eyes. I was so petrified I couldn't move.

I cursed Zavad, his henchmen, and the goddamn horses they rode in on! I cursed Antoinette for being his partner, and Theo for getting me into this fucking psycho nightmare. I cursed the trees and the darkness and my own fear. And then I started to weep. I wept and wept and wept, and then practically passed out from the terror and exhaustion of it all. I prayed to God to please get me out of this one alive. And then I thought about death, felt into death, the vast emptiness of it, the extreme unknowning behind it. I thought of my death, the death of those I loved, the fleeting preciousness of life. And I thought about love, how I had spent so much time "in love" with Maya and other women, trying to extract love *from* them instead of giving my love *to* them.

For the longest time I had felt I had little love to offer, and now as I stood weeping, tied to a tree in the middle of the night, I thought about who, and what, and which experiences I would miss, and whom I could love, and with that, an enormous sense of gratitude, a wellspring of love, flooded through me. If I ever got released from being tied to this fucking tree, I vowed to myself, I would be more loving and kind, attentive, and understanding. I would stop playing small and give myself fully to life!

\* \* \*

Over the following months, I became even more involved in this expanding community of seekers. I was desperately looking for a community, a family, a group that would accept, challenge, and love me. And so, no matter how completely crazy and insane these journeys got, I couldn't resist that primal need to be included. At Christmas that year, Antoinette and Zavad invited Theo and me to celebrate with their family. This was probably the first sign of blurring client-therapist relations, besides of course using illegal substances and the fact that I had no money to pay for most of my sessions, so they'd just "put it on my tab." I was so swept up in the magical weirdness of it all and beginning to feel as if I was part of something special, a cutting-edge community of thinkers and artists defying convention, that I didn't second-guess it. Being invited for Christmas was like being included in the inner circle, being a chosen one. Coming from a family of distance, I saw the hope for a family of connection and open feeling.

After the days we spent together around Christmas, I didn't even think twice when a few weekends later at a gathering I saw Theo and Antoinette curled up on the couch in an intimate embrace. A few weeks after that, a glossy-eyed Theo showed me pictures of him and Antoinette running around the yard together . . . naked. That's when I started to get concerned and finally ask, "What's really going on here?"

I soon learned that they were sleeping together and had been for a while. Antoinette was pregnant. Theo's girlfriend, who had gotten swept up into working with Zavad, called me in a venomous, hysterical rage, and all hell broke loose in a nasty emotional maelstrom. And there I was smack dab in the middle of it all, not knowing who to believe or not believe.

The disappointment, denial, accusations, and utter confusion overwhelmed me. It turned out that Antoinette had been sleeping with several clients in the group and that Zavad had known. Supposedly, they had an "open" relationship, and he refused to take responsibility for his part in the destruction and pain it caused. I stepped away in disbelief and sadness. I tried to forgive, but I felt better off keeping a safe distance.

I had found myself on a great journey of awakening, and this was one weird stepping stone along the brilliant path. It took me years to integrate all I learned in those sessions, and for a long time, I wasn't sure how to reconcile all the contradictions of being involved in what could only be characterized as a cult. This was my family: Antoinette and Zavad my parents, Theo, my brother, Theo's girlfriend, my sister, and there were others tied up in the inner circle. It was devastating, and yet somewhat familiar at the same time.

On the one hand, I was completely bewildered by how Antionette and Zavad had betrayed my and all their clients' trust. At times, I was so angry that I thought they should be turned in. And on the other hand, I had learned quite a bit from Antoinette and Zavad, and in some ways they were great teachers. They could be incredibly kind and generous, even sweet and loving at times, not unlike Mom and Dad. They taught me how to face my fears head on, how to work through emotional turbulence, and how to truly nurture and love myself. And yet, they were so lost in their sense of power, judgment, and professional boundaries. They themselves obviously still had a lot of emotional work to do.

After a while, I didn't see their actions as malicious, so much as a result of their ignorance, their susceptibility to the power, grandiosity, and the dramatic temptations of leadership. I soon began to see them as confused and weak, whereas previously I saw them as almighty gods and goddesses leading me to the promised land. Now that I suddenly felt more together and balanced than my therapists, I knew I had to move on.

It wasn't until recently that I also realized how my addictions, my whole path of escape through drugs and alcohol, would also be part of my salvation. At least the drugs, anyway. Alcohol always felt like *the* big problem for me. Though I did a lot of other drugs, I never grew acutely addicted to any of them. And during this whole time with Antoinette and Zavad, I felt more of an addiction to the *experiences* than to the substances. Although mushrooms are not necessarily addictive, they are, in fact, an extremely powerful mind-altering substance and should never be underestimated, as the escape and transcendence that one experiences from regular waking consciousness can become a dependency. A mushroom journey is the ultimate adrenaline rush of the mind—it always seems as if there is someplace farther you can go. And just as the community and my place in it was coming apart, I learned that a couple of people were doing several "medicine journeys" a week. This seemed extreme to me, and was another red flag that sent me running.

When I had begun with Antoinette and Zavad in 1994 at age twenty-five, I was truly desperate and lost, and now I had a deeper glimpse into my own soul, a greater sense of self-worth and emotional strength, with expanded notions of personal creativity and ultimately what was truly possible for my life.

I knew in that last session with the mushrooms that I had gone far enough with substances, with drugs, or whatever you want to call them—and I no longer needed them or anything else to get to that transcendent truth of being, of emptiness, peace, and great joy. Except perhaps, a deepening exploration of creativity via the magic of art and poetry, and a little attention to the simple fact of my own breathing. But first a little more about Mom and Dad.

15

# A Brief History of Mom and Dad

Dad loved talking about his past, despite all the tragedies. Right around this time in 1994, when I was in San Francisco for graduate school in photography, Mom and Dad came out for a visit. One day Dad and I walked up to Lafayette Square Park, sat on one of those weathered green benches talking for hours about his life. I was twenty-six then, the year Dad turned eighty.

He was born in 1914 in Brooklyn to my namesake, Albert DeSilver, a handsome lawyer and cofounder of the American Civil Liberties Union. His mother, Margaret Burnham DeSilver, was an heiress, friend, and patron to artists, and to writers such as John Dos Passos, Ernest Hemingway, Dawn Powell, and Dorothy Parker, among others. The only picture I've ever seen of her is one of her with Carlo Tresca in the early 1940s. In this photo, she's plump, with cherubic features, a small nose, and dark, nervous eyes. Dad used to say how "terrified" of children she was. That was the word he used: *terrified*. Terrified the way some people are terrified of snakes or spiders—as in a debilitating phobia.

Dad had two siblings, a sister, Anne, who was in and out of mental institutions her whole life, and a brother, Burnham. Anne had been diagnosed with schizophrenia, which is how Margaret met Dawn Powell. (Dawn Powell's son Jojo was "treated" at the same mental institution as Anne, and as the story goes, he fell in love with her while there.) We children rarely saw Dad's brother, Burnham, when we were growing up, and when we did, he rarely spoke. I often wondered why he was so quiet. Mom used to say of Uncle Burnham, "Still waters run stagnant and odd." Given what I know now about their family history, silence seems an appropriate default trait. By contrast, Aunt Anne would sit and read the paper, repeating again and again: "Isn't that the limit?" But she did often ask us how we were, and whether or not we had been playing any tennis lately. She watched a lot of tennis on TV.

When Dad was nine, his father, Albert, fell off a train as the two of them were on their way to a Harvard/Yale game in New Haven. That was the story reported in *A Liberal in War Time: The Education of Albert DeSilver* by Walter Nelles, and the one that usually got told in family conversations. However, in my research, all I could find was a Yale University article in 1924 that reported he was "killed by a commuter train." I couldn't even find an obituary for him in the *New York Times* naming the circumstances of his death.

I have often imagined the scene of Albert holding his son Harrison's hand on that September morning in 1924. In my mind, the air is thick and hazy and even early in the day the temperature was already in the upper seventies. I imagine Dad staring out into the vastness of Brooklyn, a great sea of brick and smoke with a few lingering farms in the distance. Because of the intense heat, they stand at the back of the open-ended car.

In my imagination, Albert, usually distracted by his busy law practice and its mounting demands, is delighted to finally have a day with his son. I see him wearing a thin white round-collared Brooks Brothers shirt with gray slacks and a gray bowler hat, and Dad in long black shorts, a light blue short-sleeved shirt, and a baseball cap with a big white letter "Y" that glows above his head like a bent halo. They enjoy the dramatic light and the gentle breeze as the train speeds on. Because the day was so hot, Albert may have leaned out over the back of the open car to catch more of a breeze and to accentuate the adventure of train travel for his quiet son, Harrison.

At that precise moment, Albert yells above the screech of wheels, "I'm flying!"—one hand holding onto the hot, sweaty metal pole, one hand letting go of his son's to steady himself as the train leans farther into a curve. And in the next moment, the engineer unexpectedly switches tracks, which sends the last car lurching dramatically from side to side. Albert loses his grip and is flung from the train, landing headfirst on the opposite track. He is killed instantly in the fall. It takes almost a mile for the train to stop, as the hysterical boy screams out repeatedly: "My father! My father! My father!"

In her grief and terror, Grandma Margaret sent the kids upstate to live with an obscure uncle or cousin who turned out to be physically abusive. Dad rationalized this by saying, "You know, we were pretty out of control; he had to keep us in line somehow. Sometimes, a kid needs to be smacked into shape. I was one of those kids." A few years later, Grandma Margaret married the labor leader Carlo Tresca. Dad became close to Carlo, loving him for his devotion to the cause of equal rights for workers, and for his kind and generous heart. According to the *New York Times*, and Dorothy Gallagher's book, *All The Right Enemies: The Life and Murder of Carlo Tresca*, on January 11, 1943, Tresca was crossing Fifth Avenue at 13th Street in Lower Manhattan on foot when a black Ford pulled up beside him. A short, squat gunman in a brown coat jumped out and shot Tresca in the back and the head with a handgun, killing him instantly. The black Ford was later found abandoned nearby with all four doors open. One theory at the time was that the Mafia was the suspected assassin, acting on orders from Sicily. Others have theorized that Tresca was eliminated by the NKVD as retribution for criticism of the Stalin regime of the Soviet Union.

Although Dad wasn't there at the scene, he had just had lunch with Carlo a couple hours prior, and was one of the first to be notified. Again,

Dad was fatherless. With what must have been a bewildering tide of grief and loss, Dad left New York in his late twenties when he was called to serve during World War II.

Dad was a conscientious objector during the war, an unpopular move at the time, and had a "choice" of going to the penitentiary in Danbury, or of doing two years of hard labor, with forced "medical testing." He chose the latter and was sent to work with a road-building crew in the Blue Ridge Mountains, and then to a military hospital in Tennessee, where they conducted top-secret medical tests on him. As I understand it, they were doing research on germ warfare, and he was one of the guinea pigs. As a result, he became extremely ill and almost died.

Although young-looking for his age, Dad seemed to have lived several lifetimes by the time I was born in 1968. He had already been married four times by the time he married Mom in 1962. He and his first wife, Dana, had two children when they were in their twenties. His second wife turned out to be a lesbian, which he found out after a week or so of marriage. "That one doesn't really count," he'd say. His third wife, Ruth, hung herself from the heating pipes in their Greenwich Village apartment. The fourth one couldn't have children. Two of these wives continued their presence in Dad's life throughout my childhood. Mom even became friends with Joyce, the one who couldn't have children. She remarried one of the heirs to the Johnson & Johnson fortune and stayed in touch with Dad. Mom loved the fact that Joyce and her husband had so much money. They would invite us to their fabulous houses in Southampton, St. Helena, and Pebble Beach. "Every time you use a Band-Aid, John gets fifty cents," Mom liked to say.

Dad had two sons, Richard and David, with his first wife, Dana. Richard has led a simple and undramatic life, mostly at a distance from Dad. David was a bit of a wild child, running off to Mallorca and Mexico City with his guitar and books of poems, smoking pot and drinking recklessly. He was largely a mystery to my sisters and me when we were growing up. We didn't see him much in the seventies, though occasionally he would show up with his wife, Dolores, smoke some dope, ask for money, get into an incoherent argument with Dad, and then leave. In the eighties, David disappeared. For ten years or so, no one knew where he was. He finally turned up in Jackson Hole, Wyoming, where he was working as a cook and slowly drinking himself to death. It turns out it was David who found Ruth hanging from the heating pipes in Dad's Greenwich Village apartment. He died quietly and uneventfully of alcoholism when I was in high school. No memorial service, no discussion. Dad remained solemn and quiet about David's life and death, preferring not to talk much about him, as if there were an impenetrable emotional wall around the subject built of guilt and shame.

Dad went on to study architecture, eventually graduating from Columbia in the fifties. He never needed to work, as his mother was an heiress and supported him throughout his life. Eventually, he started a small architecture practice in Connecticut, where he moved in the early sixties around the time he met Mom.

Mom never talk much about her upbringing, except to mention occasional references to growing up "poor" in Boston, and it all being "so tiresome, boring, and embarrassing." Occasionally, she would mention how "Mummy corked it early." I believe she was in her late teens when her mom died of a heart valve condition. Grampy must not have been much of a consolation, being a devout conservative Catholic and emotionally reserved in the extreme, except when it came to a particularly moving mass. Grief wasn't something you talked about in those days, or at least in her family and social circle, and it wasn't something Mom ever got comfortable expressing. And so she covered it up with her outrageous, exaggerated wit and devotion to cigarettes and alcohol. She thought that expressing true emotion was "tacky" and somehow "lower class."

Class was Mom's lifelong obsession. She seemed to long for an aristocratic place in society, just out of reach; this was expressed by an exquisite snobbery that must have given her some feeling of superiority.

Mom's father, Grampy, was a devout and practicing Catholic and had sent all three Flynn girls off to a convent/finishing school in Rome when they were in their teens in the 1940s. "They didn't give a fig" and "preferred to have us out of their hair," was what Mom used to say whenever I asked about her childhood.

Apparently, Grampy had owned a candy factory that went bust during the war after sugar rations were imposed. He then went into merchandising for banks until he retired in the seventies. Mom always complained about how poor her family was, and yet she loved to talk about how, in her day, she and her two sisters were always attending lavish debutante cotillions and being taken to the Ritz by Harvard boys. She "came out" herself in 1950 to much acclaim in the society pages of the Boston papers. I'm not sure how you send three daughters off to finishing school in Rome and have fabulous coming-out parties when you're "dirt poor."

As well as being a debutante, Mom adored the ballet and was an accomplished dancer with some of Boston's best companies. She met all the right people, including my father, who was relatively rich at the time. It must have seemed to her that she had danced her way into the perfect life.

Whenever I asked her why she stopped dancing with the ballet, she'd say, "Oh, Daddy said you just don't do that." Until she died, she kept amazing photographs of herself dancing prominently displayed in elegant frames in the downstairs bathroom of her condo. In one, she's on point, with the opposite leg perfectly bent to form the number 4; her posture is excellent, and she's wearing a huge, slightly forced, albeit brilliant, smile that displays her amazingly crooked teeth. Mom was one of those people whose teeth were crooked, yet all the same size and set at such angles that you'd hardly notice. She had a dazzling smile. She used to say she had done a swan dive off the Empire State Building to achieve her "exquisite puss." In another photo, a male dancer holds her tenderly by the waist with both hands, his biceps exploding like a choppy sea. He is flat-faced yet debonair, and she wears a bright smile with a glint of excitement, a glint of possibility. Her legs are stretched out in opposite directions, as if she's leaping into starlight.

It's amazing to me that I know so little about Mom's past and what shaped her. It's as if the pain of losing her own mother at such a young age, coupled with her shame over her family's perceived lack of social status, kept her from revealing too much. I still long to know who she was, to somehow connect to her through a deeper understanding of her past, which is now impossible. I relished the story one of her best friends once told me about when they worked together in the fifties as secretaries to Jason Epstein at Random House, and how he thought Mom was a terrible secretary, but he kept her on because she was so damn entertaining and fun to have around the office.

Mom and Dad met in 1958 or 1959 in New York. As the story goes, Dad was dating Mom's best friend and roommate, Bigoonie, who couldn't cook. One night Bigoonie "didn't pitch up" for their date at the apartment, and Dad got to chatting with Mom, who after a couple hours (and a few cocktails), decided they needed dinner. Supposedly, Mom ended up cooking Dad a superb coq au vin, and that was it. They were married in 1962.

I remember Mom telling some variation of this story fifty times or more. Sometimes it was ratatouille, sometimes beef bourguignon, and yet what was their initial connection really, I wondered. Mom used to say jokingly, "You know I married your father for his money." And I always sensed a ring of uncomfortable truth in her joke. Yet, given how many times my dad had been married, I never understood why this marriage lasted. In some ways, they were such different people. She was snobby, outrageous, and socially elitist. He was liberal, on the side of the common man, quiet and somewhat reserved, and almost folksy (albeit wealthy, for a time, anyway). He certainly wasn't working class, nor was he elite rich. In his affections and affiliations, he was a kind of intellectual bohemian, which Mom may have thought was classy, but high-society manners and glitz were not his thing. They must have complemented each other in a way that kept conflict at bay and generally suited them. After a while, I suppose a certain acceptance and surrender became habit, they loved each other in their way, and simply "muddled through," mom liked to say, as best they could at the time.

Mom and Dad seemed prisoners of their history, victims of their stories, unable to untangle the emotional knots that tied them to their respective pasts. They seemed held captive by their grief. I was starting to see beyond my story, beyond its limitations. I started seeing art and poetry as a way to transcend my story. The more art I made, the more poetry I wrote, somehow the less bound I felt to fixed definitions of myself, and the less controlled I felt by the emotions entwined in my history.

Part III

16

# Open Mic, Closed Throat

*The poet builds a castle on the moon*
*made of dead skin and glass . . .*

When I heard those words of Jack Spicer's for the first time being read by Paul Hoover at the Cowell Theater, I was stunned and mesmerized, and I knew I had to be one of those people building castles on the moon made of dead skin and glass. This was true transcendent, creative magic, and I wanted in!

It was fall of 1994, and I was still at the Art Institute flailing about with my visual artwork, when one afternoon my art history teacher (and fabulous poet), Bill Berkson, mentioned a poetry reading he was participating in at the Cowell Theater. The reading was to celebrate the release of *Postmodern American Poetry: A Norton Anthology*, edited by Paul Hoover. It was a star-studded event, featuring readings by more than twenty of the greatest living American poets of this century, including Diane di Prima, Michael McClure, Alice Notley, Lyn Hejinian, Paul, Bill, and many others.

I had never been to a poetry reading. I figured, what the heck? I'll check it out. I went alone and brought my notebook. I was awed by the variety, complexity, beauty, breadth, and humor of the work I heard that night. This was like no poetry I had ever read or heard. I didn't know poetry could be funny, or visual, or rhythmic without classically rhyming. All of this was new to me: Larry Eigner in his wheelchair, moaning forth his disjunctively odd and sublime poems, then being translated by Jack Foley; Alice Notley and her beautifully insistent lyrics; Ron Padgett with his dry wit and humor; Bob Grenier flipping through his scrawl poems, reading them upside-down in a high-pitched growl. I was hooked. Something clicked, something transcendent was happening inside me, and for some reason I thought, "I can do this, I want to do this, I *must* do this"—and by "this" I meant play with language, explore the possibilities of language and words as filtered through my own mind. From that night, I set out to become a poet.

Words had always been prominent in my photography, and I had taken a class or two in poetry as an undergrad, but it was always fleeting and peripheral. This was different. I had the bug. That night, I started scratching poetic notes and ideas in my notebooks, which eventually made their way into poems. I devoured all the poetry I could get my hands on. Bill would fill my mailbox with classic books he felt I should read: Creeley's *For Love*, Ted Berrigan's *Sonnets*, Frank O'Hara's collected poems, Lyn Hejinian's *My Life*. I gobbled them up voraciously, and spent hours at City Lights and Green Apple rummaging through the shelves like a mad librarian. And I wrote pages and pages of incomprehensible mimicry.

Eventually, a hint of a voice appeared, and then more of one, and it expanded and I pressed on. Before I knew it, I was putting together my own chapbooks, sending poems to small presses, attending readings, and then later, reading my own poems in public.

In poetry, as in photography, I found the energy of creation and some sense that I could create my life, I could write my way into existence, an existence that was inclusive, an existence that mattered somehow to the world. The word *poem* after all, means "to make," "to create," and since I had been tuned to such self-destructive behavior for so long, poetry became the catalyst for a true and lasting transformation.

Each new poem I wrote was like a new piece of self, imprinted onto the world. Language became an infinite medium that could contain the confused and endless weirdness of my emotions. I found an exciting sense of adventure in the play of language that felt real and immediate—there was a flow to it that I didn't experience even with photography. This new obsession with poetry would soon eclipse my practice of photography altogether, as I became burdened by the process and physicality of photographs. In making poems there was a mysterious simplicity, a natural rhythmic immediacy, like writing on water, or talking to God.

Images and ideas became my new addiction, yet a much healthier one. I was swept up and consumed in them the way I had gotten lost in a gorgeous woman, or a great night of drinking. I would get hooked on certain ideas, and obsess about them for weeks, until I was good and "drunk," and then finally snap out of it as I hit an intellectual, creative—or was it an emotional—wall? The wall, the hangover, was self-doubt, and it haunted me. I was constantly seeking others' approval, unable to access my own.

Where was the poetry in my family life? I had no aunts or uncles who wrote. Sure, Mom and Dad loved books, but a book of poems was hard to come by on their extensive shelves, though upon second look a few years ago, I did find a copy of John Donne's collected poems and an ancient, coffee-stained copy of Ginsberg's *Kaddish*. I'm pretty sure they never read them, or at least hadn't turned the pages in fifty years. Mom and Dad both displayed an amazing artistic sensibility as voracious readers and devoted opera-, symphony-, and museum-goers. They were great consumers of culture. I was determined to be a creator.

\* \* \*

My first "collection" of poems was called *Olive Juice,* because when you mouth the words *olive juice* silently it looks like you are saying "I love you!"

Cooooorrrnyy, okay! But hey, I was young, and trapped in a self-absorbed conceptual art-haze. I had been writing "seriously" for all of fifteen minutes when I felt compelled to "publish" *Olive Juice*. I'm impatient that way. I just noticed now, looking at the cover again, how I still called myself "Al" at the time. It was before my radical conversion to Albert-ism.

On the cover of *Olive Juice* is a contour drawing I obviously did with my eyes closed. There is the gesture of a figure sprinting into—get this, an olive. Try and make sense of that one. The olive has five little drops of juice descending from its hollow little olive hole. I Xeroxed the thing at Kinko's on Stanyan Street in 1994 and thought of it more as a conceptual art piece than a book of poems—I think. It's dedicated to "the buoyancy of the brain" and "for Fa & Ma" (as if I were born on a friggin' Iowa farm or something). The table of "con tents" (yes, with a space) includes such wonders as "I'm ha ha," "insectual," "z burning is ahhh" and "eau Duchamp." This is all slightly embarrassing to talk about now. Though some of these poems aren't half bad (if not completely finished), others are, in fact, incomprehensible. One titled "lunatic" reads:

out
    walking
the cold,
    two rainbows
circle
    the moon

Okay, and then what happened? But not awful, a kind of thirteenth-century Chinese Zen thing was happening, or beginning to happen. Another one called "vision" reads:

A lizard
A liver
A leaf

A liver
A leaf
A lizard

A leaf
A lizard
A liver

A leaf in the street that quivers.

Can you tell that I had been doing a lot of hallucinogenic drugs around this time? Oh, and here's a winner dedicated to Maya (poor girl) called "Handed the Dark Blueing Sun-setting Sky":

all the sliver fingernails
of both hands
make a full moon

It's a haiku. When I showed this poem to Bill, he wrote "Yuck" in the margin. I was undeterred. It made the final cut, and into the pages of *Olive Juice* it went. I should have stopped with the title.

*Olive Juice* was printed in an edition of about twelve copies, complete with a clear report cover and a flimsy black plastic binding. The woman at the counter at Kinko's was so sweetly impressed: "That's so great you're publishing a book of your poems . . ." she paused, "I'd never let anyone see mine!" I felt a wave of pride surge through me like a warm rain. Had she been doing hallucinogenics too? She should have snatched the poems from my hands, quickly read a few, and then kindly refused me access to her machines. She could have faked that they had instantly broken down or there was a sudden power outage or something—anything to keep these poems from entering the world! No, no; instead she encouraged me and sent me off into the world feeling good about them—good enough to even read them out loud to other people.

This delusion eventually hit me some months later at a community open mic event in San Francisco. One of the regulars insisted on doing his "Mustang Sally" routine, yet again—which was clearly the only song he knew and which he belted out with such fervor it was just plain scary. He wasn't so much playing the guitar as thwapping on the strings with his sprawling hand like a vulture with cement in its wings. In between the words *Mustang* and *Sally,* he offered a lot of grunts, mumbles, and belches and then finished in a vituperative frenzy, practically smashing the guitar over his own head. A raucous applause followed. The kicker was that he wasn't kidding. I squirmed in my chair trying to be a polite suburban WASP, getting embarrassed for him, thinking to myself, why are you all encouraging him? He clearly had no idea how terrible he was, and he was back the next week and the week after to much acclaim. I guess all you could do was enthusiastically applaud his blind courage.

This was what the woman at Kinko's was doing for me. It was as if I had just read my poems at Shea Stadium right before the Beatles were about to come on, and the crowd went fucking nuts for *me*! Holy delusional ego! I did become a bit worried that I really sucked and that people were just being nice, and this was often the case, but then again, it sometimes appeared as if I actually baffled people into enchantment with my sincerity and my charming naiveté.

Soon after I graduated from the Art Institute in my late twenties and was getting more into poetry, I got the classic call from Mom and Dad.

"For Pete's sake, Al, why don't you get a job with a photo studio and actually do something with this degree of yours?" Dad exasperatedly whined into the phone a couple months after I had graduated and was working at a bookstore.

"I don't want to work for a photographer. I haven't been taking that many pictures lately, plus I'm totally into this poetry thing right now."

"Poetry?" he said incredulously. "Well, that's certainly not going to pay the bills."

"No it's not, Dad, but I'm enjoying myself, and it's not all about paying the bills."

"Well, you have to make a living, for Christ's sake. You can't expect me to support you your whole life, plus you don't want me to. Look what happened to me, I just squandered my goddamn life away."

"No, I don't want you to support me my whole life," I said.

"Then you better get some other job besides working in a bookstore and being some kind of wandering poet. You need to make something of yourself, goddamnit! Here, talk to your mother, I don't know what else to say."

"Hello, Alberty Walberty, what's Irish and stays outside all year round?"

"Let me guess, Mom, Kevin O'Reilly?"

"Patty O'Furniture, you dumb cluck," she said laughing. "Isn't that so enchanting?" obviously hearing herself tell the joke as if for the first time. "So, what's new with you?"

"Oh, nothing. Dad was just getting on me about getting a job and all that."

"Well, how *are* you going to pay the bills, dear?"

"I'm working at a bookstore right now, Mom," I said, sighing.

"Well, that certainly isn't going to turn you into Mr. Rockefeller, is it?"

"I'm not interested in being Mr. Rockefeller, Mom. I'm interested in being Mr. Rilke. You know he had a patron, and was put up in a castle in Duino on the Adriatic coast for many years."

"Well, that does sound *dee*-vine," she said almost supportively. "Do they really do that anymore? You'd better get cracking on your patron, because for now, you still have to pay the rent."

"Yes, Mom, I know, I *am* paying the rent."

"You know when I was twenty and worked for Jason Epstein at Random House, we got paid $15 a week, hard to believe, but back then, that was a fortune."

"Is that right? Jason Epstein? What was it like working for him?" I humored her.

"Oh, it was heaven, he was lovely and brilliant of course."

I tried to imagine my mom for a second with a job, a serious job, as an assistant editor, or something important like that. The image never formed in my mind.

"We were so poor." She sighed. "Barbara and I lived on potatoes and onions every night, except when we got taken out to the Ritz by some nice boys."

"Sounds rough."

"No, honestly, we didn't have a nickel, and if it weren't for some of these nice gents, we would have starved to death."

If this was some kind of threat and or warning, it didn't work. It never worked with Mom and Dad. They would complain and hem and haw, and then forget about it, and in this case, send me another check the following month to supplement my meager income working at a bookstore. On occasion, there would be a small "distribution" from my aunt's estate that would tide me over for a few months. This just kept me from feeling self-sufficient. And yet, I was addicted to this idea of being "art guy," who didn't "have time" for a real job, because I was too busy being a poet/genius (ha!). So, for the time being I continued to live on credit cards and handouts from Mom and Dad.

I'll never forget the first time I read my poetry in front of an audience. I went with my friend Damian, who roomed with Maya's guitar player and was a terrific poet and playwright from a rough neighborhood in South Providence, Rhode Island. We couldn't have come from more different backgrounds, yet we both had a tremendous love of poetry. We met at one of Maya's gigs and spent the whole time shouting about poetry to each other. We met again at SF State, at an opening for one of Damian's plays, and then decided we would try the open mic thing together. There was a well-known open mic at a dive bar on Valencia in the Mission District of San Francisco. I think the bar was called the Amnesiac, or the Hemophiliac, or something like that. There's a terrific Greg Brown song that just about sums up the place:

> *The joint is a dump, the owner is broke*
> *at least that's what he said, the p.a.'s a joke . . .*
> *the Bellyachers played last night, everybody got sick*
> *don't even try dancing, your feet would just stick*
> *the band signs their poster "Fuck U Miguel"*
> *and that's all the good part, the bad part's the smell . . .*

And I thought we poets had it rough. Anyway, the Amnesiac featured an MC named Lucky Spinster or Spinnaker, who opened with poems about toothless transsexual vampires and the like. There were drunks and transvestites, overweight asexual gnomes with numberless piercings and tattoos, nervous housewives, and artsy college kids.

After we had bet each other $100 we'd follow through, Demian said, "I don't know, man, this is sketchy—what time does it start—this probably isn't a good idea. Is it my turn, nice shot, what the fuck, I don't know man . . ." Damian said, as we stood around the pool table tapping our feet and swallowing hard.

"You know what, it's fine. There's nobody here. We'll probably just be reading to ourselves," I said, trying to reassure myself. But I was feeling sick to my stomach, as if I was back in Boulder, up in the Flatirons standing at the top of a thousand-foot cliff, roped in and all, but being told to just lean back, let go, and rappel into the void.

"Then we don't need to get up on the stage. I mean, I can just read from my chair, you know, like with my back to the crowd. That could work for me," he said, nervously stroking his jet-black ponytail.

"I'm pretty sure they want you on the stage. Plus, you committed, man—you bail, I bail. Plus, you lose a hundred bucks."

"I don't know," he said, for the third time in as many minutes, his voice fraying.

"Stop saying that. Of course you know, and you can, and you will. Nice shot." as I watched him sink the No. 6 solid. "Can I get you another cranberry and seltzer?"

"No, get me a fucking Dr. Pepper. No ice."

When I came back with his drink, Damian had the pool cue under his chin, both hands wrapped tightly around the tip, knuckles glowing white. He appeared to be chewing on the tip of the cue. I noticed a smear of blue chalk dust on his upper lip.

"I'm not sure you want to be eating that thing. It'll screw up your singing voice."

"Your shot," he said, rapping the cue on the side of the table, then pacing back and forth. "And I'm not singing, I'm reading one short fuckin' haiku and then I'm outta here."

"What's the big freakout anyway—I mean, what are we so scared of?" I said, feeling my stomach lurch as I looked over at the stage.

"Scared? I'm not scared, I'm fucking paralytic. I'd rather jump out of a goddamn airplane right now," he yelled. His dramatic affect made me laugh and helped me lighten up slightly.

"I hate flying. I'm fine being terrified right here at sea level," I said.

"What if I suck? Then they boo me off the stage, I crawl back into my existential poetic hole with my fuckin' broken tail between my rubbery legs. It's humiliating!"

"We haven't even read yet. How do you know?"

"Trust me, motherfucker. It's like buying weed from some sketchy punks in the projects. You don't want to fuck up. They'll pepper your ass with little lead poems. That's what this crowd will do, with their razor-sharp sneers, or even worse, their silences, which are worse than bullets. I can't take the goddamn silences between words."

At that moment, Lucky Spinnaker broke the silence by announcing the first reader. And then the second, and the third. We were so nervous we didn't hear any of it, until they called out Damian's name and he ran toward the stage, waving his arms and shouting "Take me off the list!" The audience, which consisted of everyone who was there to read their own stuff, cheered him back onto the stage. He was terrific.

I was next. I stuttered through nervously, my paper rattling in my hand as if I were being sentenced to death for murdering the President's daughter and had to read my own verdict to an open session of Congress. Enormous beads of sweat like glass marbles formed on my forehead and plunged through my eyebrows, shattering on the black stage floor in slow motion at my feet. I felt a bit as if I were being slowly and gently electrocuted.

At first, this was just a tad uncomfortable, but then I was actually thrilled by the anxious rush of nervous anticipation and then the wash of cool relief as it was quickly over and people actually clapped. This was not unlike the feeling of stepping off a small plane after a turbulent flight. Were they clapping just out of sympathy or mere obligation, so that I would clap in turn for them? Whatever. The thrill tickled me and inspired me enough to want to do it again. This rush would keep me coming back to the mic over and over again.

I did the Bay Area open mic circuit for a few years from San Jose to Santa Rosa before tiring of reading to other unpublished poets and writers desperate for a warm ear. My friend, Claudia, and I were dedicated. We used to drive every week to Oakland, Berkeley, and San Francisco to read at one bar or café after the next—The Paradise Lounge, Café Colossus, Shaky Grounds, Café International— always with the incessant whizzle of milk steamers and slam of espresso arms coming down like a gunshot. And we would listen intently to the amazingly eclectic mix of humanity eager to rant into the oblivion of another foggy San Francisco night.

There was a regular guy who called himself Nursling. I guess that was his poetry stage-name. He wore black-rimmed, Coke-bottle glasses and spoke with a lisp. Apparently he was a haiku "master." He would stand up and pace nervously back and forth across the stage for several minutes before shouting "Hellwooooo, everweeebody!" his O's extending into eternity, sounding a bit like Elmer Fudd after his balls had dropped. Nursling would then smack his lips and blurt:

The purple powkchowp
windy day
Gowslings, gowslings, gowslings

Silence. And then staring into space for what seemed like half an hour. Then, he would finally shout, "That's my haiku for the evening, fowks, thank you weary much," and rush back to his chair.

There was the Great Goddess figure who called herself Lakmishka (a Russian-Indian hybrid of some sort?). She was adorned in flowing Indian wispiness garb, like a Gypsy-cum-Marin-County-therapist, though you knew she was from a suburb outside of Minneapolis. Lakmishka was short and chunky and clearly a member of the "loud family." The microphone would start to feed back before she even got to it. And she would just lurch right into her "goddess-nymph-of-the-redwoods," routine, ranting on about her sexual infusions with "Thor Thor Thor" and "trees trees trees." She loved to repeat herself, this Lakmishka did. She would get super dramatic, pumping her fists in the air, massaging her inner thighs, and spinning off on tangents about her "magical fleshy female muscles" and her "luscious moist creamy desire that fluttered forth from the pores of her eternal vaginal universe." I don't know about the rest of the audience, but I didn't know where to look. Talk about embarrassment. And she would go on and on working herself into a frenzy of what she convinced herself was "passion," but looked to me more like an episode of *Rosie O'Donnell* gone wild—on acid.

Oh, and then there was the guy who appeared to be from Pebble Beach who had clearly made waaay too much money during the tech boom and didn't know what to do with himself anymore. He probably got delirious from playing so much golf that he started reading poetry, and then, God help him, writing it. Apparently, at the same time, he got into Aristotle, Kant, and Schopenhauer, which is a bad combination. Golf, poetry, and western philosophy. That's like mixing "Mad Dog," Guinness Extra Stout, and Jaegermeister. And sure enough, the guy shows up at a café in Oakland wearing his Kelly green trousers and a pink Izod, though instead of a golf cap, he's got a white beret tilted on the side of his head, and golf shoes that are clicking across the café floor.

He begins by pacing back and forth calmly with a golf club slung over his shoulder and waxing philosophic about golf and life. There's a bit of a lilt to his voice. Soon, a rhyme or two appears in the wilderness of his rambling, and then silence. He then explains to us in the same lilting voice that he's just read us a Shakespearian sonnet about golf and life. I look back into the audience to see if anyone else is as baffled as I am. There is a sea of vibrating question marks emblazoned on everyone's heads, like the gold No. 5 on the fire engine door in that famous William Carlos Williams poem. And then, our philosopher/poet/golfer continues his pacing and reports that he has five more "sonnets" to share with us. The first one took just under fifteen minutes. And I'm thinking, "It's fourteen friggin' lines, man! Speed this sucker along!"

So this is what I would subject myself to (and presumably subject others to, with my own random "experimental" readings). I could have sworn it was a *Saturday Night Live* skit, if we hadn't all taken ourselves soooo seriously—oh, and that for the most part, the audience didn't laugh. Most of the time we weren't sure whether to laugh or cry ourselves.

I met Steve at one of these readings in the Tenderloin. Sandy, graying hair, mustache, tall and burly, confident yet sometimes mumbly, Steve would perform fifteen-minute meandering dramatic verse-songs that started out about a green chair in a hotel lobby on Ellis Street. And then people would show up in red trench coats and large white-frame sunglasses, and a choppy relationship and some stark, wild images of nature would flow in and heighten the clash of personalities, and he would ramble on in this incredibly beautiful, complex, tangential way. And you would sit there going, "What the hell?" and just as you were about to give up on him, he'd pull you back in by referencing the green chair again, and he'd loop back at the end with this perfect image of a woman's face crumpling against the dawn or something, and it would make some profound mysterious sense and the crowd would go nuts!

He would sway back and forth with a nervy confidence, grabbing the mic low around the neck, mouth rounding around the mic top itself, and he would slur slightly, sounding almost drunk, and speak liltingly, with an urgency—a bit too fast. At times, you wanted to scream out, "Wait, I missed that image, can you go back?" I was kind of in awe of him. He was unique and uncharacteristically talented for a café poet. I started seeing him at all the readings, and we soon became friends.

It turns out he was also a concert pianist, and on occasion, if there was a piano at one of these venues, he would sit down and riff beautifully—playing part of a Chopin sonata or a Mozart rondo. He played for the Unitarian Universalist church in north Berkeley sometimes. He worked the graveyard shift at 24 Hour Fitness so he could read and write, and lived part of the time in a car (unregistered), part of the time at a friend's hotel room or apartment. He was a friend of Bill W.'s, and I could tell he'd been through the wringer. This was another commonality that connected us. I knew there was some big story to his life that he politely refused to ever reveal. He was in his early to mid-fifties, and I couldn't help imagining that he'd had a prior life of family and worldly success that had come to a dramatic and possibly violent end via alcohol. I was amazed by his talent, and baffled by his lack of ambition. He never made or printed books unless people asked him for them (which they often did), and then he would dash something off at Kinko's. He was one step away from homelessness and kept odd hours, sleeping during the day and sitting around at the gym writing and reading at night.

Steve was charismatic and charming, but also jumpy and erratic. He spoke a mile a minute, was constantly tapping his foot to some internal metronome, and would bob his head around as he talked. It appeared that his secrets were tightly coiled within him, bound by constant motion. Right after a reading, he would dash off and not be heard of for several weeks. He didn't have a phone. When talking, he would sometimes break off the conversation mid-flight, saying, "I gotta jet," and simply vanish.

One summer, we decided to hit the road for a week out to the Eastern Sierra to climb Mt. Whitney. We took a sleeping bag and backpack, my old, gold Toyota, and Garp the dog. I picked Steve up at the BART station in North Berkeley and off we went. We drove Route 108 up and over Sonora Pass, through the Owens Valley along the base of the great Eastern Sierra, arriving late in Lone Pine. The first night, we ended up camping in the Alabama Hills, talking about John Wayne and the old Westerns that had been filmed in that area. We read Blake out loud to each other under an insane canopy of glittering stars as a slight warm wind swept off the mountains, filling our noses with the sweet smell of sage and dry sugar pine.

In the morning, we headed up to Whitney Portal to meet Rick, a friend who was driving in early from Colorado. We did an acclimatization hike that first day and then the three of us set out under moonlight at 4 A.M. The granite glowed and glittered in the moonlight, looking like snow, guiding us along the trail.

Steve was dressed in a sombrero the size of a full moon, with a torn orange metal-frame pack from the sixties that he got at the Salvation Army. He carried a half-gallon of orange juice, a fat hunk of jack cheese, some jerky, and a couple of cans of sardines. He walked slowly and barely spoke on the trail. The higher we climbed, the slower he got. Rick and I looked at each other with concern, but Steve trudged on with a meditative persistence. At one point, he propped himself up against a rock and started breathing hard, holding a hand to his chest. His face was a sheet of white granite. I braced myself for his collapse. He took a few labored breaths and, seeing the concern in my face, said, "Don't take yourself so damn seriously—don't take me so seriously! The poetry of the body is as fleeting as the poetry of the page. Look at this place, the goddamn majesty of build-up and erosion, of life giving way to death, and death back into life. Whitney knows how to tell a story. My story, your story, poetry's story, written in sky, in stone, in thin fucking air!"

I took in his words as I took in the sun: waves of radiant inspiration I wouldn't soon forget. I started to realize how the power of nature, the power of poetry and creativity, were a power that could guide and sustain me, see me through doubt and confusion, my desperate need for acceptance, and my need to numb the fear and pain.

I stayed with Rick and Steve until we got a thousand feet or so above Consultation Lake late in the afternoon. Garp was getting panicky and obsessive, and I decided he wouldn't do well at 14,505 feet. Garp and I hiked back down to the first lake, where I wrote poems and we swam in the lake, and I let Steve's words sink in. More than twenty-four hours later, Steve and Rick reappeared, stumbling down the trail looking haggard and exhausted, reporting that they had both gotten altitude sickness and thrown up at the peak. But they made it. They slept soundly until late morning and we headed back into Lone Pine for lunch.

We wandered around town, and sure enough, Steve found an old burlap-topped piano nestled against a brick wall in an alley behind Caffeine

Hannah's. He started to play us an exquisite Chopin piece, closing his eyes, staring up to the sky and nodding toward Whitney. He appeared to be playing as ode of gratitude to the mountain. Then he abruptly stopped mid-riff, jumped up and said, "Let's get out of here!"

\* \* \*

Eventually, I started to publish in little magazines in New York and San Francisco, and one night I went to the Bay Area Poetry Marathon Reading at New Langton Arts south of Market Street. This was a twenty-four-hour reading, featuring some of the Bay Area's best poets, many established ones, but also some younger poets, who of course were mostly booked for the midnight hour. I went to a couple of the daytime readings, and was instantly excited to somehow participate. I approached the guy who was organizing the event and asked him if there were any no-shows later that night and whether I could possibly read. He said, yeah sure, come back at three.

"In the morning?" I sheepishly asked.

"Yep."

"Okay, see you then."

I read right before Eddie Berrigan played a song/poem on the guitar. We instantly became friends. Eddie is the son of the late, great poet Ted Berrigan and current great poet Alice Notley. He and his brother, Anselm, both poets, were living in San Francisco at the time, and had a whole scene of younger poets and artists gathering around them, many of whom came out of programs at the New School and SFSU.

At the time, there were constant readings hosted and given by friends throughout the Bay Area at places like the New School, Small Press Traffic, New Langton Arts, and the Poetry Center at SFSU. We created various small magazines and presses (my press, The Owl Press, was born around this time—1996 and 1997—and published Eddie's first book), and then a small avant-garde bookstore called Blue Books sprang up. We did house readings and events at small, local bookstores in the Mission and Lower Haight.

I found myself hanging out with this younger crew of artists and poets, moving on from the café scene, rarely seeing Steve anymore. In 2000, I finally published a piece in ZYZZYVA, the crown jewel of magazines in the Bay Area for writers and artists. I felt as if I was on my way. I started to get invited to read at some of the great venues: the New College, Modern Times Bookstore, and Cody's Books, and the Poetry Project and the Zinc Bar in New York City.

During this time in the late nineties, we wrote and made art, and some of us drank and did tons of drugs. I had been sober for about six years, which normally was pretty easy, except in certain social situations. The truth was, I was still one sip of beer away from hell, and wasn't about to fall prey just to fit into another social network, no matter how committed I was to being part of an evolving "literary scene." I would often leave parties once the beer and wine were flowing too strongly or I got offered a joint one too many times. I got the feeling my friends thought I was terribly prudish or uptight, or just plain boring.

One night, I broke down after a reading and party at a friend's apartment on (appropriately named) Fell Street, in the city. I took a couple of hits off a joint and immediately started feeling panicky and paranoid. I needed a sturdy someone, a man I could trust. Normally, I would call a female friend in a meltdown, but this situation called for a different energy. I trusted the strength of Steve's sobriety; I felt he'd understand, maybe he'd have some words of wisdom to help bring me around. Steve always helped to remind me that the creative life was the sober life, nourished by spending time in wild places. I tried his number and got his voicemail. I heard his lilting speedy and dour voice say, "Hey, this is Steve, leave a message." Then I remembered that voicemail was just voicemail. I bolted out the door for some fresh air and ran around the block three times and then called Theo from a pay phone. He picked up on the third ring.

"Hey man, I 'm freaking out! I've got an army of tartan-plaid sharks in my head, my skin is prickling, I'm hearing Slavic voices coming from the street lamps, and I think I'm about to cry. I feel a little bit like I'm in medicine-journey land."

"What the hell happened? Did you take mushrooms without your Uncle Theo?"

"No, no, I'm at a party in the city and they were passing around a joint and I thought, what the hey, and now, yikes, it was strong shit, my heart won't stop racing and I'm tweakin'."

"Okay, just take a couple of deep breaths and drink a lot of water."

"Water?" I said, staring at the phone receiver, which started to look and feel like a hatchet handle.

"Yeah, it always makes me pee, and then I feel kind of normal peeing, it's like a familiar bodily function. I don't know, it somehow grounds me. Maybe go run around in some open space, some nature spot."

"I'm in the city. I just ran around the block three times."

"Try running around four more times. Lucky seven. Or, you know what, go out to the Art Institute on Russian Hill, up to the rooftop like we used to, and gawk out at the bay and all the lights—or what about the park?—or I know, Ocean Beach."

"Yeah?" I said, with an uncertainty I could taste. It tasted like dried blood.

I drove out to Ocean Beach in a panic, and sat on the seawall kicking the cement and fidgeting with my car keys. I watched the moon adrift, a fragile sliver of lemony light being eaten by a brooding, ravenous black horizon, and listened to the wildness of the waves. This was just the solace I needed to bring me down and help me feel that I hadn't fallen "off the wagon" somehow by smoking a little pot. It felt good to know that Theo was there for me in a pinch. Even though he had dragged me into the whole cult drama, he also helped knock me out, and remained a strong and supportive friend in the years following. He was forever apologetic about getting me into the middle of such a mess, and the fact that we had been through so much together solidified our bond. It was enough to inspire forgiveness and reestablish a lasting trust.

I knew that for me staying sober from alcohol was a matter of life and death. Pot was just a distraction, albeit a powerful one. Soon, nature became my drug of choice. After my experience at Whitney with Steve, I began spending more and more time outdoors: hiking in Point Reyes, mountain biking the hills of West Marin, and backpacking in the Trinity Alps or the Eastern Sierra. I felt more and more comfortable alone in the open and accepting spaces of wild nature. And then someone told me about the Sinkyone Wilderness. I knew instantly, I had to go.

# 17

# Alone in the Sinkyone

I had never ventured north of Sonoma County and was in awe driving west out of Garberville, California as I passed through a sweet little remnant old-growth redwood forest down by the Eel River, then followed the road out toward Shelter Cove, where it got more and more wiggly, meandering up and down through blond hills and densely forested patches of third-growth redwood and Douglas fir. I continued on through a couple of old settlements that have come and gone over the years. They were just clusters of houses with junk cars strewn about and old, rusty signs advertising a stopover for lunch or gas. Whitethorn is one of these places, once teeming with a tan-bark mill at the turn of the century and then for a while at mid-century, inhabited by Beats and hippies. It now appeared mostly abandoned, except for some back-to-the-land holdouts and pot growers hiding out in old school buses and VW campers being reclaimed by blackberry and wild ivy.

At Whitethorn, the road turned to dirt, met up with the headwaters of the Matole River for a while, then split at Four Corners where there used to be a stage stop and an old hotel. I took a slight right to head into the Sinkyone Wilderness, named for the native peoples that roamed this wild land for thousands of years before European settlers showed up in the late 1800s. This is known as the Lost Coast, the one section of Highway 1's coastal route that stymied the engineers. At the Usal Beach Road, Highway 1 gets diverted inland due to the exquisitely rugged terrain and the fact that this is one of the most seismically active areas of California.

I proceeded nervously down the Needle Rock Road into the heart of the Sinkyone, as the road narrowed to one lane and descended more and more steeply. I couldn't help but notice that I was at the abrupt end of the continent. The land practically breaks off there, with the Pacific thundering a thousand feet below. The Ranger had told me it might be best to leave my car at Four Corners, as there are frequent mudslides, downed trees, and rockfalls throughout the Winter and early Spring. Down I wound, vultures flying *below* me through the fog and mist while I kept an eye out for elk who were known to trot lazily across the road.

Out my rolled-down window, I heard a redtail hawk shriek and watched him ride a thermal high above a tiny meadow. Lyle Lovett was on the tapedeck singing "If I had a boat, I'd head out on the ocean, and if I had a pony, I'd ride him on that boat, and we could all together head out on that ocean, me up on my pony on my boat . . ."

It took a good thirty minutes going fifteen miles per hour before I finally arrived at an open meadow a hundred feet or so above the sea, and there in the middle of the meadow sat the Needle Rock House. Once a homestead site, it is now a visitor center with an apartment in the back for a campground host. I was that host for the month of March in 1997 and 1998—two of the most magical months of my life. After my first visit in 1994, I had asked the ranger how to get on the list to volunteer. He said there was a three-year waiting list, but that sometimes people have to back out because of personal emergencies. I put my name down and followed up some months later. Sure enough, one of the longtime volunteers had to take care of an ill relative and gave up her slot for March of 1997. I stayed in the humble little Needle Rock House through the dramatic spring weather, sipping tea, reading books, writing poetry, painting, meditating, and hiking every nook and cranny I could find in thirty days' time. I used to hike up to Chemise Mountain to watch the sunset, or head out to Bear Harbor to explore the rocks and shells. I'd walk the length of the beach (always negotiating the tides) out to Whale Gulch to birdwatch, whalewatch, or otherwise contemplate the great, infinite magic of existence. A poem from that time reads:

Needle Rock Mountain

from the tongue
of four
ravens spill cobalt cloud
shadow paintings
on the sea

The photo self-portrait (the one that ended up in my final show at the Art Institute) epitomizes my experience of being at the Sinkyone. My pale body is caught in a bright shaft of sunlight dancing blurred against the backdrop of a giant charred-black redwood trunk. I appear as an angelic forest sprite, almost lifting off the forest floor, blooming and ascending through a giant bouquet of sword ferns and into light, emerging from the darkness of the world and merging into the light of an eternal, more-awakened self.

When I arrived for my first month-long stay in 1997, the first thing I did was hike down the steep, washed-out bluff to Needle Rock. At the bottom, I was met with the bloated remains of a recently dead elk. The smell was incredible, and I couldn't help wondering how the animal had wound up there at the base of the cliff. Had it fallen and broken a leg? Had it died of old age? During the month I was there, I visited the carcass almost daily and watched it decay, from distension and bloat to rot and animal scavenge down to the bones and head, which were the only parts left as I packed up in early April to leave.

I was about a week and a half into my stay when the ranger came down one day with the news that I had an important phone call.

It was Etoile. I hadn't heard from her in years.

"Hello?"

"Al, it's me, Etoile."

"Who?"

"It's Etoile, Al, St. Luke's, remember me? Helloooo!" She said sounding frustrated and serious.

"Holy shit, Etoile, oh my God, how are you?" I said excitedly, with a pang of nostalgia sweeping through my heart.

"I'm okay, but listen . . . I need to tell you. . . I don't know how to say this, but. . . Raine's dead." Silence.

"What?"

"She died last week in a car wreck in Florida. I thought you'd want to know."

"Oh my God, I, I, I, I—wow, this is fucked up. What the . . . Jesus . . . I've been so out of touch— but I didn't even know you two were close."

"Yeah, we became friends when I was in Denver, and then we actually moved back to Connecticut around the same time. I saw her three months ago, before she left for Florida. She got back with an old boyfriend who was doing a lot of drugs, and— I don't know what exactly happened."

"I, I, I, I . . ." I couldn't stop stuttering.

"I know, I'm so sad, Al." She broke down, which inspired me to burst into tears.

"I'm so sorry, Etoile," I said, sniffling. "Is there anything I can do from here?" I was at a loss of what else to say.

"Me too," she said, "me too—I don't know, maybe you could write to her family, tell them you were a good friend, and tell them what she meant to you."

I was shocked and devastated, and flooded with reignited guilt. But I set aside all the conflicts and confusion of our past, and did write to Raine's family with awkward, yet sincere condolences, then went down to the beach and wailed and screamed into the waves.

The ocean didn't care, my dead elk friend didn't care, the sky didn't care, but somehow they all listened, and held me as I lay in the black sand, sobbing. In the days that followed, I made little altars for Raine on the beach. I prayed for her peaceful passage, and I prayed for her forgiveness. I filled my notebooks with a wobbly poetry of grief, regret, death, and rebirth.

### We Kiss Ourselves Against This Thorny Mirror

We kiss ourselves against this thorny mirror
face our punctured lips
clean up our deflated kiss          against
this thorny mirror  begin
again in the name of love . . .

. . . I will beam ecstatic float and drown
and resurface once again against that thorny mirror
upon which we kiss ourselves
release the wounds and embrace the world!

While in the Sinkyone, I kept obsessive notebooks that were not only filled with poems, but also drawings, watercolors, favorite words, journalistic drivel, and various quotes. I had endless amounts of time on my hands. The park was quiet at that time of year, though an occasional local might come by to visit. Otherwise, I just hung out and read, wrote, ate, slept, meditated, and walked or hiked. Thinking back on it now, one day at the Sinkyone was like a month in my current life. A year these days seems to fly by in the span of a single month. Out there in the Sinkyone, each day I was meeting eternity face to face, keeping time by the sun and stars, the shouting waves, and the sound of the singing rain.

The other thing I did a lot of was read. I read five hundred pages of dialogues with the obscure Indian mystic Nisargadatta Maharaj, called *I Am That*. Twice. I read Lorca's biography and collected poems forward and backward about twenty-seven times. I read Gertrude Stein until my brain started to burble and seep out my ears, until I would run naked, laughing hysterically, into the meadow, tears of confused joy streaming across my face like frayed silver ribbon. I read Henry Miller's *Tropic of Cancer,* lamenting how I had missed the boat on a life of serious Euro-bohemianism. I read books on physics and the origins of the universe, and then a terrific book called *An Everyday History of Somewhere*, about the history of this most remote stretch of Northern California coastline: the Native Americans, the miners, the loggers, the hippies, and the back-to-the-land pot growers.

All this time of reading, writing, and just being, was heavenly. There was such an intense immediacy to the landscape, and a lack of regular distractions (TV, the computer, socializing, making money). I became emotionally raw and open, clear of mind and filled with an inspired happiness and joy. Around this time, I had begun to ask those great, timeless human questions: Who am I? What is the meaning of life? What is my purpose? These questions enchanted and sometimes haunted me. In a way, I felt as if I was finally living them here in the Sinkyone, in this space of wild simplicity. And yet, like everything, it was temporary. Temporary, with a taste of the eternal.

One evening, I was hiking down Chemise Mountain at sunset when I came around a slight turn in the trail and I found myself on the edge of a steep cliff more than a thousand feet above the ocean. The waves were crashing below with their little foam doilies shifting across the sand and then disappearing—and suddenly facing me, was a huge male elk with a massive rack of antlers. Our eyes met and we stared at each other, frozen in time, suspended in the salt air in a kind of magical embrace, species to species. I don't know how long we stayed in our embrace, but it was a brilliant sliver of eternity.

At that moment, my heart burst open, and my vision became incredibly clear. The elk finally wandered into the brush and I kept walking, and my surroundings continued to glow—the ocean rushed into my eyes and receded, the redwoods laughed, the clouds breathed in sync with my lungs, the alder leaves shimmered electric green. I started to cry and I didn't know why, except that I was just overwhelmed by the sheer beauty of this merging experience, by the simple yet profound lack of separation. At that moment, the self I knew as Albert merged into elk and alder, ocean and sky. In that moment, I became awake to the immense presence and infinite beauty of this world, and instantly realized, yes, *I am that!*

After this experience with the elk, I felt like I didn't need anything or anyone to make me happy. I felt a growing contentment in my self, I finally felt at ease in my skin. This was a revelation and relief after all I went through with Maya. I was reluctant to enter in to another relationship, until it came from a sincere and grounded place of simply wanting to share my life with someone, rather than needing to be with, someone. I had my passion for poetry and art, a new interest in meditation, my love and connection to the wilderness. I had Garp the dog. I was complete. And yet open.

## 18

# A Date with the Dalai Lama in Central Park

"I have just the woman for you!" Sant said enthusiastically via phone from LA.

"Really? You know, me and Garp, we're pretty good, aren't up for complicating things—though we do get a tad lonely out here in the wilds of West Marin. I'm listening."

"She's awesome! She's my friend Mallory's sister. She grew up in Westchester, I think."

"Where does she live?" There was a long pause. "Hellooo, Sant?"

"Yeah, I'm here. . . [long pause] New . . . York . . . City . . . " Sant said hesitatingly.

"Oh great, that helps, Sant. That's all I need, another urban girl. Let me guess, she's a singer in a band in the East Village."

"Nooo, Al, she's a social worker, and I think she lives in Hell's Kitchen, Midtown, west side."

"Oh, well, shit, Midtown, practically around the corner."

"She's totally great, *and* single. You should just talk to her. I don't know, I just think you two would connect."

"Don't you have a fabulous feeling about someone a couple of thousand miles closer?"

"Not that's coming to mind right now, but I'll think about it. Just try calling her and saying hi, see what happens."

I was skeptical, but remotely curious. After living in San Rafael for a while and then bouncing around West Marin, late in 1998, I found a quiet, dark one-bedroom apartment underneath a woman's house in Forest Knolls. I was single again, teaching part-time as a poet in the schools, and writing poetry at odd hours throughout the day and night. I was in the process of trying to sever my financial dependency on Mom and Dad. Though I lived fairly simply, I still usually spent more than I made. I seemed to have inherited Mom's taste, along with Dad's earning (or lack thereof) and spending habits. This was a continuous source of insecurity, if not outright shame, for me. When my aunt died right around this time, I used that money to carry me through the year. It would be a couple more years until I finally became more financially self-sufficient, free of leaning on Mom and Dad and credit cards. I would go on to invest in a house, and then later, a successful business. Until then, much of my time was spent meditating, riding my mountain bike, recovering from my cult experience, and generally trying to live a quiet artist life.

It just so happened that I was giving a reading and having a book-release party in New York at the end of the month. I finally gathered up the courage to call Marian after repeated urgings from Sant. She was insistent (her name doesn't mean "Saint" for nothing).

Sant is another one of the angels in my life. She's always been a catalyst for insight and change, a source of inspiration, an open expression of love and friendship. I met her in Aspen at a photography workshop, and we hit it off immediately. Sant had been a devout Sikh, living for many years in an ashram in India. Now, she was a devout artist and professor of studio art at Cal State San Bernardino, with an infinite creative drive and an astounding knowledge of photography. She has long, red hair rivering down her back, a bright cheerful smile, and a glimmering sheen to her small, brown eyes. She is almost gnomic in body and movement, chatty and vibrant, wise and loving. At the time of this phone call, she had been to the Art Institute in San Francisco for a visit and a photography event with Marian's sister. That was the connection.

Marian and I had a classically awkward "we've been set up" kind of conversation that didn't seem to inspire a great future. But for some reason, I held on to her phone number, and when I got to New York I called her again. I don't know why, as I wasn't up for getting involved in a long-distance relationship with an urban girl. After Maya and another short fling or two with women in San Francisco, I was convinced I was incompatible with any woman from a city. I was "nature guy," after all. This was the identity I had been convincing myself of for some time. Thinking back on it now, the impulse to connect with Marian seemed to be coming from some larger force of the universe that was far beyond my control.

"Hi, it's Albert, from California, Sant's friend."

"Oh yeah, hi," Marian said a bit surprised, but with a remote tinge of interest.

"Well, I'm in New York and have some free time, and was just wondering if you maybe—you might want to possibly—I mean if you have any time at all, or not— It's fine. . ." I was sputtering nervously, hoping she'd interrupt or the phone would suddenly get disconnected.

"Sure, what are you doing Saturday?"

"Saturday, hmm, let's see, let me check my—Saturday's great, what time? Do you want to go to a museum or gallery or get lunch or something?"

She didn't answer and instead said, "You like cycling, right?"

"Well, kind of, I mostly ride on dirt, but yeah, sure, sort of, I could . . ."

"How about we ride over the Brooklyn Bridge?" That sounded extreme to me. Dangerous. Who rode their bike in New York City? I swallowed audibly into the phone.

"Is that your other line?"

"Huh?—as in ride through Manhattan?" I said with alarm.

"That's how you generally get to Brooklyn."

"Isn't it a bit dangerous?"

"Of course not, I ride to work to Gravesend in Brooklyn three days a week. And what, flying down a mountain on a rocky narrow trail in California isn't dangerous?"

"Good point, but wow, from Hell's Kitchen to Gravesend sounds like a ride straight out of Dante . . . You know, I've never ridden in New York, and I don't have a bike, and . . ."

"What time's good for you? And don't worry, I can come up with an extra bike." she interrupted.

Wow, a woman who rode a bike through the streets of New York City, who wanted to take me over the Brooklyn Bridge. This was getting interesting.

We chatted a bit more, and she became even more sweet and smart, witty and assertive. Our conversation felt natural and easy; it continued to flow and soon I started to relax into it. Normally, I'd be craving a drink in the midst of such a vulnerable first meeting.

The next thing I knew, I was on a bike pedaling nervously down Twelfth Avenue in New York City trying to keep up with her. It was a gorgeous June day as I pedaled frantically a half block behind her while she wove beautifully through slow cabs and double-parked trucks, standing up on her pedals, her light blue skirt, white blouse, and blonde curls all billowing in harmony as they caught a westerly breeze off the Hudson River.

Everywhere I laid my eyes—Marian on her bike, the yellow cab that just cut me off, the black brick warehouse, the spray-painted bubble letters tagging up the torn awnings—took on a soft-focus halo. Things were glowing. For a second, I felt as if maybe we had been transported into the midst of a commercial for fabric softener.

During lunch at Patsy's Pizzeria in Brooklyn, I just stared at Marian in a goofy, baffled, nervous, and clearly love struck kind of way.

"So, you grew up in Westchester?" she said, snapping me out of my trance.

"South Salem, and you in Kisco, right?" I said, biting into the cheesy tip of a new slice. "That's what my sister called it: *Kisco, duuuude*," I said with a stupid, nervous laugh. "She spent a lot of time on the bar circuit in Mount Kisco— We went to John Jay for a while," I continued.

"No way! I went to Greeley."

"I think we played you guys in sports," I said, watching an olive fall off my slice in slow motion, ride a spidery strand of white mozzarella, and then swing into my water glass. "Oh shit, nice move. Did you ever hang out at the rez in Pound Ridge?" (Not as in Indian reservation, but as in drinking reservation. It's actually an open-space preserve.)

"Oh sure, that was our major party spot, along with the quarry in Bedford and the rocks out at Lake Waccabuc."

"The rez was my sister's home away from home. 'Kegger at the rez' was her mantra on the weekends." There was a long silence. "This is great fucking pizza," I yelled a little too loudly. "Excuse my Italian."

"Wait, so how old's your sister?"

"Thirty-three," I replied.

"Okay, so she's my age, we probably knew some of the same people. We used to go to the rez all the time, and Woody's Bar in Kisco was our default hangout, they never checked IDs."

"I'm pretty sure my sister had her own barstool there, like Cliff in *Cheers*."

She laughed and then there was another long silence.

"So do you still party?" I asked.

"Who, me?" Marian said, looking around. "Actually, surprising you should ask, I just quit three weeks ago."

"You're kidding!" I said, in an alarmingly high-pitched, almost shrill voice filled with excitement. "I've been sober, I mean, I haven't had a drink in about seven years."

"Hmm, what happened?"

"Oh, geez, you got a second?"

What a relief knowing that Marian was recently sober. Normally, I would have been nervous to the point of having a slight panic attack on a blind date. But this solidified the bond beyond mere commonalities. I felt as if she just might be able to understand me—and in some ways, already did. And the way she listened as we talked. It's amazing, the simple act of listening, when you're talking with someone who is genuinely interested in hearing what you have to say and not anticipating their next line. And then, of course, the things we had in common just multiplied as our conversation deepened; we both grew up in Westchester and were weaned on trips into New York City with our parents for plays and musicals. We both loved biking, nature, good food, and traveling.

After lunch, we rode back up town, stopping at a pier on the Hudson to watch the sun descend over Jersey. In the past, I would have made a joke about the sunset over Jersey, but now I was experiencing it just as magically as if it were a sunset over the Pacific as seen from the white sands of Kauai.

As we were staring out over the river taking in the evening glow, Marian pulled out a pack of Parliament cigarettes. I thought this was almost charming in the "falling-in-love-drunk" moment. Which was odd, considering Mom's habit. In Marian's hands, a cigarette was hip, almost elegant. In my mom's hand it was a cancer stick. This was a temporary acceptance. By the time I got back to California, I had barely put my bags down when I immediately called Sant.

"She smokes!" I said harshly, practically demanding an answer.

"Shit, I forgot about that. Don't worry, she'll quit."

"Damn straight, she'll quit. But either way, I'm mad for her. We had an amazing weekend! I've already booked my ticket back to New York for July."

After this first date, it quickly became obvious the universe was actively conspiring at every opportunity to further connect us. The night after our bike ride, I invited Marian to my reading downtown on Houston Street at Zinc Bar, and then out to dinner with my parents in SoHo. After dinner, we walked more than forty blocks uptown to Marian's apartment, talking passionately the entire way. I was leaving in two days to go back to California. I was dying to kiss her goodnight at her door, but felt as if it was a tad premature, so I left the kiss squirming inside me and sprinted ecstatically back to Grand Central to catch the 1:35 A.M. train back to Westchester.

The next night, we went to Nirvana. Literally (and figuratively and spiritually, for that matter), that was the name of the ornately decorated Indian restaurant high above Central Park South. After dinner, we walked up to Sixty-eighth Street to see a Japanese avant-garde film called *After Life*. After *After Life*, we perpetuated our own dreamy nirvanic scene of romance and memory.

We stayed talking in the courtyard behind the theater until after one o'clock in the morning. No way I'd make the 1:35 train back to Westchester. There was an awkward moment about what to do next. Theoretically, I was going to stay with my sister, who lived on the Upper West Side, yet I neglected to call her before she went to bed, which meant I would have to wake her up to get in. I explained to Marian that I didn't have a key and that waking my sister at this hour would be a major drama.

She gazed at me suspiciously and then said, "You can stay at my place, but you're sleeping in the closet—and the place is a mess," she added.

"Oh my God," I said dramatically, "well, my apartment looks like the lobby of the Carlyle, twenty-four-seven." She had just taken a sip from her water bottle and practically spit it all over me in response.

Back to her apartment we walked, nervously giggling internally to ourselves. Needless to say, the closet idea didn't last long. Plus, I was thinking to myself, closet? She's going to relegate me to a closet? I don't think so! I managed, in a very gentlemanly way, to wiggle my way at least onto her bed, where we lay across the top of it crosswise talking at the ceiling tiles and occasionally turning our nervous heads toward each other until four in the morning.

Soon, my blood began to surge like a pre-storm tide and break into little red pieces, which turned into miniature butterflies with rose petal wings, which fluttered ecstatically through my veins. Eventually, by sunrise I got the kiss I so innocently desired, and the butterflies were released to the room and stayed fluttering around us for days.

Our first date when I returned to New York a month later was with the Dalai Lama in Central Park. Just the fact that she was interested in seeing the Dalai Lama had me sold. We couldn't hear a word he said that day, but it was his *presence* that sunk in. There was an incredible silence that surrounded him, as he, in turn, was surrounded by more than a hundred thousand New Yorkers. Quiet New Yorkers. The crowd was so silent, hanging on to every word. Though it was late June and we were packed among tens of thousands of people, it felt more like being alone on an early Sunday morning in February with snow falling on New York City in muffled silence, the quiet scrawling of the branches writing forth a single person who strolls along in the distance, a dark shadow moving through the cold white expanse—eerie in its beauty and emptiness.

Marian and I spent the next three weeks meandering the streets of New York, love-drunk and hungry. It was a euphoric few weeks of food, sex, more food, and walking Manhattan, followed by food, sex, sex, sex, food, walking, walking, sex, sex, food, walking, sex.

I had the summer off from teaching, so my agenda became writing poems and falling in love. For the first time in my life, I was ecstatic and happy in a sincere and grounded kind of way. I wasn't looking to extract anything from the experience or from Marian; I was content to simply share, to marvel, and to finally, truly, love.

Between trips to and from New York and California, we wrote daily letters and constantly sent packages to each other. One time, I sent Marian a box of rose petals with handwritten words on them, a kind of love-poem puzzle. No matter how you arranged the word/petals, you got the gist of the poem, the intention of love. There was one original arrangement and yet infinite possibilities arose (so to speak). I remembered back to when I was a kid playing in that dirt patch just off the driveway at the Clock Tower, beneath the tattered rosebush, looking at that collection of curled rose petals in funny piles and imagining notes I was writing to myself. I remembered Antoinette whispering in my ear during my first medicine journey, asking me to look within and surrender to the heart of the world. And here "she" was, showing up in physical form before me, reminding me of who I really was. I cried a few tears of joy into these petals, closed the box, and mailed it to Marian in New York City.

After "the campaign," as Marian called it, during which time we had expressed our perfectly balanced bright side, complete with Zen-like patience, the ability to say "yes" to anything asked of one another, and constant loving attention, we got to know each other more deeply, and our respective darker sides inevitably reared their ugly heads. Mine included leaving crud in the sink drain after doing not quite all the dishes, and responding to a request in a defensive high-pitched voice like a yelping puppy. There were also freakish emotional outbursts over a dropped utensil (which I inherited from Dad). There was Marian's occasional overly controlling micro-management, penchant for enduring bad movies, and random use of carcinogenic sweeteners. No major deal-breakers there.

Given my past, and my uncertainty about my parents' relationship (though they never divorced, they had fairly severe arguments at times and didn't appear to me to be what you'd call "in love"—they seemed more resigned to their togetherness, rather than passionately committed to each other), I almost kept anticipating some sort of high drama or big freakout to derail our relationship (Marian's parents had gotten divorced when she was just out of high school). But it never happened. Any moments of fear and doubt were soon quelled by Marian's pragmatic and emotionally balanced disposition, and my ecstasy at finally having found someone so kind, loving, and at home with herself. Sure, we had our mood swings and minor meltdowns, but they were fleeting and followed by a sincere understanding, a growing experience of trust, a capacity for forgiveness, and a loving acceptance.

So, after to-ing and fro-ing back and forth from New York to California for about eight months, we finally decided it was time to decide. Who is going to move where? It became pretty clear right away that Albert and Garp the dog were not moving to New York City. As much as we loved visiting, this was no place we could live for long, plus Marian had been contemplating a move out of the city, although perhaps not three thousand miles out of the city.

In May 2000, we packed up Marian's apartment on Forty-ninth Street and headed West in her mom's 1990 Honda Accord. We made a limited-edition chapbook of our journey, titled *Al & Marian's Coast to Coast Round Up,* which is filled with silly anecdotes, poems, botanical drawings, and random road musings. It was a fabulous drive, filled with classic mood swings, doubts, excitement, and a whole grab bag of "getting-to-know-you" moments.

\* \* \*

Being big fans of the all-American road trip, and having had a *mostly* stellar time moving Marian out to California, the next summer we agreed to hit the road with Mom and Dad and drive from Santa Fe to Carmel, California. They had been planning a trip to see my sister, Margaret's, new baby in Taos, and Marian and I were going to be in southern Colorado around that same time on a mountain biking trip. My dad thought it was a brilliant idea for us all to drive back to California—together. After all, we were headed there anyway. I wasn't so sure.

I said to Marian in a slow, weary sigh, "I dunnooow . . ."

She was clearly excited by the idea. "It will probably be the last time you get to spend such intimate time with your parents."

My dad was eighty-five at the time. I was pretty sure after a couple of hours we'd all be driving each other insane. Dad put his heart into the plans. He started mapping the route, telling me stories of his first road trip out West in the late thirties on two-lane, sometimes dirt, back roads.

We met up with Mom and Dad in Taos at my sister's after the bike trip. They had decided to take a train from the East Coast and were driving up from Santa Fe.

Mom went off on the whole train fiasco: The overweight peasants, the filthy food, the nineteen-hour layover in Gary, Indiana. "We sat there staring at rust heaps for two days. Two fucking days!" she said.

It was actually eight hours, but who's counting? Dad should have known better. There's no such thing as first class on Amtrak. After a couple days of cooing over Margaret's gorgeous new baby, we hit the road in my Subaru station wagon, traveling south to meet up with Highway 40, which would take us into Arizona and on into the Golden State.

There are a couple of great photos from this trip. In one, Marian has perched the camera on the dashboard as we are heading west into the setting sun. I'm driving, looking serious and focused on the infinite ribbon of road before me. Marian is tilted slightly toward me looking jolly and bemused, while Mom and Dad are leaning forward in the backseat, heads together like a couple of spazzy kids headed to the Dairy Queen. Which, in fact, might have been our next stop.

The first day, there were long stretches of silence, punctuated by Mom expressing her exaggerated euphoria about the whole program. "This is stunning, I mean this is absolutely marvelous, such a fabulous idea. Look at this scenery, it's simply divine!" as the blond, orange, and pink chalky cliffs outside of Gallup streamed across our eyes.

As we pulled into our first lunch stop at a family restaurant in Gallup, Mom said, "I forgot—there's nothing to eat outside of New York." Marian ordered a "lady's steak" the color of a storm cloud, and Mom, an iceberg wedge that looked like a haggard doorstop, and a stack of onion rings reminiscent of a sandstone hoodoo. The waiter asked my mom if she'd like something to drink. "What do you have?" she said, beaming.

"Well, ma'am, we have coffee, tea, soda, water, milk, and orange juice."

Her face collapsed. "That's not something to drink," she snapped. "I'll have a gin martini on the rocks with an olive and a twist."

The waiter paused, then smiled, and said, "I'm sorry, ma'am, we don't serve alcohol. I wish we did, hee hee."

She caved in to an iced tea. Mom wouldn't stop talking about the onion rings for days, because they were "soooo deeee-vine!" Even after we had been in California for a week and were staying with Joyce and John, she went on at length about the onion rings in Gallup.

For dessert, we were offered Jell-O, and when we asked what flavors, our waiter said in a stone-faced, matter-of-fact tone, "Red and green." He paused, and then continued, "I think the green has some stuff embedded in it."

"Like table scraps?" I offered.

"Oh, no, no," he said defensively, "like bits of fruits and stuff." He emphasized the *s* in *fruits*, as if he were selling a nutritional supplement.

"No, thanks," we all said in harmony, except Dad, who said, "That sounds perfectly delicious."

"Help yourself at the salad bar, the Jell-O is to the left of the olives." And that was our lunch in Gallup.

The next day, a little before noon somewhere outside of Flagstaff, Dad piped up suddenly, no doubt after being poked in the leg by Mom, and said, "Al, get off at the next exit, would you? Your mother needs to grab something at the store."

"I just need some ciggies," Mom chimed in. I looked in the rearview mirror as Mom waved her hand around as if wielding a magic wand, or orchestrating the universe to create before her excited eyes the perfect carton of Marlboros and a nice bottle of Tanqueray. We passed a billboard that read Frankie's Truckstop Country Store & Liquor.

"Can't you wait 'till this afternoon?" I said, protesting.

"Pull over here, this is lovely, darling," Mom said, ignoring me with a glazed yet determined look in her eyes. Dad sighed.

I looked at Marian, furrowing my brow, as I reluctantly pulled the car toward the offramp, the steering wheel feeling like one of those enormous dam-release valves at the top of the Hoover Dam that takes five burly men to turn. There was a deafening silence as I stopped the car and Mom bounced out like a twelve year old having just arrived at Disneyland.

Mom bought a fifth of gin and a carton of Marlboros. She was glowing with delight. We drove in silence for much of the afternoon except for an occasional euphoric outburst from Mom about the scenery and what an absolutely incredible time she was having.

We pulled into Kingman, Arizona, around dusk, with clouds thickening after descending off the plateau from Flagstaff into the Colorado River basin and the eastern Mohave Desert. We drove past wash after wash that ran under the highway in squat concrete tunnels: Rattlesnake Wash, Diamond Wash, Gila Wash, Whisky Wash. I imagined huge rivers of amber whisky flowing over the road and spilling into the car, pickling us all in the process and turning us into a kind of whisky bottle on wheels. I shook my head vigorously from side to side to rid the image from my mind, replacing it with walls of mud and water flowing through carrying dead cottonwoods, huge rocks, and debris from the rare thunderstorm during monsoon season. I secretly hoped these walls of watery mud would wash away my anxiety and discomfort with Mom's drinking. For now, they were bone dry and scattered with freeway trash, empty except for the mystique of their names.

Normally, the temperature climbs twenty to forty degrees as you approach Kingman, but we had caught a rare summer afternoon of clouds and even a sprinkle. It couldn't have been more than 65° when we pulled into the Best Western. Dark, steel-blue clouds billowed around us, contrasting beautifully with the piñon-speckled mountains to the north. A vein of lightning flashed across the mountain tops as I glanced into the distance.

The next morning, we drove over the river and into sunny California. After just a couple of hot hours on the road, we stopped at Rosarita's Mexican Restaurant in Barstow for an early lunch. We sat down and Dad and Marian ordered an iced tea, Mom, a pink lemonade, and I said I was fine with water for now. After we ordered our food, Mom suddenly jumped up and said, "I'm going to nip out for a ciggie." She grabbed her lemonade and scurried out to the parking lot. Our plates arrived filled with puddles of refried beans surrounded by an oil slick of orange cheese, the requisite pile of red-tinted rice, and a messy crimson smear of enchilada sauce. Mom came back in and sat down next to me.

We were all delicately asking each other about our respective dishes when I glanced over at Mom's delicious-looking pink lemonade shimmering through the brown mottled glass. I spontaneously leaned in, guided the straw to my lips and took a quick swill. The icy liquid flashed into my mouth with a razor-like blast and shot down my throat before I could even think to spit it out. The unmistakable viscerally jolting taste of alcohol. I felt as if I had just been electrocuted or shot with a stun-gun in the throat.

"Fuuuuuuuuuuuuuck!" I screamed. The entire restaurant turned to stare. I slammed my fist on the table, making all the silverware scatter, knocking over a water glass, and startling the shit out of Dad, who was completely absorbed in his chile rellenos. I picked up a fork, grabbing it like a javelin, thinking I might stab Mom in the shoulder, then dropped it and stormed out, hearing my dad squeal, "For Pete's goddamn sake, Albert, what the hell's gotten into you?"

I stomped through the streets of Barstow, wandering around pouting and sputtering, kicking dust and punching air. My mind was racing with images of relapse, flashbacks surging: me at the Boulder Hospital swinging at the night nurse; me under a car in Pat's driveway; me puking facedown in the wet grass at Waveny Park; me with J.T. contemplating drinking one of our concoctions from Mom and Dad's liquor lab. My mind was spinning back in time, my life of alcohol flashing before my eyes like the instant before death.

Next, it's Christmas dinner and I'm about six years old. I've just made it through the cloved ham and potatoes au gratin and am struggling through a collapsed forest of string beans, fantasizing ever more intensely about Mom's famous buche de Noël. It's so rare that she makes dessert, and this is the best. Finally, plates are cleared and the buche is served. "Albert, wait for your father," says Mom. I ignore her, pushing my silver fork into the soft, chocolate corner of my first bite. It hits my tongue with an awkward sting. Something's wrong. It's tainted. My face buckles in disappointment. My expectation of sweet and chocolatey is soiled by the sour cut of alcohol. Mom's spiked the dessert. I spit it out and begin to cry.

Then, my mind goes to one of Mom's favorite stories she used to tell her friends with pride about how she breastfed us kids. "Of course, you get the kid on your lap, martini in one hand, ciggie in the other, press the kid to your tit, and Bob's yer uncle. Darling Dr. Martinson always just reminded me not to spill the martini or knock the ashes on the kid's head."

After a while, I finally just slumped into the dust and cried into the blinding hundred-degree midday sun. It was a kind of surrender, a release that softened me. A little. By the time I got back to the restaurant, I was angry again. Marian intercepted me outside in the parking lot.

"Are you okay, honey?"

"Nine fucking years of sobriety down the tubes! Thanks, Mom. What the hell is wrong with her? I'm so sure she absolutely has to have a fucking cocktail with every goddamn meal."

"I'm pretty certain that's one of the definitions of being an alcoholic . . . I'm sure she didn't mean to . . ."

"Yeah, right, she didn't mean to. Like she didn't mean to hire someone to take care of her kids either . . .That's her problem—she's soooo well-meaning, and yet so goddamn selfishly clueless. I can't stand to be around her sometimes."

"Well here we are, honey. What are you going to do? Take a cab from here?"

"I'll fucking hitchhike. I can't believe this shit, this was your goddamn idea, a road trip with my parents—what were you thinking?"

"What was *I* thinking? — Oh, come on Al, this was *our* trip." She paused and stared at me fuming in a heap against the parking lot fence.

"If it's not one thing, it's your mother."

"Ha ha," I said, not the least bit amused.

Back in the restaurant, Mom looked like an innocently wounded little girl, staring up at me meekly with her exquisite, emerald eyes.

"What the fuck, Mom—what are you, some kind of drunken peasant, sneaking booze into your lemonade like that?"

"That's enough Albert, don't talk to your mother like that," Dad snapped, defending Mom as if she were too frail emotionally to defend herself. Which, perhaps she was. I couldn't believe I called Mom a peasant. Those were her words, turned back against her. She winced, gasped slightly, and shifted uncomfortably in her seat. I braced myself for a reply, ready for battle. I kept staring at her, hopeful she might scream at me, perhaps smack me, or better yet, break down crying, finally acknowledging she had a problem. I imagined her saying, "You're absolutely right, honey, I don't need this right now, I should really cut back on my drinking." Nothing. Instead she appeared to be retreating further into the locked Italian Villa of her self. She was wearing the frozen face of denial, of emotional paralysis, the same face she would wear the day Dad died.

"I'm so sorry, darling. I had no idea you might take a sip. If I had known you would be so upset . . ." Her voice was quivering slightly. Were her eyes welling up? She quickly excused herself and scampered back out to the parking lot for another ciggie.

For the rest of day, we drove in silence, then late in the afternoon stopped at a gas station with a Dairy Queen attached. We all stood around the car eating our Blizzards in silence. Mom and Dad were completely absorbed in their ice cream, with an almost child-like joy and obliviousness. It was slowly dawning on me that Mom would drag her bottle to the grave and Dad his disconnect, and there wasn't a damn thing I could do about it. Marian was right: no amount of rage and complaint would snap Mom out of it, would change her. I was amazed at how quietly resolved she was in her addiction, while I was over here thrashing and fuming, wrestling with the Jabberwock of my own making.

As we pulled into a restaurant that evening in Paso Robles, I looked into the dusky sky and noticed a small gang of bats circling just off the corner of the building. My mind shot back to the Clock Tower and that dead mother bat I had found outside my bedroom door, with the baby frantically peeping, and which I saw back then as crying out for help, and which I now saw trying to slip out from under his mother's dead weight and fly off into the dark on his own.

## 19

# My Father, My Father

It was a year after our road trip with Mom and Dad, and I was teaching at the California Poets in the Schools annual conference when I got the call. I had been working with CPITS for a few years by then, and this was the first time I had been invited to teach the teachers. I was also invited to show slides of my visual art and give a talk about the relationship between language and poetry. My workshop was packed, the participants loved it, and the slide show went beautifully.

I was in "seventh heaven," as Mom liked to say. I was thriving in my work and art and relationship when I got the call. I knew Dad had been sick on and off for a few months, but my mom always assured me, "Oh, he just had to nip into the hospital overnight, no biggie." But this time, she was panicked, as he had had trouble breathing in the middle of the night and was complaining of chest pain. Even though Mom was wavering about whether or not I should come, my sister Serena jumped on the phone and said with grim command, "Get on the next plane!"

I packed my things and left the conference right away, catching the next plane out of SFO to JFK. It was two weeks after 9/11, and air travel had just resumed. The airport and plane was empty—ghostly, you might say. Marian came with me. We stayed with her mom in Pleasantville, and ran over to the hospital in Dobbs Ferry early the next day.

Dad was in the ICU, tied to all the requisite tubing, but awake and somewhat coherent. The nurse had to lift off the pale green oxygen mask for him to speak. It looked almost amusing to me, like a translucent bullfrog tied to his face. I smiled at him. Dad smiled back.

The doctor came in later that day and offered Dad dialysis. "If you think it will help," was his feeble reply. This, after the charge nurse had told us he had only a day or two to live. So we hovered around the bed, going back and forth from the waiting room where we watched CNN flash images and commentary on the troop buildup in Afghanistan. Dread piled on dread.

Dad had no idea that his city was burning and that war was imminent. He was one of the few conscientious objectors to World War II, and he came from a pacifist Quaker family. He was born during the First World War, and had endured hard-labor camps and experimental government medical (bio-warfare) testing during the Second World War, and I wondered what was going through his head, between everyone chattering on about war, the dialysis, and all the testing they were doing on him—did he think he was back in an Army hospital during World War II? He seemed only slightly agitated and disoriented, almost comfortable in his unwitting surrender. He had watched Korea, Vietnam, and the first Gulf War come and go, and now, this seemed almost too much war for his pacifist being to take.

I simply sat by the bed and told him how much I loved him, and how sorry I was about the time when I was sixteen and he offered to take me to Baskin-Robbins for ice cream, and I said no thanks, because I was too embarrassed to be caught hanging out with my seventy-year-old father at Baskin-Robbins. He said it was okay, he understood.

I read Dad some of my recent poems, although my poetry had always baffled and dismayed him ("You know, son, the point is to actually communicate with your readers, so they can understand what you're saying

. . .")—though in his dazed, doped-up state, I think he actually enjoyed the poems, or perhaps it was just the cozy intimacy of being read to. I probably could have been reading him an aviation meteorology manual or Gertrude Stein, and he would have enjoyed it just the same.

I read him a poem of mine called "A Pond," and the next day he was making requests that I read "upon" to him again. He'd groan, shift a little in the bed, and then gaze out the window and ask why it was snowing. I reminded him it was late September and that the leaves were shimmering in the wind and beginning to fall to the ground.

"Oh, that's nice," he'd say. I tried to tell him what was going on in New York, and he couldn't make sense of it. This was his city. He'd grown up in Brooklyn Heights, just across the bridge from Manhattan. We'd had dinner in those towers just a couple of years before with my cousin, Johnny. None of it made any sense. I was being stormed by a stark and vast personal, as well as societal, grief.

At different points throughout my visits with him, I'd ask him how I could make him more comfortable:

"Do you need another pillow? Do you want some ice cream?"

"No, I'm fine, you don't have to do that," was the usual reply.

This one particular day, his feet were sticking out from the sheets looking like bleak sticks of petrified wood. Lisa, his favorite nurse, came by and said, "How about a foot rub, Harrison?"

"Oh no, you don't have to do that." His usual reply.

Before anyone else could respond, Lisa volunteered me. Me, who was just a tad freaked out by feet, especially my father's eighty-seven-year-old feet, complete with mashed veins, overgrown nails, and scabby plates of skin.

"Yeah, Dad, how about a foot rub," I said queasily, hoping he would insist against it. He repeated that I didn't have to, which meant, "That'd be great!" I could hear it in his voice and see it in his dying eyes.

I gulped and then slowly began warming up the greasy foot cream in my hands, and proceeded to massage my father's feet for the very first and last time. I could tell he enjoyed it, and I quickly got over the discomfort and extreme intimacy, and actually began to revel in his enjoyment. The ordinariness was astounding. I felt as if I was engaged in a small, sacred act, the act of soothing my father's dying feet, touching his dying body.

While my dad was dying, I wrote a chapbook about the process, called *Time Pieces*, which is filled with fleeting bits of poems I assembled into a chronicle of those two weeks at the hospital in New York. They are all dated as if they were journal entries. Marian's drawing of the waiting room couch is on the front cover, and the bench outside the front door next to the standing ashtray adorns the back. They are drawn in black ink on a white cover, and both float alone in a sea of empty space. There's nothing on the couch, no one sitting on the bench. One section reads:

beard smeared by
clear green mask
oxygen oxygen oxygen
maple, oak, and elm
welcome to America

* * *

45 geese on the river
116 on the lawn
One child chases the lawn clean . . .

For the next two days, Dad was unconscious and unresponsive. There was a classic grim silence about the room, as if the walls were leaning toward us, the wallpaper peeling like sheets of blackened lead. Finally, Dwyn, Dad's granddaughter from another marriage, brought in a boom box so we could play him some of his favorite classical music. Otherwise, we sat around reading and drawing. Old relatives I hadn't seen in twenty years drifted in and then left for another twenty. Marian made more drawings of the ashtrays and magazine racks. I continued to alternate between scribbled death notes for Dad in my poetry notebook, to rereading *Newsweeks* from six months prior for the eighty-seventh time. We paced around, ordered food, and when feeling particularly ambitious, went for walks along the Aqueduct Trail. My sisters and I used to do that walk with Dad whenever we visited New York.

Serena was wound up and nervous, pacing back and forth. Being local, she took on the practical, trying to busy herself with the updates from the doctors and nurses. She would waver between a fairly pragmatic sturdiness or anger about the hospital's incompetence to a fragile sadness, breaking into tears and leaning on my shoulder. With both Margaret and Serena, there was an unspoken emotional openness between us, a knowing that part of who we were as DeSilvers was vulnerable, emotionally charged, prone to denial and overwhelm. We could break down or strike out in our grief at any moment. And yet, we'd be there for each other to help soften the blow.

Serena, like me, had had her own harrowing adventures with alcohol and drugs, which partly prompted her to drop out of high school early and go straight to work instead. She went on to get her GED, and soon after a BA from Hunter College in New York City, where she now lives and works as a social worker for a family service agency. Margaret had been on her own journey of searching. After a brief stint at an art college in New York, she moved to New Mexico to study massage therapy, then spent some time in a Buddhist-affiliated retreat center in Ireland, then back to New Mexico to begin raising a family.

Being in the hospital in such an open emotional state made me feel for my sisters and consider more deeply their experience with Dad. Who was he to them, for them, and how differently were they treated by him as daughters?

On the third day, we were back at the house going over the estate details with the accountant when Dwyn called from the hospital to say, "He just took his last breath peacefully."

We rushed back to the hospital to find him oxygen-less and tubeless on the other side of the room, monitors pulled away from his bedside. I came to his bedside to see his body—now empty and completely motionless—one last time, and there it was, just a body, an empty container. "Dad" was long gone. I kissed his cold head and then quietly prayed for his peaceful passage. It all seemed so natural to me. One of the great disappointments was that we never got Dad home to die in his own bed in which he had been born.

The next day, Margaret and I went to the mortuary to arrange for the cremation. Dad's ashes were poured into a cheap box the day after that. We declined the expensive and downright tacky urns on display in the mortuary parlor room, feeling Mom might think they were not "up to snuff."

Back at the house, Mom matter-of-factly led me upstairs and asked me in a demanding voice, "Can you wear any of your father's things?—and please get rid of what doesn't fit!"

I hesitated. "He's not my size," I said, eyeing a couple of his signature thick denim and plaid flannel L. L. Bean jack shirts, floating in a sea of Brooks Brothers' button-downs from the eighties. A token keepsake, a Dad-reminder. They were a bit frayed at the collar and at the sleeve ends. They had that old musty dry-cleaned-two-years-ago smell to them. It felt so strange talking about Dad in the distant third person, grazing his shirts as if I were at a thrift store looking for a sweet deal.

"Whatever, just get rid of this stuff, will you?" She seemed to want to usher Dad's ghost out of the house as quickly as possible so as to not have to face the grief of too many reminders. A favorite shirt of his she had bought for his birthday would throw her into abrupt silence, lip quivering, and reaching for another drink.

I stayed back East for another week helping Mom out, and occasionally took walks alone in the Mianus River Gorge. Dad and I used to walk there together in the last ten years or so of his life. Dad had a sincere, yet somewhat vague appreciation for nature, among other things. *Vague* was the word. He had what I would call a soft interest, never getting seriously into things, never allowing himself to be consumed by or obsessed about them, or ever fully committing. Even architecture, which he practiced for thirty-plus years, seemed for him to just be something to do, or kind of do.

As I walked in the gorge alone, I cried off and on for a few days, and that was pretty much the geography of my grief. It started to dawn on me that I barely knew this man assigned to me as my father. We rarely had had extended passionate conversations about life; he was curious only on a surface level about my life. He was supportive in word and frustratingly so in action, and generally remote. I do remember one warm June night, a year or so before he died when I was back East visiting. We were out to dinner seated on the patio of an Italian café on the Hudson. I watched the sky darken and listened to the distant thunder. I was mindlessly fondling a little, brown packet of "Sugar in the Raw," when Mom left the table as usual, to go out front to the sidewalk and have her ciggie. "This leaving the table for her cigarette still drives me crazy, makes me feel like she doesn't want to hang out with us," I said.

"I know, but that's just your mother, Al. This is her nervous way. You really oughta stop complaining about her behavior and learn to accept her, and love her for who she is. Plus, you know at this point, she probably isn't going to change much."

I shifted a little in my chair, surprised by Dad's comments, and his sudden new role as old wise man. I couldn't remember a time he gave me any sage advice about anything, let alone how to deal with Mom. There was a slight twinkle is his eye, a small pride at having unloaded a bit of wisdom to his son. At that moment, I saw in my father an amazing capacity to adapt, and accept challenging circumstances for what they were, and be able to maintain a semblance of sanity and balance, and even love. It made me move toward a greater acceptance and appreciation of this seldom revealed, beautifully human, side of him.

All this left me feeling both distant from him and, yet, all the more curious about him when he died. There was nothing particularly devastating or dramatic about his death, as he had lived a long and dynamic, albeit somewhat tragic, life. There was no deep emotional connection between us to begin with, and I felt generally resolved about his role in my upbringing, and even grateful for what he could offer emotionally, given his own tumultuous story. In relation to Dad, it seemed the anger I felt about Miss Hedy, his obliviousness, and his general detachment, had largely dissipated.

And, yet, as I walked alone in the gorge that day kicking leaves, I found myself bundled in one of Dad's L.L. Bean jack shirts, raising the frayed collar against my neck, trying to get warm, trying to gather some protection against the cold October afternoon.

## 20

# I Am That

After Dad died, and Rebecca, my landlord in West Marin, left to move back to Colorado, Marian and I moved upstairs, and Rebecca rented the downstairs unit to a nineteen-year-old kid named Jed. I was skeptical of Jed from the get-go, but Rebecca assured me that he was super-mellow and not into the party thing. At this point, I was fully committed to my meditation practice and wanted "sacred space" to grieve, write, meditate and just be. It wasn't but a few weeks later that the music started cranking up on Saturday nights. Then, his friends would gather, and soon, the pot smoke would waft up through the vents into our bedroom where I sat to meditate in the evenings.

One night, Jed was having some friends over, the music was thumping, and all I wanted was peace and quiet. I sat down to meditate as wafts of pot smoke started seeping through the vents. I pounded on the floor—no response. I pounded louder. Still no response. I felt the anger boiling within me, skin reddening, muscles tensing. I felt a bit like a tightly wound little kernel of corn floating in a sea of hot oil, ready to explode into a demented white flower. I picked up the phone to call. No answer. The rage was searing. I called again, pounded the floor even harder, jumped up and down. I tried to breathe through this rage, to no avail. Soon, it was so smoky that I became afraid I'd get stoned and once again damage my very fragile ten precious years of sobriety, this time to pot.

I stormed out the front door in a blind rage to the sliding glass doors of Jed's apartment below. Just as I had envisioned: beer bottles everywhere, a large bong, music blasting. I was apoplectic and began smashing my fists on the sliding glass doors. Jed opened the door. I screamed into his face, "Turn down the fucking music—now!"

"What the fuck?" said Jed. "What's your problem, dude?" I lunged at him, grabbing him around the collar of his shirt right at the clavicles and began to shake madly. He was terrified and instantly enraged himself. A defensive survival instinct kicked in. He fought back. All of the sudden, I felt as if I was staring into a mirror. His shirt was my shirt, his soft clavicles were my soft clavicles, once cracked in a high school lacrosse game by a bigger, older brute. His freaked-out reactionary rage was my freaked-out reactionary rage. Instantly, Jed turned into a silvery reflective surface of mirrored cloth and I saw, standing before me, myself at nineteen: drunk, stupid, and confused—and I wanted to kill him (me). I wanted to literally annihilate that image which stood before me. I wanted to smash it like the Christmas lights I smashed as a kid on the road above the Clock Tower. I wanted to hear the hollow, muffled sound of a leg bone breaking under skin. I wanted to watch this image, this person before me, explode into a small puff of brown smoke. I wanted to shoot it with my BB gun.

Suddenly, mid-shake, I snapped out of it and came to my senses, realizing I was ready to kill this drunk little punk motherfucker, and better stop before I did—I was out of my mind. I pushed him off of me, and stormed back upstairs to call the cops. On who? Myself? I was too rattled to make any sense of it. I just dialed the sheriff's department in a panic and started sputtering into the phone. "There's been a fight and he was drunk and . . ."

"Okay, calm down, sir, is anyone hurt?"

"No, I'm just freaked out, and this kid just took off, drunk and stoned, out of my driveway!" Jed and his friends had piled into their car and literally peeled out of the driveway like Dirty Harry in a mad flight.

"Okay, sir, just hang tight and I'll send someone out."

Two weeks later, I ran into Jed in the driveway, he was moving his stuff out and dragging a bag full of empties to the trash, and I couldn't help thinking I was seeing some part of me hauled away. I tried to offer my humble apologies. Part of me wanted to reach out, to help Jed, but I knew, like Mom, he was on his own trip, had to live out his own story. He kept a safe physical distance between us, clearly thinking (rightly so) I was a nutcase neighbor. He was wearing a Budweiser T-shirt and jeans, his eyes slightly bloodshot and at half-mast.

"Hey, I'm sorry about the other night, I was totally out of my head, that was completely inappropriate."

"Yeah." He paused. His eyes darted around. "Whatever. As you can see, I'm outta here"

"Really? I hope it's not because of what happened," I said, delighted by the news. "I mean it was really my fault, I overreacted. I just want you to know that's not the way I usually deal with things. You didn't deserve to be treated that way."

"Yeah, it's cool. I need to move back in with my parents. We tried it, and I guess it didn't really work. You definitely scared me though, dude."

And while he was talking to me I was having the strange sensation of noticing that my lips were moving and sound was emanating from me but the sound was distorted and looping back on itself in a weird echoey playback, like a call and response in a jail cell, as if I was apologizing—for attacking—*me*, for poisoning my younger traumatized, oblivious self—and I was praying at the edge of a mirrored prison wall, for release.

21

# Happy, Happy, Empty, Empty

My first experiences with meditation were brutal. Besides wanting to kill people who reminded me of my former self, I found it incredibly difficult at first to focus my mind. I liken it to tilling parched, cracked earth in a mosquito-infested field with a dopey, uncooperative mule and a broken plow.

This is what it was like for me trying to sit still in a meditation hall, trying desperately to blast through the incessant chatter of my conditioned mind. Mine is a wild mind, easily seduced by luscious poetic ideas, sensual fantasy, riveting colorful memories, and a nostalgia for the past that's visceral, constantly poking at the muscles deep in my belly.

The first time I meditated was with my friend Sant, when she was teaching a photography workshop at Anderson Ranch in Snowmass, Colorado. It was the summer of 1993, and we were out on a field trip in the mountains. We had gathered in a small circle in an open meadow, surrounded by twelve thousand foot peaks spotted with shrinking snow. We were told to close our eyes and follow our breath. I recall being extremely challenged by this relatively simple-sounding task. I was easily distracted by the wind, the flies, the scenery, and needless to say, the endless chatter buzzing through my head.

It wasn't until two or three years later, when I was invited to a meditation center across the street from where I lived, that something inside me clicked. I had driven by the sign a thousand times on my way home, always wondering what a "mediation center" was. Spirit Rock Mediation Center? I imagined family counseling of some sort. Oh, *meditation*, where you sit cross-legged and contemplate your navel? I really hadn't a clue.

I went to an open community sitting one Monday evening with a friend and found myself reveling in the calm energy and peacefulness of the gathering. Jack Kornfield, one of the founding members of the Spirit Rock community, told sweet parables and wise tales, and read poetry about living from truth and love. I was hooked. He read us Rumi and Hafiz, Hildegard of Bingen and Emily Dickinson, Walt Whitman and Rilke, Anna Akhmatova, and Mary Oliver. He spoke in a soft, fatherly tone about living honestly with integrity, compassion, and kindness, of slowing down and simply *being* in the moment, attentive and loving. What a concept.

I had never heard people talk about these things in a real way and then offer a practice for living from direct experience rather than someone else's doctrinal idea. This was a deep revelation for me, and I was immediately intrigued. And though it was initially extremely difficult, the meditating got, if not easier, more tolerable, and eventually hints of ease and grace emerged.

One night, Kornfield showed a film about Nisargadatta Maharaj, who reportedly had awakened to his true nature (whatever that meant). People from all over the world (including Jack) began showing up at his modest apartment in Bombay, looking for teachings. He was dramatic, this Nisargadatta, gesticulating wildly, chain-smoking beedies, practically yelling at his students with such passion and insistence you thought he might literally smash them over the head with a bundle of incense sticks. He would repeat himself over and over again, working himself into more and more of a frenzy trying to drive home the simplicity of the teachings to these thick-headed Westerners, who just couldn't grock the concept of nonduality and nonaction.

I fell instantly for Nisargadatta because of his rowdy character and no-nonsense, passionate approach. He spoke no English, lived an extremely sparse life materially, never wrote a word, and, yet, was considered a great teacher, exuding a vitality and passion that was palpable. I picked up his classic text of interviews, *I Am That,* and read it over and over again. This was the first book I packed in preparation for my adventures to the Sinkyone back in 1997. I lived with it intimately those days, reading excerpts daily, trying to understand, *I am what, now?* His teachings were based on the idea that you can only understand what you *are* by understanding what you are *not.* I was baffled, but enchanted. I loved the mysterious and esoteric.

And as I read these interviews over and over again, I realized he was saying the same thing over and over again to different people with slightly different words. *Neti, neti,* not this, not this. The story of your past is just a story, with no intrinsic reality. The story of the future is just a story, an anticipated dream with no intrinsic reality. What's real is the eternity of this moment. Dwell there, he screamed, awaken to this reality, and you will have attained nirvana. Not that your entire life will all of a sudden become an expression of pure bliss, problem-free, but that your problems will cease to be seen as problems, and the circumstances of your life will become neutralized as an expression of your acceptance of, and attention to, the present moment.

I began to attend regular sittings and then day-longs at Spirit Rock, and found the practices to be incredibly healing and grounding for me. Spirit Rock hosts teachers from all over the world from many denominations, though mostly Buddhist.

Ajahn Jumnian was my first direct experience with a Buddhist monk. He started coming to Spirit Rock in the early 1990s, initially for day-longs, which is where I first met him. He was a teacher of Jack Kornfield's from Thailand in the Theravada Vipassana tradition. A few years ago, he started teaching eight- to eleven-day silent retreats.

He struck me as not too unlike a baby, with his rosy cheeks and bald head, his exuberance and joy, his absolute innocence, his divine curiosity, his peace and certitude! I knew instantly, this was my guy; I want to learn from him! For a long time, I thought he was just this fat, jolly monk, until he finally started to tell us about all these weird talisman doodads hanging from his goldenrod-colored robes. It turns out that for many years, he studied shamanic healing and mysticism. Often during one of his talks, one of the dangling talismans would start to sound. It turned out to be an alarm in distorted Thai announcing the time. How embarrassing, we thought. He always just stared out into the crowd and laughed. When he walked, he jingled and clacked—people kept asking, what's with all the dangling thingamajiggies? Finally, one day in the midst of a talk, he started to unravel his robes. Layer upon layer. Was this some kind of Buddhist striptease? We were alarmed. Is he going to undress right here before us?

It turned out that he was quite slim. Underneath his robes he wore a simple monk jumpsuit undergarment, which had pockets and belt loops, and from which dangled dozens of wands, prayer sticks, tiger claws, feathers, flashlights, scissors, and all manner of tchochkes, all of which together, he told us, weighed more than a hundred pounds. He wore this stuff on his body every single day, wherever he went, and had done so for more than thirty years. He said he never had a problem getting through airport security; they just ushered him through as if he was a dignitary, which of course he is, just not an "official" one.

Ajhan Jumnian still knew only two words of English, *happy* and *empty,* so in between his long rambling dharma talks in Thai, he would stare out lovingly into the audience, wiggle his pinkies and exclaim with glee: "Happy, happy, empty, empty," and then burst into fits of giggles. I've finally figured out that those are the only two words worth knowing in any language, except maybe *love* and *poetry.*

He was a passionate storyteller, and would often drone on in Thai for hours with fanciful, convoluted stories about his exploits as a young monk. The entire exchange needed to be translated from the Thai, which was sometimes excruciating, as it would be often twenty minutes between paragraphs while the translator confirmed the gist of the story. One was about noticing a woman on a moped whose skirt flew up exposing her bright red panties, which he said inspired all kinds of exciting thoughts and sensations that needed to be simply witnessed and let go of.

He also told us this hilarious story of the two monks who were traveling a long way from one monastery to the next. One night, they were sitting around the fire deep in the jungle when one went off to relieve himself. The other one, left alone, started to panic when, after a few long minutes, he heard rustling in the bushes. He was convinced a tiger must be crashing through the bushes. After a few more minutes of mounting panic and worry he set out looking for the other monk, only to come around a corner and see an actual tiger. He screamed in horror and fear and ran in the other direction, convinced a tiger was after him. It turned out it wasn't a tiger at all, but his friend looking a bit like a tiger as he was positioned squatting down with his robes over his head, butt face up, testicles dangling in the moonlight. Ajahn just sat there giggling for five minutes straight.

He also told us about first being asked to teach as a young monk at a monastery in southern Thailand in the late seventies. The monastery was situated in an area of dense forest and rubber tree groves and had been mired in years of violent conflict between government forces and communist insurgents. When he arrived, he was told to leave the area immediately or he would be shot. He stayed and began teaching people from both sides of the conflict. Soon, government soldiers showed up for his teachings, then communist insurgents. The power of his presence, his teachings of loving-kindness and compassion, inspired a coming together from both sides. They soon both offered to protect his monastery. I was heartened and moved by this story, the courage of heart and commitment to his community, his fearlessness in confronting authority.

In 2004, after much encouragement from my therapist and inspiration gathered from numerous day-longs, I committed to my first eight-day silent retreat with Ajahn Jumnian. On the first day, for the first half-hour of meditation after lunch, I felt a few sparks of insight, followed by annoyance and frustration from sitting so long—the aches and pains started to kick in. I came for silence and meditation, but the lectures were made up of incessant babble in a language I couldn't understand, with translations that were fragmented and repetitive. After three days of uncomfortable meditation, my mind settled a bit, but then the commentator in my head showed up with a vengeance. He was loud and righteous, bellowing about this and that. The commentator had a bizarre story about everything and everyone. He had fallen in love with at least three other practitioners and proceeded to have mad sprawling passionate sex with all three of them at once, right there in that pile of multicolored zafus at the back of the room.

Meanwhile, Ajahn Jumnian babbled on with grace and ease, vying for attention. Now, the commentator moves onto that fat guy at the back of the room. The commentator has him nailed. All he needs is just a bit more commitment to his meditation practice and to get off his lard ass and start exercising and stop eating chicken-fried steak cooked in bacon grease. The poor guy must be freaking out on all this vegetarian food.

Then the commentator is on to that angry and embittered trophy wife with the facelift and bleached-blonde hair. She's nervy and self-absorbed, wound as tight as a bale of barbed wire; one surprising tap on the shoulder and she'd explode into a million serrated pieces. And then, there's a bookish androgynous creature I've named "Pat," definitely a lesbian, having a hard time getting over the cold disappointment of her parents. I know she hates me; she hates all men. It all goes back to her cold and distant father.

And there's that fat lady who works here. I've seen her around, hovering like a spiritual groupie, always hanging around the senior teachers like a paparazzi photographer. She's a wannabe, an insatiable *consumer* of enlightenment. She's always talking loudly, and I've noticed that she takes a left when leaving the driveway of Spirit Rock, where there's a big sign that says "No Left Turn." That'll get her eaten by the wrathful deities! She knows this is a silent retreat, so why is she talking so goddamn loud? It's like she's on a cell phone in the giant echoing bathroom of my mind. Perhaps she's out to torture me with her squealing fat-lady voice. It's as if she's commandeered my head. Her voice is taking over; she's oblivious to anyone else's need for a voice, or for silence. I'm getting *aggravated.* Suddenly J.T.'s mom's word feels so, so, so . . . so damn necessary! This fat lady is making me so *aggravated,* says the commentator. Is she even signed up for this retreat? The commentator is on a rampage.

Have I always been this judgmental—for no reason whatsoever? And what's with this hangup about fat people? I ask the commentator. The commentator pauses, and then goes off on a weird babbling rampage about that overly skinny anorexic who showed up late for the retreat. She's so beautiful, can't she see that? She never should have listened to her drunk friend last weekend who called her an ugly, fat slut. Yadda, yadda, the commentator drones on and on.

I mean, I don't even *know* these people; I've never spoken a word to them in my entire life. What must I be doing under my breath to those I *do* know? Uh oh! Surrounded by the endless sea of silence, the commentator has free rein of my mind and decides to just take over, his voice becoming like the screaming rattle of the A train express to Queens. The first couple of days of the commentator are excruciating and then endlessly hilarious, as I finally get a bit of distance and perspective.

One day, I shuffle over to the bulletin board where we can post anonymous messages to the teachers, and I write in big bold letters "I THOUGHT THIS WAS SILENT RETREAT. PLEASE TELL EVERY ONE TO SHUT

THE HELL UP WHEN IN THE FOYER!" I post it on the bulletin board and march off in a huff. Once back in the hall for our next session, I regret writing it, and feel as if I'm complaining, which of course I am. That's not particularly spiritual, I muse to myself.

A few minutes later, I shuffle back to the bulletin board to remove my note, but it's not there. One of the teachers has gathered the notes. Back in the hall before lunch, there is an announcement from one of the teachers asking us all to be silent in the foyer. I beam with righteousness. And then I think, should I have used the word *hell*?

On the second-to-last day of the retreat, with my commentator on temporary hiatus, I wandered off into the woods to do some lying-down meditation. I hiked up into the small canyon and found a perfectly flat spot of clean sand in the middle of a dry creek bed.

I began by following my breath, and then tried one of Ajahn's body scans he had taught us the day before. I was drifting deep into a spacious meditative zone, when suddenly my mind was overtaken by what I can only describe as a vision. It was sort of like an intense dream at night, in which you wake up screaming or sweating, or at the very least are freaked out for days afterward. The weird thing was, I was awake, but clearly in a completely *different* state of awareness after days of intensive meditation. It was quite similar to one of the medicine journeys, but without the psychedelia, nausea, and intense anxiety.

I'm in the cold, tiled, downstairs hallway just outside my bedroom at the Clock Tower. I'm four or five years old. Miss Hedy is there, rage in her eyes, venom in her voice. She's wearing a blue nightgown, torn, frayed, and full of holes. Instead of skin underneath, I see tiny points of light, and what appears to be smoke spilling through the tatters. The hallway is dark and hazy. Miss Hedy is screaming at me to pick up my clothes. She's apoplectic; starts freaking out about the mess, hollering in demonic German tongues. I can't understand what she's saying; it's just pure, garbled, angry yelling. It's as if all the words have gotten sliced into incoherent pieces on the rusty blade of her tongue and have shattered all around me. The sound is making my ribcage rattle.

Suddenly, she lunges at me and grabs my arm to show me what an incredible mess I've created. She's pulling me into the mess, ready to push my face in it like she did with my cat, Snowy, the time he peed in my bedroom closet. But my arm comes off in her hand. More frustrated than shocked, she throws it aside like a worthless mop handle, blood spewing, veins wriggling. She, then, reaches for my ear. This, too, comes off in her hand, peeled from my head with a slurping sound, and is also tossed aside as if it's a broken dessert plate. Then, she goes for the hair on my head, tufts of it filling her sweaty hands as if she's pulling dead weeds. She throws this aside as well, like so much tangled yarn. She moves on to the other limbs, each time filled with a more virulent rage, until I've been reduced to a ragged, limbless stump. And I'm just wobbling there, torn and bloody, utterly useless to her. And she has bloated up and turned from a fuming red to dark purple, and is about to burst the seams of her tattered nightgown, when she explodes, vaporizes, into a puff of pale blue smoke.

She is cast into the Outer Void, beyond this world, and I am immediately jarred awake, sitting up in the creek bed filled with a sensation of absolute spaciousness and release. A profound sense of freedom and complete relief has overtaken me. My body is airy, filled with light and a weightlessness that's impossible to describe. I grab onto a couple of large rocks to keep my body from drifting up into the canopy of trees above. Then, I'm sobbing into the riverbed the tears of a thousand lifetimes. I'm convinced there has been an exorcism of sorts, that something dark and metallic, horrific and sticky, has been released, and along with it, my story of abuse and abandonment, neglect and disconnection. Those pages, that fiction, that book of illusions is burned up in the roiling blue smoke with Miss Hedy. And I realize in that moment, in both body and mind, that I am definitely *not* my story.

\* \* \*

The next day, I find myself stumbling around with a massive grin on my face, practically blinding people with the glint off my teeth—I am so spontaneously happy for no reason that I burst into tears of joy at the slightest thing. A leaf of lettuce at lunch takes on an exquisite, shimmering, emerald significance, and I cry tears of joy into the little green boat of it before placing it lovingly into the dark sea of my mouth. "I'm definitely becoming enlightened now!" shouts the commentator, puffing up his chest.

For the rest of the retreat everyone continues to ignore my request for not talking in the foyer, especially my fat lady friend. My bliss is beginning to eclipse my agitation and rage. One morning, I'm late to breakfast, and I'm rushing, a bit distracted by my hunger, and notice there's only one muffin left in the basket. I practically lunge for it when I see another hand intersecting mine. It's hers. I retract and open both hands as a gesture, as if to say, "No, no, you take it." She gestures back silently, puts a hand to her heart, smiles, and walks off. I start to cry. I break down further as my commentator has finally been relegated to a more distant retreat center of his own, and she's one of the first people my heart cracks open to. She is the first one I cry to and for, the first one I ask forgiveness of. You'd think it would be Marian, my mom or dad or sisters, or even Miss Hedy. Nope, it's "what's her name." I've vowed a thousand prostrations at her feet. She's become my angel of awakening, my deva of enlightenment.

Here I was, a wounded, aspiring artist/poet trying to cobble together an identity for myself, a story of significance, with all this crap flying around in my head, crap that I took so seriously. I was trying to find a place in the world, trying to show the world that I matter, that I exist, that I have a gift for the world, and Ajahn Jumnian in his dharma talks keeps referring to "nonexistence" and letting go of the ego and the persona—letting go of your story. This is exactly what Nisargadattta had been screaming about in his interviews, in words he never even wrote down. This is what crazy Antoinette had said to me after that first medicine journey, and Bibi Makena on the balcony of the YMCA in Nairobi. And all this time, I've been desperately trying to *create* a persona, to *create* an identity that I can show off to the world, a story that I can name and imagine, one that says: *see what happened to me.* I'm realizing that the story had been filled with blame and complaint, confusion and limitation. It has been clouding out the creativity.

How will I live? How will I exist? How will I matter to the world without my persona, without my story? This was the question that began to haunt me throughout the rest of the retreat until I realized that the persona is just a fiction, along with the story that the persona acts out. Ultimately, it's not real. It's not to be clung to. Otherwise, you get completely caught up in the story, in the drama, and want to have more drinks or dope or sex or more unhealthy relationships to make yourself feel more alive and real.

Most of my earlier relationships with women seemed a kind of addiction to the drama, and to a solidified—albeit limited—identity that gets created within a relationship. What I actually want is true peace and balance, connection, love and inspiration. And that comes from inside of me, not from the story in my head, not from the wife or lover or teacher, or book or poem, or great work of art, or bottle of hand-crafted beer, or Maui-Wowee bong hit. It comes from that great mysterious blob of creation-energy inside each one of us. It goes by so many names: Buddha, Mohammad, Yahweh, Jesus, the Great Mystery, God, life force, whatever, but it's all happening within me—*now*, as a kind of expansive energy sensation.

So, I am finally starting to see how I am not that chaos of the outer world and its manifestations, and I never was. I am not the boy cowering in terror under the hand of a brutish governess while bats swirl overhead, and screams for my parents' attention are swallowed by the chunky dark of suburbia. I am not the boy in his mother's lap beaming somewhere over that rainbow, wishing upon a star. I am simply the beauty and mystery of awareness itself. I have become rainbow and star, and in this moment of release and insight, my dreams have come true. This feels like a great relief and a great illumination, and then simultaneously I remember I must come back to the challenges (and joys) of daily life, into the cut and thrust of the world, no matter how seemingly ordinary and boring, thrilling or euphoric, and practice there—be awakened right there, moment to moment, remembering that my only ambition, my only reason for being, is to love.

# 22

# Epilogue: Beamish Girl

So there it was, my perfect little ending, all sewn up with my profound meditation/awakening experience where I slay the monster (the Jabberwock), merge into divine love and everything's hunky dory, neat as a pin, book over. Done.

Not. By now (2010), it was several years later and Mom was suddenly struck with severe bleeding episodes, wound up in the ICU, not once, but twice, and then was quickly and matter-of-factly, diagnosed with stage 4+ cervical cancer. As in terminal. I flew back to New York several times in the winter and spring of 2010 as the news got worse and worse. I would visit her at St. John's Riverside Hospital in Yonkers (which, of course, she referred to as a leper colony) and in between bedside visits, would stare out over the Hudson River watching the hazy sunlight glint off sharp chunks of ice that had piled up along the banks like huge plates of broken glass. As the terminal diagnoses was confirmed and Mom refused treatment, I felt as if I were being buried beneath those thick slabs of dirty ice, blurrily watching Mom slip off into a choppy current of nameless ocean.

She was so kind and almost upbeat in the hospital, giving me her copy of *Tattler*, the special luxury travel issue to keep me distracted on the plane back to California. (We shared a devout love of traveling, and simultaneous manic fear of flying.) Normally, she was hyper-possessive about her magazines. (Don't touch my *New Yorker*, she would snap sometimes when I came to visit, as if it were an original Degas monotype.)

We were shocked, but not surprised by the news, given the fact that Mom hadn't been to the gynecologist since the nineteen seventies ("It's all so tiresome and unattractive," she would say), and how she had subsisted on a diet of cigarettes, cocktails, and an occasional peanut butter sandwich, half an egg and toast, a bite or two of steak and fries, and all too rarely, a vegetable.

She kept up with the stories to the very end reflecting on various poets and literary figures to keep the conversation going, or to drum up yet another witty anecdote. "I was trapped in a stuck elevator once with Tom Eliot," (I loved how she called him "Tom," as if they were old buddies) she said one day at the hospital. "There was a long silence, and I was anticipating some profound poetic comment, when he said, 'Shit, we're stuck.'"

This cracked me up to no end, and then moments later as I wandered down the hallway to get her another pillow, made me burst into tears, wondering who I will ever go to for such priceless, goofy stories. And the answer was no one. Mom was an original genius of the wacky anecdote. In these moments I found a renewed understanding of her sadness, and a deep appreciation for who she was and what she, too, had suffered in her lifetime. A few months later when I was cleaning out her condo, I found a paper she had written in 1947, when she was seventeen. "When in Rome" was written on her first trip abroad, as she was sailing alone on the *Queen Mary* to a convent school in Rome. I was delighted by what a good writer she was. I had always been enchanted by her witty and hyperbolic letters, but writing as a practice was something she never talked about having much of an interest in, though I rarely saw her without a book in her hand. She was an incredible reader of such diverse material; from architecture and antique magazines to Russian novels, to dime-store mysteries. For a school assignment at seventeen she wrote about her first Atlantic crossing:

> The Kevin and Kelly football teams were returning to Ireland and were rendering nostalgic Irish ballads for the benefit of the crowd. I expected to feel something—excitement, sorrow, nausea—anything. At home, the very thought of going back to school had me homesick, even before I left and here I was sailing to Europe for the first time, and I felt simply nothing. Phenobarbital is the best invention since the wheel, I thought.

This, after she describes how nervous she and her parents were at the prospect of letting her to sail alone to Europe. She mentions taking an "extra dose" of Phenobarbital (normally taken to manage seizures and anxiety), presumably with her mom, as they were both "feeling just a little numb." I'm not exactly sure why they had this sedative in the first place, except that Mom sometimes described her mother as a "nervous Nellie." She went on to write:

"The cabin was the size of an annex to a telephone booth, and occupying the only floor space was my wardrobe trunk, and horrors! A baby's bassinet." And then describing a man she met one night at dinner:

> He was a wiry fellow with small, round tortoise-shell glasses perched on an eagle-beak nose, and with a sleek receding hairline. He had a very prominent upper plate, which loosened itself whenever he smiled or laughed. Both, he did often after an unceasing number of little gems of witticisms. This very toothy laugh started out sounding like an agonizing moan and gradually worked itself up to a hysterical pitch.

I can hear her voice as if she were retelling this as an adult at a dinner party at the Clock Tower, gesticulating with her ciggie in one hand, glass of wine in the other, complete with her exquisite hyperbole and exaggeration, rousing the whole table to explode with laughter.

This was the Mom who inspired a social sensibility in me, an inventive, exaggerated use of language (AKA poetry), the Mom who showed up at the Zinc Bar for my poetry readings (it helped that you could smoke and they had a terrific liquor selection), the Mom who had a great heart despite her hurts and denials, who insisted on putting on a lunch party for her gym pals two days before she died, choreographing Marian, my sisters, and her caregiver, into a kind of frenzied dance regarding which silver to use, what table cloth to display, how to arrange the flowers properly. This Mom, my mom, was dying, and so too were pieces of me; pieces of an old, enraged and resentful self were lifting, and in their place, acceptance, appreciation, and love were taking root.

We had her transferred home and she was immediately put on hospice care. We set up a bed in her library downstairs. Almost tomb-like, the library was her favorite room in the condo with its dark green walls framed in gold-leaf molding, the great wall of art, interior design, and architecture books, low glass tables stacked with *Architectural Digest* and *Vanity Fair* from the nineties—the *Brunschwig & Fils* floral curtains with their pink epaulets, the ashtrays of crushed ciggies, the worn-out sofa where she spent thousands of hours reading the *Times*, Evelyn Waugh, Agatha Christie or Tolstoy, and watching Judge Judy, sometimes simultaneously. There were the dark paintings of the ancestors we could never identify, the fake marble fireplace she had shipped from London for $1,800. We shifted things around just so, bringing her favorite furniture pieces from upstairs to make it all okay. "Very *House & Garden*," she said in a weak whisper once we had everything arranged.

We managed to keep her comfortable and virtually pain-free, and as she was dying, I sat and listened to her stories get weaker, and then disintegrate into random fragments, blurred memories, and crazier than normal anecdotes. At one point she told her Ugandan Caregiver how she once dined with the vice president of South Africa in Kenya in 1954, and then asked her if she knew some obscure "Tanganyikan" diplomat named Sir Wasabu. (She still insisted on calling Tanzania by its pre-colonial name.)

Meanwhile, I offered to read to her, shift her pillow, bring her grapefruit juice, told her I loved her ten times a day, thanked her for putting up with me staying out all night in high school drunk with the car, apologized for my horrific hospitalizations, my phase of blame and maternal rejection, my baffling poetry. And I thanked her for sending me those thousands of *New York Times* clippings related to poetry. Then, I simply held her hand, tried not to cry too much as I whispered "I love yous" and kissed her on the head goodbye, all the while quoting T.S. Eliot in my mind. . .

. . .*Home is where one starts from. As we grow older*
*The world becomes stranger, the pattern more complicated*
*Of dead and living. Not the intense moment*
*Isolated, with no before and after,*
*But a lifetime burning in every moment. . .*

# ACKNOWLEDGMENTS

Many thanks to Elsa Dixon, Adair Lara, Janis Cooke Newman, Dana Lomax, Karen Benke, Karen Evans, and all those who read excerpts and provided invaluable feedback on the initial drafts. Thanks to Rachel Howard, who hosted a terrific couple of classes at the SF Writers' Grotto, and went on to help me usher the book through the toughest midway point of the process. Thanks to Ivory Madison who helped me bring the book to a state of suspended finality. Thanks to Holly Payne and Skywriter Books, neighbor, friend and teacher Molly Giles, and Doug Childers, who all provided invaluable editing and feedback on the final, final drafts. And to my gourmet dinner readers, Sarah, Lisa, Cyndy, Nicole, and DB. You are true angels! Thanks also to copyeditors Carolyn Miller and Elizabeth Berstein for their keen eyes.

Much gratitude and love to Magpie and Serena for your patience, memories, and insights, and especially for your understanding of my version of events.

And to Marian, love of my life, for *not* reading the book in progress and providing any feedback whatsoever. You have done me, and our marriage, a great service. And more than anything thanks for your patience with me in this time of great obsession. I love you.

Infinite gratitude to my teachers and guides named and un-named, in physical form and beyond, especially Megan Freeman, Ajahn Jumnian, James Baraz, Heather Sundberg, and the Teen Council at Spirit Rock, Adayashanti, Nisargadatta Maharaj, and Jerry and Esther Hicks.

# ABOUT THE AUTHOR

**Albert Flynn DeSilver** is an internationally published poet, author, artist, teacher, and speaker. He served as the very first Poet Laureate of Marin County, California from 2008-2010. Albert is the author of several books of poetry including *Letters to Early Street*, and *Walking Tooth & Cloud,* and his work has appeared in dozens of literary journals and anthologies worldwide. He presents at literary conferences nationally, directs a homecare agency, and teaches in the Teen and Family program at Spirit Rock Meditation Center near his home in Northern California. Please visit the author's website at www.albertflynndesilver.com

CPSIA information can be obtained at www.ICGtesting.com
Printed in the USA
LVOW040740311212

313850LV00002B/265/P